A1

READING DETECTIVE®

Using Higher-Order Thinking to Improve Reading Comprehension

SERIES TITLES

Reading Detective Beg.   Math Detective Beg.   Science Detective Beg.
Reading Detective A1   Math Detective A1   Science Detective A1
Reading Detective B1   Math Detective B1
Reading Detective Rx

Written by Cheryl Block, Carrie Beckwith, Margaret Hockett, and David White

Pen and Ink Illustrations by Susan Giacometti

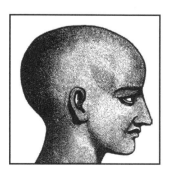

© 2001
THE CRITICAL THINKING COMPANY
www.CriticalThinking.com
P.O. Box 448 • Pacific Grove • CA 93950-0448
Phone 800-458-4849 • FAX 831-393-3277
ISBN 0-89455-767-X
Printed in United States

TABLE OF CONTENTS

TEACHER INTRODUCTION

Teacher Overview v
Skills Matrices vii

STUDENT SKILLS LESSONS

What is *Reading Detective?* xi
Making Inferences xii
Making Generalizations xiv
Using Figurative Language xvi
Developing Vocabulary Using Context xviii

STUDENT ENRICHMENT

Enrichment: Literature Essay Questions xx

PRETESTS

Fiction Pretest: A "Dog-gone" Day 2
Nonfiction Pretest: Quartz: Our Most Common Mineral 6

LITERATURE EXCERPTS and ACTIVITY PAGES

1. *Fudge•a•mania* 10
2. *Mr. Popper's Penguins* 12
3. *Maniac Magee* 14
4. *Owls in the Family* 16
5. "Rikki-tikki Tavi" from *The Jungle Book* 18
6. *Where the Red Fern Grows* 20
7. *Island of the Blue Dolphins* 22
8. *Blue Willow* 24
9. *The Witch of Blackbird Pond* 26
10. *Charlie's House* 28

FICTIONAL SHORT STORIES and ACTIVITY PAGES

11. Iggy 32
12. Caught White-Handed 34
13. Letter from the Mother Lode 36
14. Bad Reputation 38
15. A Shot at Problem Solving 40
16. Capsized! 42
17. A Uniform Approach 44
18. The Bear and the Bees: A Fable 46
19. My First Alien Sighting 48
20. Farm Girl 50

21. Riddle Time 52
22. Pet Overpopulation 54
23. A Tale of Two Boarders 56
24. Little Squirt, Big Squirt 58
25. No Show 60
26. Truth or Dare 62
27. Case of the Missing Diamond 64
28. Buttered Up 66
29. It's All Downhill 68
30. Teacher Turns Eleven 70

NONFICTION ARTICLES and ACTIVITY PAGES

31. "Pokey-pines" 74
32. Making "Sense" Out of Poetry 76
33. Defining Geometry 78
34. Cesar Chavez: a Biography 80
35. How to Make Dough Ornaments 82
36. All Around the Sun 84
37. What Do Owls Eat? 86
38. Comanche Horsemen 88
39. Blowing Hot and Cold 90
40. The Challenger Disaster 92
41. Little Green Food Factories 94
42. Ancient Egyptian Hieroglyphs 96
43. Almonds for Sale 98
44. The Food Chain 100
45. Who Was Benjamin Banneker? 102
46. The Land Down Under 104
47. Dress Like an Egyptian 106
48. Natural Rhythm 108
49. Jackie Robinson, All-star 110
50. Magellan's Voyage Around the World 112

POSTTESTS

Fiction Posttest: Half Dozen to Go 116
Nonfiction Posttest: The Good in Forest Fires 120

ANSWER KEYS
.... 123

GLOSSARY
.... 206

LITERATURE CITATIONS
.... 207

SAMPLE ACTIVITY FROM READING DETECTIVE™ B
.... 209

TEACHER OVERVIEW

This program uses higher-order thinking skills to develop students' reading comprehension. The reading skills are based on state reading standards and assessment tests for grades 5 and 6.

The goal of the program is to teach students how to analyze what they read. Students answer questions based on a passage then provide supporting evidence from the text for their answers. Each sentence is identified with a superscripted number; each paragraph has a letter. Students use these numbers and letters to cite specific sentences and paragraphs as evidence.

The purpose in asking for evidence is to

- encourage students to go beyond simple recall of information.
- require students to support their answers by drawing on specific information from the passage.
- clarify for the teacher a student's thinking about and understanding of the material
- require students to analyze the passage in greater depth

Contents

The book contains three types of reading passages:

- nonfiction articles on a variety of topics in the different content areas
- fictional stories in a variety of writing styles
- literature excerpts from award-winning and well-known authors frequently read in schools

Each exercise provides a passage the student must read followed by a series of questions. Most of the question are multiple choice or short answer, the formats used on state reading assessments. Each question requires students to use one of the skills listed on the reading skills matrix. Definitions are given for key vocabulary words and technical terms.

Pre-and posttests are included to offer a general assessment of students' skills prior to starting the program and after completing it. Two passages, one fiction and one nonfiction, are offered for each. These tests are NOT intended as a diagnostic tool to assess an individual student's reading abilities. They are simply meant to give you an idea of your students' general level in reading comprehension. They should be used only for determining which skills and lessons to focus on.

We have included student lessons to introduce and/or review some of the higher level skills that students may not be as familiar with, such as inference. All the lessons can be given prior to starting the program, or specific lessons can be used on pretest results.

A key component in this book is discussion of answers. The teacher's manual gives suggested answers with supporting evidence. However, many of the questions (inference and prediction for example), are open to interpretation. It is important to discuss with students how they came up with their answers and how the evidence supports their answer. If you feel a student has made a good case for his response, accept that answer. The key to this program is encouraging students to think about what they read in order to better understand it. We give what we consider to be the best possible answer based on the evidence, but this does not mean that there is only one right answer. The evidence that a student gives is the key to pinpointing his understanding, and some of the evidence is subtle and open to interpretation.

The Use of Inferences in this Book

Students can be taught to make good inferences without actually knowing the word "inference." In this book, most of the inference questions in the student activities do not use the term "inference." However, it is a good idea to introduce the terminology along with the concept.

The Use of Generalization in this Book

Students can be taught to make good generalizations without actually knowing the words "generalization" and "generalize." In this book, the questions requiring generalization in the student activities do not use the term "generalization." However, it is a good idea to introduce the terminology along with the concept.

In the lesson, students are asked to answer the following question on their own. What general statement could you make about Lisa based on the information given below?

1.   Every day, Lisa greeted the neighbors on her way to school. She waved at the milkman and brought old Mrs. Newcomb her morning paper. She smiled at the joggers as they ran through the park. She knew the doorman at the hotel and the crossing guard by name. Everyone knew and liked Lisa.

Possible Answer: Lisa was a friendly person. She greeted people. She helped people. She made friends with people, and they liked her.

The Use of Figurative Language in this Book

At this level of the Reading Detective series, the questions usually avoid asking for specific figures of speech except for simile and metaphor. Most questions ask students to identify the use of figurative language or to tell how a figure of speech is used, without requiring a specific term. For example, idioms are used in the excerpt from "Rikki-tikki Tavi." Students are asked to explain what they think the idiom means, but not to identify it as such. Even so, it is a good idea to introduce the terminology along with the concept.

In the lesson, students are asked to answer the following question on their own. Can you identify how figurative language is used in the next passage?

2.   I watch the daffodils poke their sleepy heads through the soil. In a matter of days, bright yellow daffodils are nodding cheerfully in the garden. Clusters of purple hyacinth stand at attention between them.

The writer describes the spring flowers in human terms. The daffodils "poke their sleepy heads" and "nod cheerfully." The hyacinths "stand at attention."

SKILLS FOR READING COMPREHENSION/LITERARY ANALYSIS GRADES 5–6

LITERATURE PASSAGES

READING COMPREHENSION SKILLS	Charlie's House	Witch of Blackbird	Blue Willow	Blue Dolphins	Red Fern	Rikki-tikki Tavi	Owls in the Family	Maniac Magee	Mr. Popper's Penguins	Fudge-a-mania
READING										
Compare/contrast	■				■					
Define vocabulary in context			■		■				■	
Distinguish cause/effect	■				■		■	■		■
Distinguish fact/opinion										
Draw conclusions	■	■	■	■		■	■	■	■	■
Find supporting details	■	■	■	■	■			■		
Identify author's purpose					■					■
Identify main idea		■								■
Make inferences	■	■	■	■	■	■	■	■	■	
Make generalizations									■	■
Make predictions										
Read for details	■	■				■	■		■	
Sequence facts, steps										
Use tables, illustrations, etc										
LITERARY ANALYSIS										
Analyze character traits				■	■			■		■
Identify key events in plot	■									
Identify theme									■	
Identify figurative language		■			■	■	■	■	■	
Identify setting				■						■
Predict outcome/resolution							■			
Recognize conflict				■						
Recognize point of view										
Sequence events		■								■

SKILLS FOR READING COMPREHENSION/LITERARY ANALYSIS GRADES 5–6
FICTION PASSAGES

READING COMPREHENSION SKILLS	Iggy	Caught White-Handed	Letter from Mother Lode	Bad Reputation	Problem Solving	Capsized	Uniform Approach	The Bear and the Bees	My First Alien Sighting	Farm Girl	Riddle Time	Pet Over-population	A Tale of Two Boarders	Little Squirt, Big Squirt	No Show	Truth or Dare	Missing Diamond	Buttered Up	It's All Downhill	Teacher Turns Eleven
READING																				
Compare/contrast								■						■					■	
Define vocabulary in context						■				■			■		■	■		■		
Distinguish cause/effect	■	■	■	■	■	■	■		■	■	■			■		■	■		■	■
Distinguish fact/opinion							■	■											■	
Draw conclusions			■	■	■	■	■	■		■	■	■	■	■	■	■	■			■
Find supporting details	■		■	■	■	■						■				■	■			
Identify author's purpose												■	■							
Identify main idea			■	■													■	■	■	■
Make inferences	■	■	■	■	■	■	■	■	■	■	■		■	■	■	■	■	■	■	■
Make generalizations			■								■		■				■			■
Make predictions								■			■	■						■	■	■
Read for details		■			■															■
Sequence facts, steps			■																	
Use tables, illustrations, etc			■																	
LITERARY ANALYSIS																				
Analyze character traits	■		■			■	■						■	■			■	■		
Identify key events in plot						■														
Identify theme		■						■												
Identify figurative language			■	■		■			■		■		■	■	■		■		■	■
Identify setting									■	■						■		■		
Predict outcome/resolution							■	■	■				■			■	■			
Recognize conflict				■			■													
Recognize point of view												■		■		■	■			■
Sequence events	■	■								■	■			■		■			■	■

SKILLS FOR READING COMPREHENSION/LITERARY ANALYSIS GRADES 5–6
NONFICTION PASSAGES

Passage	Compare/contrast	Define vocabulary in context	Distinguish cause/effect	Distinguish fact/opinion	Draw conclusions	Find supporting details	Identify author's purpose	Identify main idea	Make inferences	Make generalizations	Make predictions	Read for details	Sequence facts, steps	Use tables, illustrations, etc	Analyze character traits	Identify key events in plot	Identify theme	Identify figurative language	Identify setting	Predict outcome/resolution	Recognize conflict	Recognize point of view	Sequence events
Magellan's Voyage			■	■		■	■		■	■		■											■
Jackie Robinson			■	■		■			■			■											■
Natural Rhythm		■	■					■		■		■						■					
Egyptian Dress			■						■	■	■												
Land Down Under		■		■	■			■				■		■									
Benjamin Banneker					■	■		■				■							■				■
Food Chain	■				■	■					■	■	■	■									
Almonds for Sale					■		■		■	■			■										
Egyptian Hieroglyphs	■		■		■			■	■			■											
Green Food Factories	■	■			■			■				■	■										
Challenger Disaster	■				■	■	■					■											
Blowing Hot and Cold	■		■		■			■	■				■					■					
Comanche Horsemen			■		■	■		■															
What Do Owls Eat?	■	■	■					■				■	■										
All Around the Sun	■								■	■	■	■	■	■									
Dough Ornaments			■	■			■				■	■	■										
Cesar Chavez			■	■		■		■						■									
Defining Geometry	■					■	■					■		■									
Sense Poetry					■	■	■				■	■	■										
"Pokey-pines"		■	■		■			■				■											

READING COMPREHENSION SKILLS

READING

LITERARY ANALYSIS

WHAT IS READING DETECTIVE?

Reading Detective has stories and questions that will help you read and think better. After you read a story, you will answer questions that will help you improve not only basic reading skills (such as reading for detail) but also thinking skills. One of the best ways to learn is by discussing your answers with your teacher and other students. By comparing your interpretation of the story with other people's ideas, you will learn to see new relationships (between story events and characters, for example).

Types of Reading Passages

There are three types of stories: (1) literature passages from books written by highly acclaimed authors you may have read before; (2) factual articles; and (3) a variety of short fiction stories. The passages include a variety of story types: mystery, science fiction, humor, adventure, etc.

Types of Questions

Each activity asks you 6–8 questions about the passage. Types of questions include multiple choice, short answer, and fill-in-the-blank. Multiple choice questions include four choices. Usually, you must pick only one; once in awhile, there will be more than one correct answer, and you must list all answers that are correct.

Reading for Evidence

When you answer questions, you will often be asked to list sentences or paragraphs from the story to support your answer choice. When giving evidence, you must choose the best sentences to support and explain your answer.

The sentences in each passage are numbered with a small number at the beginning of the sentence. In some stories, a letter is used to indicate each paragraph in the story. You will use these numbers and letters to identify your evidence.

Key vocabulary words and technical terms in some of the passages are highlighted with a star (asterisk). A definition of the word is then given at the end of the passage.

Using the Glossary

At the end of the book is a glossary of terms you will need to know when answering the questions. You may refer to this glossary at any time.

MAKING INFERENCES

Inferences and Facts

In many of the activities in this book, you will be asked to draw a conclusion from information that is suggested in the passage. This is called *making an inference.* There is a difference between making an inference and identifying a fact. When you identify a fact, you are simply finding information that is stated in the passage. When you make an inference, you are drawing a conclusion based on information that is not directly stated in the passage.

In the following passage, see if you can tell the difference between an inference and a fact.

1.   [1]The sun was shining; the birds were singing. [2]There wasn't a cloud in the sky as the bus went along. [3]It was going to be a beautiful day. [4]"A perfect spring day to be biking," thought Chai, as the bus brought him into the school parking lot.

Fact: Birds are singing.
Fact: Chai is on a bus.
Inference: Chai is a student.
Inference: Chai would rather be biking.

The facts are stated in the passage. The inferences require the reader to use information suggested by the story to draw a conclusion.

Examine the Evidence

When you make an inference about information from a story, look at the events described and the actions and words of the characters. Often an author uses the events and characters to lead you towards an inference he or she wants you to make. The events described and the characters' words and actions become evidence for your inferences. The more evidence you have to support your inference, the more likely your inference will be true. However, you must be careful when making inferences to identify and carefully examine your evidence. Otherwise, you may make an inference that turns out to be false.

For instance, in the passage above, the author never directly says that Chai is a student who is riding to school in a school bus, but you can infer this. Your inference may be true. However, another possibility is that Chai is the bus driver. You need more evidence to determine who Chai is.

Read the next passage. What can you infer (or conclude) about Charlie's behavior?

2. [1]Charlie had taken my lunch box again and was holding it over his head. [2]"Come on, kid," he said. [3]"Try and get it." [4]We'd been through this before. [5]I knew it was no use trying to get it, but Charlie just loved to keep playing this game. [6]As I grabbed for the box, Charlie tripped me, and I went sprawling on the concrete. [7]"Missed again, loser!" yelled Charlie, as he dumped the contents of my lunch box on top of me.

The passage doesn't state that Charlie is acting like a bully. However, the author gives you evidence in the words and actions of both Charlie and the narrator. In sentence 1, Charlie takes the narrator's lunch box. Both sentences 1 and 4 tell us he has done this before. In sentence 6, Charlie trips the boy. In sentence 7, Charlie dumps the boy's lunch on his head. Charlie teases the boy in sentences 2 and 3. In sentence 7, he calls him a name.

Using Your Own Knowledge

Sometimes when you make an inference, you combine your own knowledge with the information that is suggested or given in the text. It is common knowledge that some snakes eat rodents. In the following passage, can you make an inference about what happened to the gerbils? Is there enough evidence to support your inference?

3. [1]Amanda was pet-sitting Alejandro's pet boa constrictor. [2]When she went to check on him in the morning, the snake was missing. [3]There also seemed to be fewer gerbils in the next cage.

It is possible that the snake and the gerbils escaped together. It is more likely that the snake escaped and ate the gerbils. It is a fact that boa constrictors eat small animals. Although the author doesn't give us this fact, we can use our own knowledge of boas to support this conclusion. In this case, our inference is probably true, but might be false. There is not enough evidence in the story to make a definite conclusion about the gerbils.

MAKING GENERALIZATIONS

Generalizations

Some of the questions in this book ask you to make a general statement about a group of things. This is called making a *generalization*. When you make a generalization, you take specific information about something and apply it to *all* similar things. For example, let's say you've never tasted Brussels sprouts. You try one Brussels sprout, and it tastes bad to you. What do you decide about Brussels sprouts? Do you figure they *all* taste bad and decide not to eat them again? Such a decision is a generalization, but it may not be a good generalization.

A Good Generalization

To make a good generalization you need plenty of evidence. Could you be sure all Brussels sprouts taste like the one you ate? Maybe the sprout you got was spoiled. How could you be sure about the taste of Brussels sprouts in general? Let's say you tried all the sprouts in the batch and they all tasted bad. Would that mean all Brussels sprouts taste bad? What if that whole batch had been spoiled? Or what if your sense of taste were "off" due to illness? To make a good generalization, you should try to gather more evidence about how Brussels sprouts taste.

Read the following passage. Could you make a general statement about all cats, based on the information given?

1. [1]Whenever Nancy has a glass of chocolate milk, her cat Archie wants to share it. [2]He comes running when he hears her open the refrigerator. [3]If she pulls out the chocolate milk, he meows until she pours some for him.

Even though Nancy's cat likes chocolate milk, this does not mean that *all* cats like chocolate milk. Saying that all cats like chocolate milk would not be a good generalization because there is not enough evidence. One cat is not a large enough sampling.

The following passage gives information about several similar animals. What general statement might you make about all animals of this kind?

2. [1]Squirrels are rodents that use their strong front teeth for breaking nuts. [2]Beavers are rodents that use their front teeth for gnawing wood. [3]Rats and mice are rodents that can use their front teeth for gnawing through plaster walls. [4]Even pet

rodents, like hamsters and gerbils, chew on sticks of wood to keep their teeth strong.

Since all of these animals are rodents and all of them use their front teeth for gnawing on hard objects, you might decide that most rodents have strong front teeth. You would be making a generalization about rodents. Since your statement is based on more than one type of rodent, it is probably a good generalization.

Besides making general statements about groups of things, you can also make a general statement about an individual. For example, you can make a generalization about a character's traits based on his or her actions. When you do this, you are applying what you know about the character's actions in one or more situations to his or her behavior in all other similar situations. What might you decide about Amanda after reading the following description?

3. [1]Amanda prepared dinner every night this week. [2]She did all her homework. [3]She scrubbed the kitchen floor, cleaned the bathrooms, and delivered papers each morning.

From her actions, you might decide that, in general, Amanda is a hard-working person. When you do this, you are making a broad statement about Amanda's behavior in all similar situations. However, it is possible that she worked hard only this week. The more evidence you have to support your general statement, the stronger it is.

Look at the following example. What general statement could you make about Lisa based on the information given below?

4. [1]Every day, Lisa greeted the neighbors on her way to school. [2]She waved at the milkman and brought old Mrs. Newcomb her morning paper. [3]She smiled at the joggers as they ran through the park. [4]She knew the doorman at the hotel and the crossing guard by name. [5]Everyone knew and liked Lisa.

USING FIGURATIVE LANGUAGE

Figurative Language

Sometimes writers use words in a special way to make their writing more interesting or to create an image in the reader's mind. Often, figurative language uses words to mean something other than their dictionary or *literal* meaning. Literal language describes how something actually looks, feel, or sounds. For example:

Literal: He looked strong.
Literal: She is flying through the air on her hang glider.

Figurative language describes something by comparing it to something else or by using words in creative ways.

Figurative: The muscles in his arms looked like bowling balls.
Figurative: She is a bird riding gently on the breeze.

Of course, his arms are not really the size of bowling balls, and she is not *really* a bird. Figurative language helps the writer to make a point and to make the writing more imaginative.

Simile and Metaphor

Two specific kinds of figurative language are used in the activities in this book.

Simile: A simile uses the word "like" or "as" to compare two things.
Metaphor: A metaphor makes a comparison by suggesting that one thing *is* the other.

Look at the two examples below. Which one is a simile? Why?

1. She floated in the air like a feather.
2. Her lined face was a map of her life.

Sentence 1 is a simile. It makes a direct comparison between two things, a girl and a feather. It says she floated *like a feather*. Sentence 2 is a metaphor; it suggests that her face is a map.

Figurative language is used in the following passage to describe a spring garden. Can you identify which kind of figurative language is used in the following sentences?

3. [1]New green leaves appear on the trees. [2]The leaves slowly unfold like the tiny fingers on a newborn baby's hands. [3]Pink and white blossoms burst open like popcorn popping on the branches. [4]Spring is here!

Other Ways of Using Figurative Language

Figurative language is more than similes and metaphors, however. There are other ways an author might use figurative language to describe something. When you say, "My father blew his stack last night," you don't really mean that your father has a stack on his head or that he blew up. You mean he was angry. Figurative language can include using words to mean something other than their actual meaning. There are many common phrases that do this such as it "weighs a ton" or he "lost track" of the time. These phrases are called *idioms*.

Identify where this kind of figurative language is used in the following passage. What do you think the phrase means?

4. [1]Mom was fit to be tied when she heard I was going to be late for dinner. [2]I tried to explain, but she wouldn't listen.

Sentence 1 uses the expression "fit to be tied." It means that Mom was mad.

Sometimes a writer will describe an object in human terms. This is called *personification*. Can you identify how this type of figurative language is used in the next passage?

5. [1]I watch the daffodils poke their sleepy heads through the soil. [2]In a matter of days, bright yellow daffodils are nodding cheerfully in the garden. [3]Clusters of purple hyacinth stand at attention between them.

DEVELOPING VOCABULARY USING CONTEXT

Using Context Clues within the Sentence

Context is the words or sentences that surround an unfamiliar word. If you understand the other words in a sentence, you can often figure out the meaning of an unfamiliar word.

1. Long *festoons* of flowers were strung along the railings of the balconies as decorations.

In the sentence above, we know that the festoons were long, made of flowers, and were strung up as decorations. The word *strung* also gives you a clue that a festoon is probably a kind of string or garland of something, in this case, flowers.

Sometimes a sentence will describe the meaning of the word for you, as in the following example:

2. She spoke in such a soft whisper that her voice was barely *audible*, and I had to bend down to hear her.

The second part of the sentence helps to define the word for you. Since the person had trouble hearing her, the word *audible* probably means able to be heard. The definition is also supported by the fact that since she spoke in a whisper, she was barely <u>heard</u>.

Using clues in the sentence, what do you think the word in the following sentence means?

3. The evening finally *culminated* with the arrival of a huge, flaming dessert carried in on a silver tray by two waiters.

Using Context Clues within the Passage

The surrounding sentences in a passage can also give you clues as to the meaning of an unfamiliar word. Look at the following example:

4. [1]The phone had rung unexpectedly very early in the morning. [2]It was a short call, but Uncle Art seemed *perturbed* after the call. [3]He wouldn't talk to anyone. [4]He just kept lighting one cigarette after another and pacing back and forth in the kitchen.

The sentence using the word *perturbed* does not give you much information about the word's meaning. However, there are clues in the surrounding sentences that can help you define the word. In sentence 1, we know that it was the unexpected phone call that caused Uncle Art to be perturbed. In the last two sentences, we learn that Uncle Art reacted to the call by not talking, by smoking constantly, and by pacing. This information suggests that Uncle Art was upset or disturbed by the phone call. So upset or disturbed would be a good definition for the word *perturbed*.

ENRICHMENT: LITERATURE ESSAY QUESTIONS

The following optional essay questions give students the opportunity to explain in greater depth their thinking about a particular topic or issue in the story.

Fudge-a-mania: Contrast Peter's and Fudge's feelings about Sheila Tubman. Use supporting evidence from the story.

Mr. Popper's Penguins: Describe in detail the setting of the story then compare the setting with a penguin's natural habitat.

Maniac Magee: a. Describe the attitude of Mars Bar and his friends toward white people. Provide evidence from the passage to support your view.
b. How do you think Maniac's behavior was different from that of other white kids that Mars Bar knew?

Owls in the Family: Explain the differences between this story and *Mr. Popper's Penguins*. Consider setting, character, plot, and theme.

"Rikki Tikki Tavi": a. Summarize the story in one five-sentence paragraph.
b. How might Rikki have reacted to this situation if he had been frightened instead of curious?

Where the Red Fern Grows: Describe how the author uses the crowd's reactions to build tension in the story.

Island of the Blue Dolphins: a. Explain the conflict the woman was having in deciding whether or not to make weapons. Provide supporting evidence from the passage.

Blue Willow: How does the author use Bounce's behavior to reinforce Janey's first impression of his character? Give specific examples to support your answer.

The Witch of Blackbird Pond: In the excerpt, the author uses imagery to suggest that the land was valuable. Identify these images and explain why they do or do not work.

Charlie's House: Describe Mr. Chapman's conflict about Charlie's leaving. Provide supporting evidence from the passage.

pretests

FICTION PRETEST—A "Dog-Gone" Day

A   [1]It was no fun staying behind the fence of my person's backyard while she was at school. [2]Just beyond those wood boards was a whole world of activity. [3]There were squirrels to be chased, dogs to be sniffed, fire hydrants to be marked, cats to be had! [4]What else could I do? [5]It was the call of the wild, so I jumped the fence!

B   [6]I headed for the park first. [7]The squirrels didn't even see me coming! [8]I chased them from rock to rock and hole to hole. [9]I heard a few people yell, "Get that dog on a leash!" so I decided I had better get going before I got caught. [10]My next stop was down the street from the park, where my good friend Lucky lives. [11]We greeted each other with all the proper sniffings.

C   [12]"Lucky," I said, "you can jump this gate. [13]It's only three feet high." [14]But Lucky wouldn't do it. [15]She had been a stray and wanted nothing to do with getting out of the yard.

D   [16]"You'll get lost, Blazer," she warned with a bark, but I didn't listen. [17]Instead, I kept going and going and going until nothing looked familiar. [18]I was really on my own. [19]At first, I panicked. [20]Then, being the intelligent dog that I am, I decided to play the "helpless

animal routine." [21]I found a sweet young girl walking along the street and looked up at her with my big brown eyes. [22]I played shy to gain her sympathy, then moved in a little closer. [23]Licking and tail wagging followed. [24]I ended up in her car. [25]A short time later, I was right back where I started.

E   [26]My person was not thrilled with me. [27]I was forced to use the "please forgive me routine." [28]My sad eyes and wagging tail worked like a charm. [29]Once again, everything was okay. [30]I was at home, at least until the next call of the wild!

DIRECTIONS: Choose or write the best answer to each of the following questions using the evidence presented in the passage. When required, list specific sentence numbers or paragraph letters from the story to support your answer.

1. What is the theme of the story?

   A. Getting lost is fun.
   B. Live life adventurously.
   C. Don't depend on people.
   D. Tame your wild instincts.

Give the letter of the paragraph that best supports your answer. _____

2. Where does the story begin?

   A. at the park
   B. in the backyard
   C. on the street
   D. at Lucky's house

Give the number of the sentence that best supports your answer. _____

3. Compare Lucky's view of getting out of the yard to Blazer's view.

_____

_____

_____

_____

List the numbers of the 2 sentences that best support your answer. _____,

_____

4. In general, Blazer

   A. likes to sleep during the day.
   B. knows how to get what she wants.
   C. is a little out of shape.
   D. listens to advice.

Using paragraph D, give the number of the sentence that best supports your answer. _____

5. Put the following events in their correct time order.

_____ Blazer jumps the fence.

_____ Blazer makes it home.

_____ Blazer goes to the park.

_____ Blazer gets lost.

6. In sentence 28, what does Blazer mean when she says the routine "worked like a charm"?

_____

_____

_____

_____

7. How did some people at the park feel about Blazer's running loose?

_____

_____

_____

_____

Give the number of the sentence that best supports your answer. ____

8. Give one example of what Blazer did when she needed the help of people.

_____

_____

_____

_____

Give the number of the sentence that best supports your answer. ____

9. What resulted from Blazer's meeting the young girl?

  A. Blazer was taken to the pound.
  B. Blazer was given a bath.
  C. Blazer was taken home.
  D. Blazer was punished.

Give the number of the sentence that best supports your answer. ____

10. Do you think Blazer will jump the fence again? Explain your answer.

_____

_____

_____

_____

Give the number of the sentence that best supports your answer. ____

NONFICTION PRETEST—Quartz: Our Most Common Mineral

[1]Quartz is the most common mineral on earth. [2]You can find different kinds of quartz almost everywhere.

[3]Most of the sand on beaches and deserts is actually tiny pieces of quartz. [4]Through a process called weathering,* rocks gradually break down into pebbles, then gravel, and finally become sand. [5]Quartz does not dissolve or wear away like most other rock materials. [6]So when rocks that contain quartz are weathered, only little bits of quartz are left. [7]In fact, there are few minerals harder than quartz. [8]Take a close look at some grains of sand. [9]The many different colors and shapes you see show the rocks the grains originally came from.

[10]There are many kinds of quartz. [11]Some of the best known are the quartz crystals used in watches and jewelry. [12]Most people are familiar with the clear quartz known as rock crystal. [13]Amethyst is a deep purple gemstone that is actually purple quartz. [14]The color comes from impurities** in the quartz.

[15]Flint is another common type of quartz. [16]Nearly half a million years ago,

quartz crystal

cavemen in the early Stone Age used flint to make cutting tools and weapons. [17]Although quartz is hard, it is also brittle, so it breaks easily. [18]Small pieces of the flint could be chipped away to shape a tool. [19]This shaping left a sharp edge good for cutting. [20]Examples of these flint tools have survived to the present day.

[21]There are many kinds and forms of quartz, from large crystals to tiny grains of sand. [22]It is a mineral that withstands both weather and time.

*weathering: gradually wearing down by heat, wind, and rain

**impurities: things mixed in that don't belong to the original object

DIRECTIONS: Choose or write the best answer to each of the following questions using the evidence presented in the passage. When required, list specific sentence numbers or paragraph letters from the story to support your answer.

1. Why does the quartz remain when a rock becomes weathered?

_____

_____

_____

_____

Give the number of the sentence that best supports your answer. _____

2. Why is there such variety in sand particles?

_____

_____

_____

_____

Give the number of the sentence that best supports your answer. _____

3. Why do you think flint was useful for tools and weapons?

_____

_____

_____

_____

List the numbers of the 2 sentences that best support your answer. _____

4. How does amethyst get its purple color?

_____

_____

_____

_____

Give the number of the sentence that best supports your answer. _____

5. What is the main idea of this passage?
   A. Sand comes from many different rocks.
   B. Quartz is the hardest mineral.
   C. People have used quartz for centuries.
   D. There are many kinds of quartz found worldwide.

6. How is rock crystal different from amethyst?

_____

_____

_____

_____

List the numbers of the 2 sentences that best support your answer. _____,

_____

7. Which of the following statements can you make about quartz in general?

A. Quartz crystals are colorless.
B. Quartz is made from sand.
C. Quartz is hard to find.
D. Quartz lasts a long time.

List the numbers of the 2 sentences that best support your answer. _____,

_____

8. As a rock breaks down, what stages does it go through?

A. Rock, gravel, sand, pebble
B. Rock, sand, pebble, gravel
C. Rock, gravel, pebble, sand
D. Rock, pebble, gravel, sand

Give the number of the sentence that best supports your answer. _____

9. How do rocks become sand?

_____

_____

_____

_____

Give the number of the sentence that best supports your answer. _____

literature excerpts___

1. *Fudge•a•mania*
by Judy Blume (Excerpt)

[1]"Guess what, Pete?" my brother, Fudge, said. [2]"I'm getting married tomorrow."

[3]I looked up from my baseball cards. [4]"Isn't this kind of sudden?" I asked, since Fudge is only five.

[5]"No," he said.

[6]"Well...who's the lucky bride?"

[7]"Sheila Tubman," Fudge said.

[8]I hit the floor, pretending to have fainted dead away. [9]I did a good job of it because Fudge started shaking me and shouting, "Get up, Pete!"

[10]*What's this* Pete *business?* I thought. [11]*Ever since he could talk, he's called me Pee-tah.*

[12]Then Tootsie, my sister, who's just a year and a half, danced around me singing, "Up, Pee...up."

[13]Next, Mom was beside me saying, "Peter...what happened? [14]Are you all right?"

[15]"I told him I was getting married," Fudge said. [16]"And he just fell over."

[17]"I fell over when you told me *who* you were marrying," I said.

[18]"Who are you marrying, Fudge?" Mom asked, as if we were seriously discussing his wedding.

[19]"Sheila Tubman," Fudge said.

[20]"Don't say that name around me," I told him, "or I'll faint again."

[21]"Speaking of Sheila Tubman..." Mom began.

[22]But I didn't wait for her to finish. [23]"You're making me feel very sick..." I warned.

[24]"Really, Peter..." Mom said. [25]"Aren't you overdoing it?"

[26]I clutched my stomach and moaned but Mom went right on talking.

DIRECTIONS: Choose or write the best answer to each of the following questions using the evidence presented in the passage. When required, list specific sentence numbers or paragraph letters from the story to support your answer.

1. Which of the following statements gives the main idea of the passage?
   A. Fudge is worried that something is wrong with Peter.
   B. Peter clutches his stomach and pretends to be sick when he hears the name Sheila Tubman.
   C. Peter reacts strongly to the mention of Sheila Tubman's name.
   D. Fudge talks about marrying Sheila Tubman.

2. Peter notices a change in the way his little brother speaks to him. Explain the change.

   _____

   _____

   _____

3. Which of these words best describes Peter?
   A. dramatic
   B. mean
   C. worried
   D. tired

   List the numbers of the 4 sentences that best support your answer. ____,
   ____, ____, ____,

4. What caused Peter to fall to the ground?
   A. Fudge told him he was getting married.
   B. He had a bad stomachache.
   C. Fudge told him he was marrying Sheila Tubman.
   D. He saw Sheila Tubman walk in.

   Give the number of the sentence that best supports your answer. ____

5. Put the following events in their correct order.
   ____ Mom enters the scene.
   ____ Mom says Sheila Tubman's name, and Peter holds his stomach and moans.
   ____ Peter falls to the ground, pretending to have fainted.
   ____ Fudge tells Peter he is getting married.

6. How do you think Fudge and Tootsie will react if Peter faints again?
   A. They will think he's very sick.
   B. They will be afraid and very worried.
   C. They will know he's pretending.
   D. They will play a trick on him.

   Explain your answer.

   _____

   _____

   _____

   _____

7. Which sentence from the passage makes you think that Fudge is not actually getting married?
   A. I hit the floor, pretending to have fainted dead away.
   B. "Isn't this kind of sudden?" I asked, since Fudge is only five.
   C. "Well...who's the lucky bride?"
   D. "Speaking of Sheila Tubman..." Mom began.

2. *Mr. Popper's Penguins*
by Richard Atwater (Excerpt)

A [1]The penguins all loved to climb the stairs that led up to the kitchen, and never knew when to stop unless they found the kitchen door closed. [2]Then, of course, they would turn around and toboggan down the steps again. [3]This made rather a curious noise sometimes, when Mrs. Popper was working in the kitchen, but she got used to it, as she had got used to so many other strange things this winter.

B [4]The freezing plant that Mr. Popper had got for the penguins downstairs was a large and good one. [5]It made very large blocks of ice, instead of small ice cubes, so that soon Mr. Popper had made a sort of ice castle down there for the twelve penguins to live in and climb over.

C [6]Mr. Popper also dug a large hole in the cellar floor and made a swimming and diving pool for the birds. [7]From time to time he would throw live fish into the pool for the penguins to dive for. [8]They found this very refreshing, because, to tell the truth, they had got a little tired of canned shrimps. [9]The live fish were specially ordered and were brought all the way from the coast in tank cars and glass boxes to 432 Proudfoot Avenue. [10]Unfortunately, they were quite expensive.

D [11]It was nice that there were so many penguins because when two of them (usually Nelson and Columbus) got into a fight, and began to spar at each other with their flippers, the ten other penguins would all crowd around to watch the fight and make encouraging remarks. [12]This made a very interesting little scene.

E [13]Mr. Popper also flooded a part of the cellar floor for an ice rink, and here the penguins often drilled like a sort of small army, in fantastic marching movements and parades around the ice. [14]The penguin Louisa seemed especially fond of leading these marching drills. [15]It was quite a sight to see them, after Mr. Popper had the idea of training Louisa to hold a small American flag in her beak while she proudly led the solemn parades.

DIRECTIONS: Choose or write the best answer to each of the following questions using the evidence presented in the passage. When required, list specific sentence numbers or paragraph letters from the story to support your answer.

1. This story could best be classified as a
   A. mystery.
   B. comedy.
   C. adventure.
   D. science fiction.

2. In sentence 13, how did the author use figurative language to describe the penguins?

   _____

   _____

   _____

   _____

3. In sentence 11, what does the word *spar* mean?
   A. to wave
   B. to swim
   C. to box
   D. to argue

4. Which of the following statements can you make about penguins in general?
   A. Penguins like to be alone.
   B. Penguins will eat anything.
   C. Penguins are easily trained.
   D. Penguins like a cold environment.

5. What did Mr. Popper feed the penguins?

   _____

   _____

   _____

6. Which of the following actions of the penguins supports the idea that their behavior was unusual?
   A. The penguins would dive for live fish.
   B. The penguins liked to climb over the blocks of ice.
   C. The penguin Louisa liked to lead the marching drills.
   D. The penguins liked to climb up the stairs and toboggan down them.

   Give the number of the sentence that best supports your answer. ____

7. From paragraphs B and C, give three examples that support the conclusion that the penguins were expensive to care for.

   _____

   _____

   _____

   _____

   _____

   _____

   _____

   Give the number of the sentence that best supports each example. ____,
   ____, ____

3. *Maniac Magee*
by Jerry Spinelli (Excerpt)

A [1]"Where you goin'?" he said. [2]Candy bar flakes flew from his mouth.

B [3]"I'm looking for Sycamore Street," said Maniac. [4]"Do you know where it is?"

C [5]"Yeah, I know where it is."

D [6]Maniac waited, but the kid said nothing more.

E [7]"Well, uh, do you think you could tell me where it is?"

F [8]Stone was softer than the kid's glare.

G [9]"No."

H [10]Maniac looked around. [11]Other kids had stopped playing, were staring.

I [12]Someone called: "Do 'im, Mars!"

J [13]Someone else: "Waste 'im!"

K [14]The kid, as you probably guessed by now, was none other than Mars Bar Thompson. [15]Mars Bar heard the calls, and the stone got harder. [16]Then suddenly he stopped glaring, suddenly he was smiling. [17]He held up the candy bar, an inch from Maniac's lips. [18]"Wanna bite?"

L [19]Maniac couldn't figure. [20]"You sure?"

M [21]"Yeah, go ahead. [22]Take a bite."

N [23]Maniac shrugged, took the Mars Bar, bit off a chunk, and handed it back. [24]"Thanks."

O [25]Dead silence along the street. [26]The kid had done the unthinkable, he had chomped on one of Mars's own bars. [27]Not only that, but white kids just didn't put their mouths where black kids had had theirs, be it soda bottles, spoons, or candy bars. [28]And the kid hadn't even gone for the unused end; he had chomped right over Mars Bar's own bite marks.

P [29]Mars Bar was confused. [30]Who *was* this kid? [31]*What* was this kid?

DIRECTIONS: Choose or write the best answer to each of the following questions using the evidence presented in the passage. When required, list specific sentence numbers or paragraph letters from the story to support your answer.

1. List two sentences from the passage that best support the idea that Maniac was not welcome in the neighborhood.

   Sentences ____, ____

2. What does the author mean when he states "Stone was softer than the kid's glare"?

   A. Stone *is* actually softer than the glare of an angry kid.
   B. The kid's glaring eyes were gray like stone.
   C. The kid's glare was really intense.
   D. The kid's glare was beginning to soften.

3. What does the author mean when he writes "Mars Bar heard the calls, <u>and the stone got harder</u>"?

   _____

   _____

   _____

   _____

4. Why was Maniac confused when Mars Bar quit glaring at him and then offered him a bite of his candy bar?

   _____

   _____

   _____

   _____

5. What was a key event in the story?
   A. Maniac bit Mars Bar's candy bar.
   B. The kids stopped playing.
   C. Mars Bar glared at Maniac.
   D. Mars Bar didn't answer Maniac.

6. What do you think Mars Bar was doing when he offered his candy bar to Maniac?
   A. He was trying to get rid of his candy bar.
   B. He wanted to share his candy bar with Maniac.
   C. He was testing Maniac to see what he'd do.
   D. He wanted to prove he didn't mind a white kid eating his candy bar.

   Give the letter of the paragraph that best supports your answer. ____

7. What two things caused Mars Bar to become confused?

   _____

   _____

   _____

   Give the number of the sentence that best supports each example. ____, ____

4. *Owls in the Family*
by Farley Mowat (Excerpt)

A   [1]Mother and Dad and I were having dinner. [2]The dining room windows were open because it had been such a hot day. [3]All of a sudden there was a great *swooooosh* of wings—and there, on the window sill, sat Wol. [4]Before any of us had time to move, he gave a leap and landed on the floor beside my chair. [5]And he hadn't come empty-handed. [6]Clutched in his talons was an enormous skunk. [7]The skunk was dead, but that didn't help matters much because, before he died, he had managed to soak himself and Wol with his own special brand of perfume.

B   [8]"Hoo-hoohoohoo-HOO!" Wol said proudly.

C   [9]Which probably meant: "Mind if I join you? [10]I've brought my supper with me."

D   [11]Nobody stopped to answer. [12]We three people were already stampeding through the door of the dining room, coughing and choking. [13]Wol had to eat his dinner by himself.

E   [14]It was two weeks before we could use the dining room again, and when Mother sent the rug and drapes to the cleaners, the man who owned the shop phoned her right back and wanted to know if she was trying to ruin him.

F   [15]Wol didn't smell so sweet either, but he couldn't understand why he was so unpopular all of a sudden. [16]His feelings must have been hurt by the way everybody kept trying to avoid him. [17]After two or three days, when even I wouldn't go near him, or let him come near me, he became very unhappy. [18]Then an idea must have come into his funny head. [19]He must have decided we were mad at him because he hadn't shared his skunk with us! [20]So one day he went down to the riverbank and caught a second skunk, and brought it home for us.

G   [21]By this time he was so soaked in skunk oil that you could smell him a block away. [22]Some of our neighbors complained about it, and so finally my father had to give Wol a bath in about a gallon of tomato juice. [23]Tomato juice is the only thing that will wash away the smell of skunk.

H   [24]Poor Wol! [25]By the time Dad was through with him he looked like a rag mop that had been dipped in ketchup. [26]But he got the idea, and he never again brought his skunks home to us.

DIRECTIONS: Choose or write the best answer to each of the following questions using the evidence presented in the passage. When required, list specific sentence numbers or paragraph letters from the story to support your answer.

1. Why did the cleaner think Mother was trying to ruin him?

   _____

   _____

   _____

   _____

   Give the number of the sentence that best supports your answer. ____

2. Which of the following sentences best describes the family's reaction to Wol's arrival with the skunk?

   A. They were thrilled.
   B. They were angry with Wol.
   C. They thought it was funny.
   D. They were surprised.

   List the numbers of the 3 sentences that best support your answer. ____,

   ____, ____

3. Which of the following explains why the family was unable to use the dining room for two weeks?

   A. Wol's supper was still lying there.
   B. The room still smelled of skunk.
   C. It was too hot to eat in there.
   D. Mother wanted to wait for the rug and drapes.

4. In sentence 3, why is it more effective for the author to use *swooooosh* to describe Wol's arrival than to simply say he flew in the window?

   _____

   _____

   _____

5. Which of the following is the most likely reason that Wol never brought a skunk home again?

   A. He didn't want the neighbors to get mad at him.
   B. He decided to bring home squirrels instead.
   C. He didn't want another tomato juice bath.
   D. He didn't want to mess up the house.

   Give the number of the sentence that best supports your answer. ____

6. Based on his behavior, you can conclude that Wol

   A. did not like getting dirty.
   B. wanted to please the family.
   C. was afraid of people.
   D. did not like to share.

   List the numbers of the 3 sentences that best support your answer. ____,

   ____, ____

7. In paragraph F, the narrator presents Wol's point of view in human terms. Give one example of how the narrator thought Wol was feeling.

   _____

   _____

   _____

   _____

   Give the number of the sentence that best supports your example. ____

5. "Rikki-tikki Tavi" from *The Jungle Book* by Rudyard Kipling (Excerpt)

[1]One day, a high summer flood washed him out of the burrow where he lived with his father and mother, and carried him, kicking and clucking, down a roadside ditch. [2]He found a little wisp of grass floating there, and clung to it till he lost his senses. [3]When he revived, he was lying in the hot sun on the middle of a garden path, very draggled indeed, and a small boy was saying, "Here's a dead mongoose. [4]Let's have a funeral."

[5]"No," said his mother, "let's take him in and dry him. [6]Perhaps he isn't really dead."

[7]They took him into the house, and a big man picked him up between his finger and thumb and said he was not dead but half choked. [8]So they wrapped him in cotton wool, and warmed him over a little fire, and he opened his eyes and sneezed.

[9]"Now," said the big man (he was an Englishman who had just moved into the bungalow), "don't frighten him, and we'll see what he'll do."

[10]It is the hardest thing in the world to frighten a mongoose, because he is eaten up from nose to tail with curiosity. [11]The motto of all the mongoose family is "Run and find out," and Rikki-tikki was a true mongoose. [12]He looked at the cotton wool, decided that it was not good to eat, ran all around the table, sat up and put his fur in order, scratched himself, and jumped on the small boy's shoulder.

[13]"Don't be frightened, Teddy," said his father. [14]"That's his way of making friends."

[15]"Ouch! He's tickling under my chin," said Teddy.

[16]Rikki-tikki looked down between the boy's collar and neck, snuffed at his ear, and climbed down to the floor, where he sat rubbing his nose.

[17]"Good gracious," said Teddy's mother, "and that's a wild creature! [18]I suppose he's so tame because we've been kind to him."

[19]"All mongooses are like that," said her husband. [20]"If Teddy doesn't pick him up by the tail, or try to put him in a cage, he'll run in and out of the house all day long. [21]Let's give him something to eat."

[22]They gave him a little piece of raw meat. [23]Rikki-tikki liked it immensely, and when it was finished he went out into the veranda and sat in the sunshine and fluffed up his fur to make it dry to the roots. [24]Then he felt better.

DIRECTIONS: Choose or write the best answer to each of the following questions using the evidence presented in the passage. When required, list specific sentence numbers or paragraph letters from the story to support your answer.

1. Why do you think the boy thought the mongoose was dead?

   _____

   _____

   Give the number of the sentence that best supports your answer. ____

2. What do you think the author means in sentence 10 when he says a mongoose is "eaten up from nose to tail with curiosity"?
   A. He is interested in everything.
   B. He is afraid of people.
   C. He is always looking for food.
   D. He is full of fleas.

3. What did Teddy's father think Rikki-tikki was trying to do when he jumped on Teddy's shoulders?

   _____

   _____

   _____

   Give the number of the sentence that best supports your answer. ____

4. What did Rikki-tikki do that made Teddy's mother think he was tame?

   _____

   _____

   _____

   _____

   List the numbers of the 2 sentences that best support your answer. ____, ____

5. In sentence 2, the author says that Rikki-tikki "lost his senses." What does this mean?
   A. He lost his way.
   B. He fell asleep.
   C. He was unconscious.
   D. He went crazy.

   Give the number of the sentence that best supports your answer. ____

6. Why do you think Rikki-tikki felt better after he fluffed up his fur?

   _____

   _____

   _____

   Give the number of the sentence that best supports your answer. ____

6. *Where the Red Fern Grows*
by Wilson Rawls (Excerpt)

A   [1]Mr. Kyle and I were told to go to one end of the table. [2]Our dogs were placed at the other end. [3]Mr. Kyle snapped his fingers and called to his dog.

B   [4]The big hound started walking toward his master. [5]What a beautiful sight it was. [6]He walked like a king. [7]His body was stiff and straight, his head high in the air, his large muscles quivered and jerked under his glossy coat, but something went wrong. [8]Just before he reached the end, he broke his stride, turned, and jumped down from the table.

C   [9]A low murmur ran through the crowd.

D   [10]It was my turn. [11]Three times I tried to call to Little Ann. [12]Words just wouldn't come out. [13]My throat was too dry. [14]The vocal cords refused to work, but I could snap my fingers. [15]That was all I needed. [16]She started toward me. [17]I held my breath. [18]There was silence all around me.

E   [19]As graceful as any queen, with her head high in the air, and her long red tail arched in a perfect rainbow, my little dog walked down the table. [20]With her warm gray eyes staring straight at me, on she came. [21]Walking up to me, she laid her head on my shoulder. [22]As I put my arms around her, the crowd exploded.

F   [23]During the commotion I felt hands slapping me on the back, and heard the word congratulations time after time. [24]The head judge came over and made a speech. [25]Handing me a small silver cup, he said, "Congratulations, son. [26]It was justly won."

DIRECTIONS: Choose or write the best answer to each of the following questions using the evidence presented in the passage. When required, list specific sentence numbers or paragraph letters from the story to support your answer.

1. In sentence 19, the author uses a simile and a metaphor to describe Little Ann. Write one of these below and identify which kind of figurative language it is.

   _____

   _____

   _____

   _____

2. Choose the two sentences that best show how the crowd supported the boy and his dog.

   A. During the commotion I felt hands slapping me on the back...
   B. There was silence all around me.
   C. As I put my arms around her, the crowd exploded.
   D. A low murmur ran through the crowd.

3. Which word best describes the main feeling the author is trying to create?

   A. enthusiasm
   B. tension
   C. indifference
   D. sadness

   Explain your answer.

   _____

   _____

   _____

4. What causes Little Ann to start walking across the table?

   A. The crowd murmurs quietly.
   B. The boy snaps his fingers.
   C. The boy calls to her.
   D. The big hound barks.

   Give the number of the sentence that best supports your answer. ____

5. Compare the big hound's performance to Little Ann's.

   _____

   _____

   _____

   _____

   List the numbers of the 3 sentences that best support your answer. ____, ____, ____

6. Give two examples from paragraph D that suggest the boy might be nervous.

   _____

   _____

   _____

   _____

   Give the number of the sentence that best supports each example. ____, ____

7. In sentence 23, what does the word *commotion* mean?

   A. excitement
   B. calm
   C. contest
   D. discussion

7. *Island of the Blue Dolphins* by Scott O'Dell (Excerpt)

A [1]That night they came back to the headland. [2]I had buried what was left of my supper, but they dug it up, snarling and fighting among themselves over the scraps. [3]Then they began to pace back and forth at the foot of the rock, sniffing the air, for they could smell my tracks and knew that I was somewhere near.

B [4]For a long time I lay on the rock while they trotted around below me. [5]The rock was high and they could not climb it, but I was still fearful. [6]As I lay there I wondered what would happen to me if I went against the law of our tribe which forbade the making of weapons by women—if I did not think of it at all and made those things which I must have to protect myself.

C [7]Would the four winds blow in from the four directions of the world and smother me as I made the weapons? [8]Or would the earth tremble, as many said, and bury me beneath its falling rocks? [9]Or, as others said, would the sea rise over the island in a terrible flood? [10]Would the weapons break in my hands at the moment when my life was in danger, which is what my father had said?

D [11]I thought about these things for two days and on the third night when the wild dogs returned to the rock, I made up my mind that no matter what befell me I would make the weapons. [12]In the morning I set about it, though I felt very fearful.

DIRECTIONS: Choose or write the best answer to each of the following questions using the evidence presented in the passage. When required, list specific sentence numbers or paragraph letters from the story to support your answer.

1. Which of the following statements best shows the main conflict in the passage?
   A. They snarl and fight among themselves over the scraps.
   B. She wonders what will happen if she goes against the laws.
   C. She decides to make weapons.
   D. She wonders how she will find food.

2. In paragraph A, who do you think are "they"?

   _____

   Give the number of the sentence that best supports your answer. ____

3. The woman decides to make the weapons because she probably believes
   A. defending herself is more important than her tribe's laws.
   B. she is above her tribe's laws.
   C. her tribe would understand if they found out.
   D. her tribe will never find out.

   Give the number of the sentence that best supports your answer. ____

4. Give two examples from paragraph C that explain why the woman was afraid to make weapons.

   _____

   _____

   _____

5. Why was the woman fearful in Paragraph A?

   _____

   _____

   _____

   _____

   List the numbers of the 2 sentences that best support your answer. ____, ____

6. What does the rock provide for the woman?

   _____

   _____

   Give the letter of the paragraph that best supports your answer. ____

7. What can you tell about the tribe based on the woman's concerns?
   A. The tribe believes the earth is flat.
   B. The tribe believes man has power over a woman's ability to make weapons.
   C. The tribe is watching what the woman is doing.
   D. The tribe believes in forces that respond to human misbehavior.

   Give the letter of the paragraph that best supports your answer. ____

8. What does the woman's decision tell you about her character?
   A. She is unconcerned.
   B. She is brave, but fearful.
   C. She is unsure of herself.
   D. She is fearless.

   List the numbers of the 2 sentences that best support your answer. ____, ____

8. *Blue Willow*
by Doris Gates (Excerpt)

A [1]"Hello buddy," he called jauntily as Mr. Larkin rose and started toward the open door. [2]"When did you move in?"

B [3]It was still broad daylight and Janey had plenty of opportunity to study their visitor. [4]And what she saw she did not like. [5]She couldn't decide exactly what there was about him to make her feel distrust. [6]"It must be his eyes," she concluded. [7]They moved shiftily about, never seeming able to rivet themselves on any one thing for more than a second. [8]Moreover, his attitude seemed to indicate plainly that he held the destiny of the Larkins in the hollow of his very dirty right hand. [9]The manner with which he stalked boldly into the house and looked casually about couldn't have made it any plainer. [10]Janey had the feeling, even, that if there were anything in sight which he considered worthy of his interest it would become his on the spot. [11]For once, she was extremely thankful that the blue willow plate was safely out of sight.

C [12]"Something I can do for you?" [13]Janey could tell that Dad was indignant. [14]His voice was hard and even. [15]Evidently he felt exactly as she did toward this intruder.

D [16]"I'll say there is," returned the stranger. [17]"You can just hand over five dollars a month rent for this shack. [18]Rent starting from the day you moved in, whenever that was."

E [19]"We've been here a week," said Mr. Larkin.

F [20]The man narrowed his eyes for an instant while he thought rapidly. [21]"Yeh," he finally said, "I guess that's about right. [22]The last time I was out this way, there wasn't nobody here."

G [23]Mr. Larkin, ignoring this remark, walked away to speak in low tones to his wife, who had remained at the stove, her back to the room. [24]Now he faced that man again and said, reaching into his pocket and drawing forth a buckskin bag:

H [25]"Here's your money, and I'll take a receipt."

I [26]For just a second the man hesitated, then [27]"That ain't necessary, buddy. [28]I'm Bounce Reyburn, everybody knows me around here."

J [29]"Just the same," said Mr. Larkin quietly, but drawing up the strings of the buckskin bag, "I'll take a receipt from you, or you won't take any money from me."

K [30]An ugly light came into Bounce's eyes, and Janey, catching it, felt a queer little shiver run along her spine. [31]The glint remained for the merest instant and then Bounce shrugged and grinned, a little too broadly, Janey thought.

L [32]"O.K.," he said, "give me a scrap of paper, somebody, and I'll put my John Henry* on it."

*John Henry: signature

DIRECTIONS: Choose or write the best answer to each of the following questions using the evidence presented in the passage. When required, list specific sentence numbers or paragraph letters from the story to support your answer.

1. In sentence 7, what does the word *rivet* mean?

   A. find
   B. stay put
   C. balance
   D. move about

2. From Janey's description of the visitor in paragraph B, how do you think the visitor felt towards the family?

   A. He felt friendly towards them.
   B. He felt threatened by them.
   C. He felt power over them.
   D. He felt sorry for them.

   List the numbers of the 3 sentences that best support your answer. ____,
   ____, ____

3. In sentence 30, what do you think is the "ugly light" Janey sees in Bounce's eyes?

   _____

   _____

   _____

   _____

4. In sentence 29, why do you think Mr. Larkin wanted a receipt for the money?

   A. He did not trust Bounce.
   B. He always kept receipts.
   C. He wanted to make Bounce angry.
   D. He needed Bounce's signature.

   Give the number of the sentence that best supports your answer. ____

5. What was it about the visitor's eyes that made Janey distrust him?

   A. He seemed to be looking for something.
   B. He squinted a lot.
   C. He never looked at anything for very long.
   D. He stared at her.

   Give the number of the sentence that best supports your answer. ____

6. What might have made Bounce finally agree to give Mr. Larkin a receipt?

   A. He planned to sign a different name.
   B. He didn't really mind giving Mr. Larkin a receipt.
   C. He agreed with Mr. Larkin that a receipt was important.
   D. He thought that Mr. Larkin wouldn't change his mind.

   Give the number of the sentence that best supports your answer. ____

7. In sentence 11, why do you think Janey was glad that the blue willow plate was hidden?

   _____

   _____

   _____

   _____

   Give the number of the sentence that best supports your answer. ____

9. *The Witch of Blackbird Pond*
by Elizabeth George Speare (Excerpt)

A [1]"After the keen still days of September, the October sun filled the world with mellow warmth. [2]Before Kit's eyes a miracle took place, for which she was totally unprepared. [3]She stood in the doorway of her uncle's house and held her breath with wonder. [4]The maple tree in front of the doorstep burned like a gigantic red torch. [5]The oaks along the roadway glowed yellow and bronze. [6]The fields stretched like a carpet of jewels, emerald and topaz and garnet. [7]Everywhere she walked the color shouted and sang around her. [8]The dried brown leaves crackled beneath her feet and gave off a delicious smoky fragrance. [9]No one had ever told her about autumn in New England. [10]The excitement of it beat in her blood. [11]Every morning she woke with a new confidence and buoyancy she could not explain. [12]In October any wonderful unexpected thing might be possible.

B [13]"As the days grew shorter and colder, this new sense of expectancy increased and her heightened awareness seemed to give new significance to every common thing around her. [14]Otherwise she might have overlooked a small scene that, once noticed, she would never entirely forget. [15]Going through the shed door one morning, with her arms full of linens to spread on the grass, Kit halted, wary as always, at the sight of her uncle. [16]He was standing not far from the house, looking out toward the river, his face half turned from her. [17]He did not notice her.

[18]He simply stood, idle for one rare moment, staring at the golden fields. [19]The flaming color was dimmed now. [20]Great masses of curled brown leaves lay tangled in the dried grass, and the branches that thrust against the graying sky were almost bare. [21]As Kit watched, her uncle bent slowly and scooped up a handful of brown dirt from the garden patch at his feet, and stood holding it with a curious reverence, as though it were some priceless substance. [22]As it crumbled through his fingers his hand convulsed in a sudden passionate gesture. [23]Kit backed through the door and closed it softly. [24]She felt as though she had eavesdropped. [25]When she had hated and feared her uncle for so long, why did it suddenly hurt to think of that lonely defiant figure in the garden?"

DIRECTIONS: Choose or write the best answer to each of the following questions using the evidence presented in the passage. When required, list specific sentence numbers or paragraph letters from the story to support your answer.

1. What do you think Kit's uncle is doing when she sees him?

   A. crying
   B. playing
   C. working
   D. thinking

   Give the number of the sentence that best supports your answer. ____

2. Which of the following does the author describe with a simile?

   A. the sun (sentence 1)
   B. maple tree (sentence 4)
   C. oak trees (sentence 5)
   D. brown leaves (sentence 8)

3. Which of these sentences from the passage best expresses the main idea?

   A. "She felt as though she had eavesdropped."
   B. "No one had ever told her about autumn in New England."
   C. "In October any wonderful unexpected thing might be possible."
   D. "Before Kit's eyes a miracle took place, for which she was totally unprepared."

4. How had Kit felt about her uncle before she saw him in the garden?

   A. She had been scared of him.
   B. She had been jealous of him.
   C. She had been grateful to him.
   D. She had been worried about him.

   Give the number of the sentence that best supports your answer. ____

5. Which of these events happens first?

   A. Kit sees her uncle.
   B. Kit closes the shed door.
   C. Kit gathers up linens.
   D. Kit stands in the doorway of the house.

6. How do you think Kit felt after watching her uncle scoop up the dirt and squeeze it with a passionate gesture?

   A. She hated and feared him.
   B. She was worried about him.
   C. She felt sympathy toward him.
   D. She wished she hadn't seen anything.

   Give the number of the sentence that best supports your answer. ____

7. In paragraph A, which of the following is described as though it were human?

   A. leaves
   B. color
   C. maple tree
   D. fields

   Give the number of the sentence that best supports your answer. ____

8. In paragraph A, what do you think was Kit's first reaction to the changes in her surroundings?

   A. amazement
   B. surprise
   C. concern
   D. fright

   List the numbers of the 2 sentences that best support your answer. ____,

   ____

10. *Charlie's House*
by Clyde Robert Bulla (Excerpt)

A   [1]When he had his own farm, he would still be near the Chapmans, he thought. [2]He would always help them if they needed him.

B   [3]Charlie came to know the neighbors. [4]He went to barn dances with other young people. [5]He listened to the fiddle music and watched the dancers and pretended he was dancing, too.

C   [6]When the rivers and ponds froze over, he went to moonlight skating parties. [7]But almost every night he was at home with the Chapmans. [8]Mistress Chapman was teaching him to read and write.

***

D   [9]A visitor came—a man named Oliver Greer. [10]He was Master Chapman's cousin from Carolina. [11]He had come north on business.

E   [12]He was slim and dark, with a neat, black mustache. [13]He dressed like a gentleman, and he seemed proud of the way he looked.

F   [14]He thought the Chapmans were much too good to Charlie.

G   [15]"That boy thinks he's one of the family," he said.

H   [16]While Master Greer was there, Charlie never ate at the table with the others.

I   [17]Master Greer gave him work to do, and he never called him by name. [18]"Boy," he would say, "shine my boots. [19]Boy, light my pipe."

J   [20]"Do as he says, Charlie," said Mistress Chapman. [21]"It won't be for long."

K   [22]But Master Greer stayed on and on. [23]Every night he and Master Chapman sat up, drinking and playing cards.

L   [24]"I do wish he would go," said Mistress Chapman. [25]"Sometimes I'm so afraid—"

M   [26]There was a change in Master Chapman. [27]He took to staying in his room all morning. [28]He looked ill. [29]He often stumbled when he walked.

N   [30]Master Greer had been there almost a month when Mistress Chapman called Charlie into the kitchen. [31]She said, "Master Greer is leaving today."

O   [32]He thought she would be glad. [33]Instead she began to cry.

P   [34]Master Chapman came in. [35]His face was gray, and his hands shook. [36]"Charlie, I must talk to you."

Q   [37]"Yes sir," said Charlie.

R   [38]"My cousin is going home," said Master Chapman, "and you—you are going with him."

S   [39]Charlie heard the words, but he did not believe them. [40]He waited.

T   [41]"You are going with him," Master Chapman said again. [42]"I lost you. [43]I lost you in a game of cards."

U   [44]"But you—" began Charlie.

V   [45]Master Chapman turned away from him. [46]"I'm sorry."

W   [47]"I came to work for *you*," said Charlie. [48]"*You* bought my bond."

X   [49]"That's true, but Cousin Oliver won it from me. [50]The bond will be the same. [51]You'll still have your land when you've worked for it—only you'll work for him instead," Master Chapman said. [52]"Now go. [53]Cousin Oliver is waiting."

DIRECTIONS: Choose or write the best answer to each of the following questions using the evidence presented in the passage. When required, list specific sentence numbers or paragraph letters from the story to support your answer.

1. Which of the following supports the idea that Master Greer thought he was better than Charlie?

   A. He gave him work to do.
   B. He didn't call him by name.
   C. He dressed like a gentleman.
   D. He treated Charlie like family.

   List the numbers of the 2 sentences that best support your answer. ____,

   ____

2. Give an example of how Master Chapman changed.

   _____

   _____

   Give the number of the sentence that best supports your example. ____.

3. Which of the following caused Charlie's having to leave?

   A. Master Chapman's gambling loss.
   B. Master Chapman's kindness to Charlie.
   C. Master Chapman's ill health.
   D. Master Chapman's apology to Charlie.

   List the numbers of the 2 sentences that best support your answer. ____,

   ____

4. Which was a key event in the story?

   A. Charlie came to know the neighbors.
   B. Charlie went moonlight skating.
   C. Master Greer came to visit.
   D. Master Greer bought Charlie's bond.

   Give the number of the sentence that best supports your answer. ____

5. Compare Charlie's life before and after Master Greer came.

   _____

   _____

   _____

   _____

   List the letters of the 4 paragraphs that best support your answer. ____,

   ____, ____, ____

6. Charlie is a bonded servant. Which of the following statements can you make based on Charlie's experience? A bonded servant

   A. could make his or her own decisions.
   B. was controlled by whoever owned his or her bond.
   C. was always considered part of the family.
   D. was always dependable.

7. From the information given, which of the following is true about a bond?

   A. You can buy land in exchange for working.
   B. You are given land after you work for it.
   C. You become a landowner right away.
   D. You remain a servant all your life.

   Give the number of the sentence that best supports your answer. ____

fiction _____

11. Iggy
by Cheryl Block

[1]Iggy, my pet garter snake, is a lot of fun, but he always seems to be getting into trouble. [2]I never know where I'm going to find him next. [3]He has his own special bed in my room. [4]It's a cardboard box with a towel on the bottom to keep him warm. [5]But Iggy is always climbing out of his box to explore.

[6]Iggy likes warm places. [7]He loves to lie beneath the window when the sun is shining. [8]One day, he discovered the clothes dryer. [9]Mom had just finished unloading some laundry, and the dryer was nice and warm. [10]Iggy wriggled inside and went to sleep. [11]His pleasant nap was quickly cut short, however. [12]Mom didn't see him curled up inside and proceeded to pile another load of clothes in the dryer and turn it on. [13]Poor Iggy! [14]He was tossed and tumbled all around. [15]When Mom opened the door, Iggy quickly slithered out. [16]I could hear Mom's scream clear out in the backyard. [17]Iggy seemed okay after his tumble in the dryer, but I did notice that he was going around in circles more for the next few days. [18]He never did go in the dryer again.

DIRECTIONS: Choose or write the best answer to each of the following questions using the evidence presented in the passage. When required, list specific sentence numbers or paragraph letters from the story to support your answer.

1. What are two things that Iggy does that get him into trouble?

_____

_____

_____

_____

   List the numbers of the 2 sentences that best support your answer. ____, ____

2. Why did Iggy climb inside the dryer?

_____

_____

_____

_____

   List the numbers of the 2 sentences that best support your answer. ____, ____

3. In sentence 17, why do you think Iggy was going in circles more?

_____

_____

_____

_____

4. Iggy's actions show that he is
   A. shy.
   B. curious.
   C. friendly.
   D. noisy.

   List the numbers of the 2 sentences that best support your answer. ____, ____

5. What happened just before Mom turned on the dryer?
   A. Iggy wriggled into the dryer.
   B. Mom piled in a load of clothes.
   C. Iggy went to sleep.
   D. Mom unloaded some laundry.

6. Why do you think Mom screamed when Iggy came out of the dryer?
   A. She doesn't like snakes.
   B. She was startled by Iggy.
   C. She thought the clothes were ruined.
   D. She had to redo the laundry.

   Give the number of the sentence that best supports your answer. ____

12. Caught White-Handed
by Cheryl Block

A   [1]Police today reported the capture of the man who has been robbing doughnut shops in the area. [2]The robber would break in during the early morning hours while employees were getting ready to open shop. [3]He would tie up the workers, then empty the cash register and steal a bag of freshly made doughnuts. [4]By the time customers found the workers and called police, the robber was long gone.

B   [5]There were still two stores in the area that the robber hadn't hit. [6]Police decided to set a trap for him. [7]They knew he always stole a bag of powdered sugar doughnuts. [8]Police coated several dollar bills with a special glue that left the surface slightly sticky. [9]When the robber touched the money with his sugarcoated fingers, the sugar would stick to the bills. [10]The trap was now ready.

C   [11]Two days later, the robber struck again. [12]Police had told store owners in the area to be on the lookout for the sugary bills. [13]The next day, police caught their man at a local grocery store. [14]He had paid for his groceries in cash, and the clerk had noticed white spots on all the bills.

D   [15]As he was led away, the robber said, "My mother always said sugar was bad for you."

DIRECTIONS: Choose or write the best answer to each of the following questions using the evidence presented in the passage. When required, list specific sentence numbers or paragraph letters from the story to support your answer.

1. What were the white spots on the bills?

_____

_____

_____

_____

Give the number of the sentence that best supports your answer. ____

2. What do you think the robber meant in sentence 15 when he quoted his mother?
   A. He was overweight from eating doughnuts.
   B. He became a robber because he liked doughnuts.
   C. He was unhealthy because he ate too much sugar.
   D. He got caught because of the powdered sugar doughnuts.

List the numbers of the 2 sentences that best support your answer. ____,

____

3. The police coated the money with glue so
   A. the bills would stick to the robber's fingers.
   B. the robber would leave sugar on the bills.
   C. the robber would leave his fingerprints.
   D. the robber wouldn't be able to pick up the bills.

Give the number of the sentence that best supports your answer. ____

4. From the time they set up the trap, how long did it take the police to capture the robber?

_____

_____

_____

_____

List the numbers of the 2 sentences that best support your answer. ____,

____

5. Which moral is best supported by the story?
   A. Crime doesn't pay.
   B. Life is short; eat dessert first.
   C. Life is full of sticky situations.
   D. Doughnuts are bad for you.

List the letters of the 2 paragraphs that best support your answer. ____,

____

6. What did the thief do to make sure he wasn't caught while robbing?

_____

_____

_____

_____

List the numbers of the 2 sentences that best support your answer. ____,

____

13. Letter from the Mother Lode
by Carrie Beckwith

Pacific Ocean

Daniel's ocean route

Sacramento

San Francisco

CALIFORNIA

December 5, 1849

Dearest Lillian,

A [1]I have finally arrived in Gold Country after nearly eight months of sailing, three of which were spent on land in South America during poor weather. [2]I am now living in a makeshift tent in Sacramento along a vein of quartz known as the Mother Lode. [3]The gold is rich here, and I am finding almost $20 worth every day! [4]However, food and clothing are unreasonably high—nearly $10 for a dozen eggs and $40 for a shirt! [5]For some men, the costs are enough to break them, and they have gone home penniless. [6]For more successful miners, these costs are only a drop in the bucket.

B [7]I work every day but Sunday, from sunup to sundown. [8]Three of us sit by the river with what is called a cradle, a wooden box that is set on rockers. [9]On top of the box lies a tray with wooden slats. [10]One man shovels gravel from the river bed into the tray and another pours water over the gravel. [11]The large rocks are caught in the tray, and the rest flows down to the cradle. [12]It is my job to then shake the cradle until the dirt has washed away, and all that is left is the precious gold. [13]We do this all day, and it is exhausting.

C [14]When we are not working, we are playing cards or chess. [15]Other men prefer the fights—boxing, wrestling, even animal fights. [16]They are bloody, horrible things to watch, but it is wild here and so too are the games.

D [17]I hope it will not be long before I can afford to send for you and little Joe. [18]I look forward to seeing you again.

All my love,

Daniel

DIRECTIONS: Choose or write the best answer to each of the following questions using the evidence presented in the passage. When required, list specific sentence numbers or paragraph letters from the story to support your answer.

1. Give two examples of some of the hardships Daniel is *now* experiencing.

   _____

   _____

   _____

   _____

   Give the number of the sentence that best supports each example. ____, ____

2. In paragraph B, what happens just after the men have put the gravel and water into the tray?

   _____

   _____

   _____

3. What has caused some miners to go home penniless?

   _____

   _____

   _____

   Give the number of the sentence that best supports your answer. ____

4. In what region of the country is Daniel living?
   A. North
   B. Midwest
   C. South
   D. West

5. During what period in American history is the writer of the letter living?
   A. The Revolutionary War
   B. The Civil War
   C. The Gold Rush
   D. The Dust Bowl

   Using paragraph A, list the numbers of the 3 sentences that best support your answer. ____, ____, ____

6. What can you say about Daniel?
   A. He is rich.
   B. He is bored.
   C. He is frightened.
   D. He is hard working.

   List the numbers of the 3 sentences that best support your answer. ____, ____, ____

7. In sentence 6, what does the phrase "a drop in the bucket" mean?

   _____

   _____

   _____

   _____

14. Bad Reputation
by David White

A [1]"My name is Wolf, and I've been given a bad name. [2]I hope that when I am finished speaking to you today, you will see my side of the story.

B [3]"First off, Little Red Riding Hood and her grandmother are alive and well. [4]In fact, they're living in Australia right now. [5]They said they couldn't stand the cold and wanted to live in a warmer climate. [6]They also said they were tired of sneezing. [7]They had developed severe allergies from all those leaves. [8]Why they stayed in the forest for so long I don't know, but they have a nice little hut in the Outback now. [9]They love it—not a tree for miles.

C [10]"Secondly, that girl was a spoiled child. [11]Her grandmother gave her everything she wanted. [12]Sure, she was bringing food to 'dear old Granny.' [13]But what did Little Miss Riding Hood expect in return? [14]I'll tell you—she wanted a new set of clothes. [15]She was tired of the red outfit. [16]When I talked to her in the woods that day, she said she hoped her grandmother would have a nice new green outfit all ready for her. [17]The last time she visited, she brought a few small cakes and left with a big shiny bracelet. [18]She does nothing 'just because.'

D [19]"OK, let's get another thing straight—I'm not exactly big. [20]I'm not even four feet tall. [21]People just say that I'm big because they think I was a bully to an innocent girl. [22]I'm just an ordinary animal trying to get by on what nature allows me. [23]I don't eat people, I don't wear women's clothing, I don't even talk to people that often.

E [24]"Let me pause here. [25]Does anyone have any questions?

F [26]"Yes, I know it looks like I did all those terrible things, but that's because you're reading that from a book, aren't you? [27]And who published that book? [28]It wasn't Wolves and Coyotes Press, now was it? [29]You people are all alike. [30]You always take the people's point of view.

G [31]"All I ask is that you compare what you've been told all these years with what I've said today. [32]Make up your own minds. [33]After all, those stories say I'm dead. [34]But I'm here talking to you now. [35]Isn't that enough to make you start to doubt?"

DIRECTIONS: Choose or write the best answer to each of the following questions using the evidence presented in the passage. When required, list specific sentence numbers or paragraph letters from the story to support your answer.

1. Which of these statements best describes the main idea of the story?
   A. Wolf questions facts.
   B. Wolf wants revenge.
   C. Wolf makes his case.
   D. Wolf pleads for mercy.

   Give the number of the sentence that best supports your answer. ____

2. Which of these conclusions is best supported?
   A. Wolf wants people to believe him.
   B. Wolf wants people to dislike Grandmother.
   C. Wolf wants to see his own book published.
   D. Wolf wants to see Little Red Riding Hood again.

   Give the number of the sentence that best supports your answer. ____

3. Give three examples of how Wolf tries to restore his good name.

   _____

   _____

   _____

   _____

   List the numbers of the 3 sentences that best support your answer. ____, ____, ____

4. Whose viewpoint is Wolf trying to change?
   A. his own
   B. Little Red Riding Hood's
   C. Grandma's
   D. the public's

   List the letters of the 2 paragraphs that best support your answer. ____, ____

5. In Sentence 18, Wolf says of Little Red Riding Hood, "She does nothing 'just because.'" Explain what this means.

   _____

   _____

   _____

   _____

   Give the letter of the paragraph that best supports your answer. ____

6. Why did Little Red Riding Hood and her grandmother leave the forest?

   _____

   _____

   _____

   _____

   List the numbers of the 2 sentences that best support your answer. ____, ____

7. Which of these words best describes what Wolf thinks he is?
   A. heroic
   B. forgotten
   C. unrewarded
   D. misunderstood

   List the letters of the 2 paragraphs that best support your answer. ____, ____

15. A Shot at Problem Solving
by David White

[1]"Catalina, leave your shoes here!" my brother called as he stopped dribbling the basketball.

[2]I was putting my sneakers back on so I could go home and fix dinner. [3]"Mom will be home soon," I said. [4]Sitting on the grass barefoot was OK, but I wasn't going home that way, not in this heat.

[5]"But we're using your shoes as the boundary line," my brother said, wiping his forehead with his shirt. [6]It was so hot that my brother and his friend kept stopping to wipe the sweat from their heads and hands.

[7]"You can use a big rock or something else instead," I said. [8]"You'll figure it out."

[9]Mom encouraged us to solve our own problems. [10]So it didn't surprise me that when my brother asked for a basketball hoop, she told him to invent his own. [11]That's right—a basketball hoop.

[12]See, Jose (that's my brother) and his friend Tyrone had found this old ball and then wanted their own hoop. [13]In a flash of brilliance, Jose had said, "What about that plastic trash can in the garage?" [14]Mom had then carved out the bottom and used wire to hang the can from a telephone pole down the street. [15]She had a big smile on her face the whole time.

[16]Today, they were playing Make It–Take It, this game where you get to keep control of the ball as long as you keep scoring. [17]Each basket was a point. [18]Jose was ahead 32–26. [19]The first player to score 50 won the game.

[20]I headed home. [21]An hour later, Jose came home—with Tyrone and another boy.

[22]"Can Tyrone and Masako stay for dinner?" Jose asked, grinning.

[23]"They can if you all wash up first," Mom said. [24]"Jose, let them go first."

[25]As the two others headed off, Mom said, "Jose, have I seen Masako before?"

[26]"No, Mom. [27]We said he could play if he gave us an out-of-bounds line. [28]So he took off his belt and we used that."

[29]"You made him play in jeans that were falling down?" Mom said, laughing.

[30]"Well, they weren't that loose," he said with a smile. [31]"Besides, we couldn't let him win the first time. [32]He's good!"

DIRECTIONS: Choose or write the best answer to each of the following questions using the evidence presented in the passage. When required, list specific sentence numbers or paragraph letters from the story to support your answer.

1. Who was winning when Catalina left?
   - **A.** Jose
   - **B.** Tyrone
   - **C.** Masako
   - **D.** Catalina

   Give the number of the sentence that best supports your answer. ____

2. Give one reason why Masako took off his belt.

   _____

   _____

   Give the number of the sentence that best supports your answer. ____

3. Why do you think Mom was smiling, as described in Sentence 15?

   _____

   _____

   Give the number of the sentence that best supports your answer. ____

4. Which two details support the idea that it was a hot day?

   _____

   _____

   _____

   Give the number of the sentence that best supports each detail. ____, ____

5. If the boys hadn't wiped the sweat from their hands during the game, how would that have affected their ability to play basketball?

   _____

   _____

   _____

   _____

6. Show two ways in which Jose demonstrates his problem-solving skills.

   _____

   _____

   _____

   _____

   List the numbers of the 2 sentences that best support your answer. ____, ____

7. According to the game description in sentence 16, what would happen if Jose missed a shot, Tyrone got the ball, and then Tyrone put the ball through the hoop?

   _____

   _____

   _____

   _____

16. Capsized!
by Cheryl Block

A [1]Fusako kept checking her helmet and life vest to make sure they were tight. [2]It was her first time white-water rafting. [3]Even though it was a cold day, her hands were sweating. [4]The guide gave them instructions on handling the raft. [5]Then they all climbed aboard and slid the raft into the water. [6]The water was calm at first, but the raft soon began to pick up speed as the currents* became stronger.

B [7]As they rounded a bend, she saw them. [8]Rapids! [9]The swirling waves looked like a pot of boiling water. [10]She felt her stomach churning the same way. [11]She took a deep breath and dug in her paddle as they plunged into the rapids.

C [12]The raft rode up and down the waves like a roller coaster. [13]Each time the waves lifted it a little higher out of the water until it was nearly upright. [14]Fusako felt exhilarated. [15]This was better than any ride at the amusement park. [16]As the raft started to rise again, it suddenly slammed down hard and hit a large rock, making the boat flip over. [17]Fusako was thrown into the rushing water. [18]She was carried along, bobbing up and down like a cork. [19]Waves threw her against rocks and logs. [20]Thank goodness she was wearing a helmet and life vest! [21]Finally she came to a section of river where the water was calm. [22]Bruised and exhausted, she climbed onto the shore.

*current: water flowing in a definite direction

DIRECTIONS: Choose or write the best answer to each of the following questions using the evidence presented in the passage. When required, list specific sentence numbers or paragraph letters from the story to support your answer.

1. Which of the following sentences from the story best supports the idea that Fusako is nervous?
   A. It was Fusako's first time white-water rafting.
   B. The guide gave them instructions on handling the boat.
   C. Even though it was a cold day, her hands were sweating.
   D. She took a deep breath and dug in her oar as they plunged into the rapids.

2. In paragraph C, how does the narrator describe the raft ride?

   _____

   _____

   _____

   _____

   Give the number of the sentence that best supports your answer. ____

3. The raft flipped over because it
   A. was gradually filling with water.
   B. rose up too high in the water.
   C. slammed down against a rock.
   D. was overloaded.

   Give the number of the sentence that best supports your answer. ____

4. In sentence 14, what does the word *exhilarated* mean?
   A. joyful
   B. frightened
   C. timid
   D. unhappy

5. Choose the two sentences that best show how the author builds tension in the story.
   A. As they rounded the bend, she saw them.
   B. Fusako felt exhilarated.
   C. Fusako was thrown into the rushing water.
   D. Then they all climbed aboard and slid the raft into the water.

6. How did the helmet and life vest help Fusako?

   _____

   _____

   _____

   _____

   List the numbers of the 2 sentences that best support your answer. ____, ____

7. In paragraph B, what one thing does the author compare to both Fusako's stomach and the rapids?

   _____

   _____

8. Which two of the following sentences support the idea that you can be hurt while white-water rafting?
   A. The raft rode up and down the waves like a roller coaster.
   B. The swirling waves looked like a pot of boiling water.
   C. Thank goodness she was wearing a helmet and life vest!
   D. Waves threw her against rocks and logs.

17. A Uniform Approach
by Carrie Beckwith

A [1]"Having to wear school uniforms violates my right as an individual to express myself," fourteen-year-old Maya argued from her seat in the cafeteria. [2]"I attend a public school, and I don't think anyone should be able to tell me what to wear."

B [3]"Yes, Maya, but we've had *four* gang-related fights on campus because someone was wearing the 'wrong' color. [4]We need to make our school safe. [5]Not to mention the fact that it's hard for kids whose parents can't afford to buy them a closetful of nice clothes," Juan said.

C [6]The group of Compton Middle School students had gathered to discuss a solution to the problem of lunchtime fights on campus. [7]Some students thought school uniforms were the answer. [8]Others, like Maya, disagreed.

D [9]"But where do we draw the line, Juan? [10]First you take away the right to wear what we want. [11]Next, you'll be telling us what we can and cannot read or say!"

E [12]"Who's to say wearing uniforms is going to stop fights?" a usually quiet boy asked from the back of the room.

F [13]"Yeah! How is a uniform going to end that?" Maya added.

G [14]"It may not, Maya. [15]But I think it's worth trying." [16]The school's student body president turned to his classmates. [17]"What if we wore school uniforms on a trial basis? [18]If it ends fighting on campus,

LET YOUR VOICE BE HEARD!

Compton Middle School Student Body invites you to a meeting about on-campus fighting. Bring your ideas, opinions, and solutions!

MONDAY, JANUARY 5

2:30 P.M.

CAFETERIA

we'll wear school uniforms. [19]If not, we'll meet again and work out another solution. [20]How does that sound?"

H [21]Vi spoke up quickly. [22]"That sounds like a great idea, Adam. [23]We could try it out for a year and see how it works." [24]Nods of approval could be seen throughout the cafeteria. [25]Maya saw the positive response from her classmates.

I [26]"Wearing uniforms helped end fights at Central Elementary School and East Town High School, Maya," another boy added.

J [27]"All right, we can give it a try," Maya finally accepted. [28]"But don't expect me to wear plaid pants!" she finished with a grin. [29]Laughter broke the tension of the room. [30]A show of hands made the decision final: School uniforms would be worn on a trial basis for a year.

DIRECTIONS: Choose or write the best answer to each of the following questions using the evidence presented in the passage. When required, list specific sentence numbers or paragraph letters from the story to support your answer.

1. Give two reasons from paragraph B that support the argument for wearing school uniforms.

   _____

   _____

   _____

   _____

   List the numbers of the 2 sentences that best support your answer. ____,

   ____

2. What does the comment the boy made in sentence 12 suggest?
   A. He is for school uniforms.
   B. He doesn't agree that every school needs rules.
   C. He is unconvinced that school uniforms are the solution.
   D. He doesn't understand the argument.

3. What is the main conflict in the passage?

   _____

   _____

   _____

   List the numbers of the 2 sentences that best support your answer. ____,

   ____

4. Which of the following traits best describes Maya?
   A. outspoken
   B. shy
   C. agreeable
   D. confused

   List the letters of the 2 paragraphs that best support your answer. ____,

   ____

5. What caused students to call the meeting?

   _____

   _____

   _____

   Give the number of the sentence that best supports your answer. ____

6. Which of the following quotes from the passage is a fact?
   A. "That sounds like a great idea, Adam."
   B. "We've had four gang-related fights on campus."
   C. "I don't think anyone should be able to tell me what to wear."
   D. "Next, you'll be telling us what we can and cannot read or say!"

7. What do you predict will happen to the campus as a result of wearing school uniforms?

   _____

   _____

   List the numbers of the 2 sentences that best support your answer. ____, ____

18. The Bear and the Bees: A Fable
by David White

A [1]In the forest there lived a big bear. [2]The bear was often hungry but didn't want to work for his food. [3]"So much is available, why should I waste my energy?" the bear would say to any animal that listened.

B [4]The other animals were careful to guard their food as best they could, but the bear always seemed to find a way to discover where their food was hidden. [5]Since the bear was bigger than all the other animals in the forest, the bear got his way.

C [6]Not even the bees were free from the bear. [7]They learned the hard way that the place to build their hive was high up in a tall, thin tree that the bear couldn't climb. [8]The bees worked hard all summer long, taking nectar from flowers and making honey so they would have something to eat in the winter. [9]The bear, meanwhile, did nothing to prepare for winter.

D [10]As the days grew shorter and colder, the bees enjoyed their honey and didn't worry about running out. [11]Many other animals, such as the squirrels and the ants, had stored food as well. [12]Taking a tip from the bees, the squirrels and ants had stored their food in tall, thin trees. [13]Other animals had moved away. [14]It seemed that the bear was on his own.

E [15]Time went by, and the bear grew hungry. [16]He followed some bees to their home tree one day and tried and tried to climb to the top of the tree. [17]But he was too tired and weak from not eating

to go more than a few feet up. [18]Seeing this, the bees buzzed with laughter.

F [19]"Please, share some of your food with me," the bear groaned. [20]"It's mighty cold out here, and I have nothing to eat. [21]I've tried hibernating, but I just can't stay asleep."

G [22]"You should have thought of that in the summer," an angry squirrel chattered in reply. [23]"You depended on stealing our food then. [24]You can't get it now. [25]No nuts for you!"

H [26]Knowing he was beaten, the bear hung his head and walked sadly out of the forest. [27]The bees, squirrels, and ants felt not a bit sorry for him.

[28]Moral: Cheaters get what they deserve.

DIRECTIONS: Choose or write the best answer to each of the following questions using the evidence presented in the passage. When required, list specific sentence numbers or paragraph letters from the story to support your answer.

1. What is the main conflict in the story?
   A. The bear can't stay asleep.
   B. The bees won't share their food with the squirrels.
   C. The bees argue over where to hide their food.
   D. The other animals object to the bear stealing their food.

   Give the number of the sentence that best supports your answer. ____

2. Why did the bees laugh at the bear?
   A. He was cold.
   B. He was hungry.
   C. He was asking them for food.
   D. He was too weak to climb the tree.

   List the numbers of the 2 sentences that best support your answer. ____, ____

3. Which of these sentences is an opinion?
   A. The bear was often hungry but didn't want to work for his food.
   B. Not even the bees were free from the bear.
   C. "You should have thought of that in the summer."
   D. "No nuts for you!"

4. In the last half of the story, the author uses sounds to describe the animals' speech. Below, fill in the word used to describe the sound made by each animal.

   bear   _____

   bees   _____

   squirrel _____

5. Tell how the bear's attitude is different from the bees' attitude.

   _____

   _____

   _____

   _____

   List the numbers of the 4 sentences that best support your answer. ____, ____, ____, ____

6. Based on what you know about the bees, ants, and squirrels, what do you think they might say if the bear came back a week later and asked for food?

   _____

   _____

   _____

   _____

   Give the number of the sentence that best supports your answer. ____

7. How does the story support the moral?

   _____

   _____

   _____

   _____

   List the letters of the 3 paragraphs that best support your answer. ____, ____, ____

19. My First Alien Sighting
by Cheryl Block

A   ¹Carlos and I had been planning this campout all summer. ²We didn't want to sleep in a tent in the fenced back yard, as Mom would have preferred. ³We wanted "real" camping. ⁴Mom finally agreed to let us spend the night in the woods behind our yard. ⁵We were only a few yards from the house, but to us it seemed like another country.

B   ⁶We set up the tent and rolled out our sleeping bags. ⁷Mom had packed us sandwiches for dinner. ⁸It was getting dark, so we turned on the lantern. ⁹We told stories and joked around for awhile, then we went to bed. ¹⁰We left the lantern outside and turned on, just in case there were any wild animals around.

C   ¹¹I don't know how late it was when I was awakened by someone talking in a high, squeaky voice. ¹²I figured some of the guys were trying to scare us, so I woke up Carlos. ¹³We decided to crawl out the back of the tent and surprise them.

D   ¹⁴As we came around the tent, we both got a shock. ¹⁵A small, glowing green creature was standing next to the lantern. ¹⁶All eight arms were waving and pointing wildly as he carried on in that high-pitched voice. ¹⁷He seemed to be upset that the lantern wasn't responding. ¹⁸Grabbing it, he shook the lantern.

E   ¹⁹He wouldn't have seen us if Carlos hadn't sneezed. ²⁰The alien creature slowly turned and stared directly at us. ²¹The green glow came from a green globe attached to the end of his nose (or what we thought was his nose). ²²But we didn't have time to get a good look at him. ²³Whirling around, he squealed and disappeared into the trees, leaving a glowing green trail behind him.

F   ²⁴Carlos wanted to follow him, but I wasn't so sure it was a good idea. ²⁵As we were arguing about it, we heard a roar and looked up just in time to see a shining silver disk rise from the woods into the dark sky. ²⁶It was gone in a flash. ²⁷Carlos and I ducked into the tent and hid in our sleeping bags until morning. ²⁸When we got up, there was no sign of the little creature or his slimy trail. ²⁹Luckily, Mom didn't notice the glowing green spots that had baked onto the lantern.

DIRECTIONS: Choose or write the best answer to each of the following questions using the evidence presented in the passage. When required, list specific sentence numbers or paragraph letters from the story to support your answer.

1. Why do you think Mom preferred that the boys sleep in the back yard?

_____

_____

_____

_____

Give the number of the sentence that best supports your answer. ____

2. In sentence 5, what did the narrator mean when he said "it seemed like another country"?

_____

_____

_____

_____

List the numbers of the 2 sentences that best support your answer. ____,

____

3. Why did the boys think that some of their friends were outside?

_____

_____

_____

Give the number of the sentence that best supports your answer. ____

4. What do you think happened to the little green creature?
   A. He took off in the shining disk.
   B. He went back to his home in the woods.
   C. He was eaten by a wild animal.
   D. He disappeared without leaving a trace.

   Give the number of the sentence that best supports your answer. ____

5. What probably caused the alien to disappear into the trees?
   A. He heard an animal in the woods.
   B. He was startled by the boys.
   C. The lantern wouldn't respond.
   D. It was getting late.

   List the numbers of the 3 sentences that best support your answer. ____,

   ____, ____

6. How do you think the green spots got on the lantern in sentence 29?

   _____

   _____

   _____

   _____

   List the numbers of the 2 sentences that best support your answer. ____,

   ____

20. Farm Girl
by Margaret Hockett

A [1]Step, slosh, step, slosh. [2]Gloria cautiously placed one foot in front of the other, just like Papa showed her, her left arm outstretched to balance her burden. [3]At 15 pounds, the pail of life-giving liquid weighed nearly a fifth of her own weight.

B [4]She had left her father 20 yards behind, where he was transferring the big sucking machine from Betsy to Moovystar. [5]The end of the barn was still a good thirty yards away. [6]There she would steel herself for the effort of pouring out her pail in the milkhouse. [7]She knew she would struggle to raise the pail high enough, without spilling a drop, to empty it into the bulk tank, its opening just above the level of her shoulders. [8]She paused to catch her breath and wipe off the sweat that trickled down her neck. [9]It was hard work for a girl of her age.

C [10]Even so, she looked protectively at the farm product in the bucket at her side. [11]She knew every drop was precious, and would become money used to buy any of the food they did not grow themselves, any clothes they did not make at home. [12]Each drop would also help her older brother finish college; eventually, it would allow her, too, to go to college.

DIRECTIONS: Choose or write the best answer to each of the following questions using the evidence presented in the passage. When required, list specific sentence numbers or paragraph letters from the story to support your answer.

1. What sentence from paragraph B suggests that the pail contains milk?

   Sentence ____

2. Choose the two best answers to complete the following sentence: Gloria most likely felt that her work was

   A. hard but worth the effort.
   B. a necessary thing.
   C. something to do for fun.
   D. a waste of time.

   List the letters of the 2 paragraphs that best support your answer. ____,

   ____

3. Which of these actions was completed within the story?

   A. carrying the pail to the end of the barn
   B. entering the milkhouse
   C. dumping the milk in the bulk tank
   D. carrying the milk twenty yards

   Give the number of the sentence that best supports your answer. ____

4. You can conclude that Gloria is probably

   A. a preschooler.
   B. a preteenager.
   C. a high school senior.
   D. a college freshman.

   Give the number of the sentence that best supports your answer. ____

5. The contents of the bulk tank most likely will be

   A. fed to farm animals.
   B. donated to the homeless.
   C. sold for money.
   D. fed to the family.

   Give the number of the sentence that best supports your answer. ____

6. Why did Gloria walk so carefully?

   A. to protect the product she carries
   B. to keep herself from getting hurt
   C. so her father wouldn't criticize
   D. so her walk would take longer

   Give the letter of the paragraph that best supports your answer. ____

7. As used in sentence 6, the word *steel* most likely means

   A. strengthen
   B. remind
   C. sneak away
   D. cover with a metal

21. Riddle Time
by Margaret Hockett

A [1]Greg and Nan enjoy making up games. [2]Yesterday, they played DescriptoPict, in which one would draw an object and the other would guess it. [3]Today, they were playing DescriptoRhyme. [4]It was Nan's turn.

B [5]"It's often wide but very long; it's hard to see the end. [6]It can be curved, but sometimes straight; it often needs a mend. [7]Sometimes it comes, sometimes it goes; it crosses many others. [8]Use it on vacation or go home to see your mother."

C [9]Greg took only a minute to recognize what she was describing.

D [10]"It's the road!" he shouted.

E [11]"Right! [12]Now you have to try your hand at it," Nan said, eager to guess his riddle.

F [13]It took Greg a few minutes because, of course, he had to plan it so it would rhyme. [14]Finally, he started:

G [15]"It carries several members; all end in something hard. [16]It hangs around in all the joints and sometimes in the yard. [17]A tool you use in many ways, you raise it for attention; it should be easy now to guess—it's something you just mentioned!"

H [18]Nan was stumped at first. [19]She racked her brain thinking of different parts of her "road" riddle. [20]A road is hard, but what are the joints? [21]The road crossings? [22]No—you raise it for attention. [23]Road workers raise flags…but she never mentioned those. [24]She gazed at her fingers as they drummed on the table. [25]Fingers…are attached with joints…to hands…which are raised for attention…

I [26]"I've got it!" she exclaimed.

DIRECTIONS: Choose or write the best answer to each of the following questions using the evidence presented in the passage. When required, list specific sentence numbers or paragraph letters from the story to support your answer.

1. What clue probably gave Nan the answer to Greg's riddle?

   _____

   _____

   _____

   _____

   List the numbers of the 3 sentences that best support your answer. ____, ____, ____

2. Which of the following are rules of the game Greg and Nan were playing? (Choose all that apply.) You have to
   A. describe an object.
   B. draw an object.
   C. make the clues rhyme.
   D. use at least 5 sentences.

   List the letters of the 3 paragraphs that best support your answer. ____, ____, ____

3. What is the answer to Greg's riddle?

   _____

   List the numbers of the 2 sentences in which Nan mentions the answer to Greg's riddle. ____, ____

4. Which one of the following is NOT referred to in Greg's rhyme? (Hint: some of these are referred to by other names.)
   A. fingernails
   B. joints
   C. bones
   D. hand

5. In general, Nan and Greg
   A. try to outdo each other.
   B. make up and play games.
   C. play DescriptoRhyme.
   D. draw objects for each other.

6. If Nan and Greg made up a game called DescriptoSong, what would the players have to do?

   _____

   _____

   _____

   _____

   Give the number of the sentence in paragraph A that best supports your answer. ____

7. In sentence 18, "Nan was stumped" meant that Nan
   A. needed to make a choice.
   B. was sitting on a tree.
   C. had stubbed her toe.
   D. couldn't think of an answer.

8. Number the following according to the order given in the passage.
   ____ Nan wonders about Greg's riddle.

   ____ Greg guesses "the road."

   ____ Greg describes a hand.

   ____ Nan gives a description.

   ____ Greg thinks about his riddle.

22. Pet Overpopulation
by Carrie Beckwith

Dear Editor:

A   ¹Dog and cat overpopulation is a serious problem. ²Most people don't realize that every day in the United States, almost 100,000 puppies and kittens are born. ³Compare this to the 11,000 humans that are born each day. ⁴As you can see, there simply aren't enough homes for them all.

B   ⁵An easy way to lessen the problem of pet overpopulation is to have your pets spayed or neutered, or "fixed." ⁶Spaying or neutering an animal is a simple surgery that prevents your pet from having a litter of kittens or puppies. (⁷Females are spayed and males are neutered.)

C   ⁸I know some people argue that fixing a pet is dangerous to the animal. ⁹They believe that it shortens the animal's life and causes health problems. ¹⁰They also worry that the surgery itself is too risky. ¹¹However, studies have shown that animals who are fixed live just as long and are just as healthy as animals who have not been fixed. ¹²There will always be some risk with surgery, but fixing a pet is a fairly simple operation. ¹³The real risk is *not* spaying or neutering your animal and having to find homes for 6 to 8 new puppies or kittens!

Don't Litter!
Have your pets spayed and neutered

D   ¹⁴If you still haven't been convinced to have your pets spayed or neutered, imagine this: You purchase a cat at the pet store. ¹⁵Your new cat, Fluffy, has a litter of 6 kittens. ¹⁶If each of those 6 kittens has 6 kittens, there will be 36 new kittens. ¹⁷If those 36 kittens each have 6 kittens, there will be 216 new kittens! ¹⁸Female cats as young as 6 months of age can give birth to kittens. ¹⁹That means that after only a year and a half, Fluffy could have 258 offspring! ²⁰As you can see, the problem can get out of hand very quickly.

E   ²¹So become a solution to the problem of pet overpopulation—spay or neuter your animal friends!

Sincerely,

A concerned
member of the
community

DIRECTIONS: Choose or write the best answer to each of the following questions using the evidence presented in the passage. When required, list specific sentence numbers or paragraph letters from the story to support your answer.

1. What is the writer trying to convince you to do?

   _____

   _____

   _____

   _____

   List the numbers of the 2 sentences that best support your answer. ____,

   ____

2. Using paragraph A, give the numbers of the two sentences that best support why the author believes you should have your pets fixed.

   Sentences ____, ____

3. What can you conclude from the example of Fluffy in paragraph D?

   A. Cats should be left indoors.
   B. Cats reproduce quickly.
   C. Cats can't have kittens until age one.
   D. Cats should be watched carefully.

4. Give two reasons why people might NOT spay or neuter their pets.

   _____

   _____

   _____

   _____

   List the numbers of the 2 sentences that best support your answer. ____,

   ____

5. What type of math did the author do to find out Fluffy could have a total of 258 offspring?

   A. addition and subtraction
   B. multiplication and addition
   C. multiplication and division
   D. square root

6. What do you think would happen to the problem of pet overpopulation if more people spayed/neutered their pets?

   A. Pets would have more litters.
   B. The problem would get worse.
   C. More animals would end up in shelters and pounds.
   D. The problem would get better.

   Give the number of the sentence that best supports your answer. ____

7. Why does the writer bring up the views of people who disagree with having their pets fixed?

   A. He wants to defend their position.
   B. He doesn't know how to make an argument.
   C. He doesn't understand their views.
   D. He wants to explain why he thinks they're wrong.

23. A Tale of Two Boarders
by Margaret Hockett

A   [1]I, Su Kapo, was ready for a change. [2]My skateboard was only two months old but I was tired of it. [3]At first, I loved the blue design highlighted with bright colors. [4]After awhile, the graphics "got old" and everyone else's board looked better to me. [5]What could I do? [6]I couldn't afford a new one. [7]Then I saw it! [8]An ad for a used skateboard that sounded really cool.

B   **[9]Check out the hottest skate in town! [10]Gold and crimson bands form a dragon that appears and disappears in the misty aqua background of this rolling winner. [11]Only $85! [12]Call 303-6578.**

C   [13]I called the number. [14]Like me, the owner was tired of her board, and she suggested a trade! [15]If she liked my board and I liked hers, we would exchange boards and both be happy.

D   [16]Skating to her house, I gazed at the top of my board. [17]Maybe the idea that someone else might want my board made me see it in a new light. [18]I had never noticed how those yellow and red stripes curved back and forth through the blue-green haze. [19]Or how they could come together to form the shape of some kind of…beast?

E   [20]I was at her front door. [21]Before I could knock, the door swung open and revealed a girl about my age and size. [22]We both shouted with surprise as we each looked at the other's skateboard.

DIRECTIONS: Choose or write the best answer to each of the following questions using the evidence presented in the passage. When required, list specific sentence numbers or paragraph letters from the story to support your answer.

1. What is the best explanation for the girls' surprise?
   A. Their boards looked alike.
   B. The girls were the same size.
   C. They didn't expect to see each other.
   D. The door swung open too suddenly.

   List the letters of the 2 paragraphs that best support your answer. ____,
   ____

2. In sentence 4, Su says the graphics "got old," though the board was only two months old. What do you think she really meant?

   _____

   _____

   _____

   _____

   Give the number of the sentence from paragraph C that best supports your answer. ____

3. Explain why Su didn't recognize the description of the board in the ad.

   _____

   _____

   _____

   List the numbers of the 3 sentences that best support your answer. ____,
   ____, ____

4. What was the "beast" mentioned in sentence 19?

   _____

5. In sentence 2, Su says she was tired of her board after only two months. If she also said "I never finish books because I lose interest," you might say that Su is a person who
   A. keeps her interest in things.
   B. becomes bored quickly.
   C. takes good care of things.
   D. sticks to her decisions.

6. The word *reveal*, in sentence 21, most nearly means
   A. hit.
   B. uncover.
   C. hide.
   D. enclose.

7. Predict what Su will likely do next.

   _____

   _____

   _____

   List the numbers of the 3 sentences that best support your answer. ____,
   ____, ____

8. Describe two ways the writer of the ad tries to persuade the reader to buy the board.

   _____

   _____

   _____

   _____

24. Little Squirt, Big Squirt
by Carrie Beckwith

A [1]I was facing another hot, boring day in the valley. [2]Normally, I didn't allow my little brother to step one foot near me, but I decided this day would have to be different. [3]I came up with the idea of turning Mom's clothesline into a theatre of sheets, and I let A.J. help me. [4]"This time," I told him, "I will be a beautiful Arabian belly dancer." [5]With golden bells around my waist and billowy lavender pants, I danced to the snakes. [6]They coiled themselves as if to attack, but were powerless under the spell of my dancing. [7]"Hissss…"

B [8]"Stop! [9]You're spitting on me." [10]My brother screamed and fell backwards in a fit of laughter, knocking over the picnic bench that was supposed to be front row seating.

C [11]"You have no imagination, A.J." [12]Of course, why did I expect an eight year old to know raw talent when he saw it?

D [13]"Well maybe if you did something besides squirm around with the garden hose I'd be interested!" A.J. joked. [14]Then he picked himself up and began cartwheeling around the yard, amused by his own humor.

E [15]I did not take kindly to insult, especially from my own brother. [16]So I did what any self-respecting sister would do to keep her brother in line…I played a little trick on him. [17]"You're right, A.J," I said. [18]"I'll start over. [19]This time I'm going to enter the stage from behind this bush. [20]You won't be able to see me right away, but just sit on the bench and wait, okay? [21]I'm going to act out a mystery, and I want you to be part of it, too."

F [22]When A.J. heard he could participate in one of my plays, he raced to the picnic bench, sat down, and folded his hands. [23]Within seconds, I had the hose. [24]POW! [25]Right to the gut! [26]Front row seating was soaking wet. [27]"How did you like that mystery, A.J.?" I cackled. [28]But A.J. was quick. [29]He leaped up, grabbed the hose at its neck, and squirted it right back at me.

G [30]"Not as much as I like squirting you with this hose, Tameeka!"

H [31]Nothing was left dry when we were through. [32]As I look back now, maybe it wasn't such a boring day after all.

DIRECTIONS: Choose or write the best answer to each of the following questions using the evidence presented in the passage. When required, list specific sentence numbers or paragraph letters from the story to support your answer.

1. Why do you think Tameeka "allowed" A.J. to play with her?

   A. She always played with her brother.

   B. She needed an actor for the play.

   C. She didn't have anything better to do.

   D. She liked A.J.'s ideas.

Give the number of the sentence that best supports your answer. ____

2. From whose point of view is the story written? Explain your answer.

   A. An unnamed narrator

   B. A.J.'s

   C. Mom's

   D. Tameeka's

_____

_____

3. What caused A.J. to race back to the picnic bench?

_____

_____

_____

Give the number of the sentence that best supports your answer. ____

4. What does A.J's reaction to being in his sister's play tell you about him?

   A. He is afraid of his sister and will do whatever she asks of him.

   B. He is excited about being part of the play.

   C. He has his own plan to trick his sister.

   D. He's not sure if he wants to be part of his sister's play.

Give the number of the sentence that best supports your answer. ____

5. Compare Tameeka's opinion of the day at the beginning of the story to her opinion at the end.

_____

_____

_____

List the numbers of the 2 sentences that best show this comparison. ____, ____

6. Put the following events in their correct order.

____ A.J. sprays Tameeka with hose.

____ A.J. knocks the bench over.

____ Tameeka pretends to be a belly dancer.

____ Tameeka tells A.J. she will act out a mystery.

7. What conclusion about Tameeka is NOT supported in the story?

   A. She likes to dance.

   B. She is shy.

   C. She is playful.

   D. She is imaginative.

8. Using paragraph A, describe the setting of the story.

_____

_____

_____

_____

List the numbers of the 2 sentences that best support your answer. ____, ____

25. No Show
by Margaret Hockett

A [1]"Look," I said, sitting on Jeremy's bed, "everyone's going to be there. [2]And Mr. Grimes says some kid is doing some really cool magic tricks this year." [3]But my best friend was making some lame excuse about going to the library first. [4]I was afraid he was going to miss "Talent on Tap" at the high school gym. [5]The variety show was so funny last year we both thought we'd bust a gut laughing.

B [6]I tried once more. [7]"Come on! [8]"You even have your dress shoes on—and shined," I said. [9]"Let's go *now*!"

C [10]"Nah, I'll catch up with you later, Sid."

D [11]I gave up and left to meet Andy. [12]Come to think of it, I'd been doing a lot with Andy lately. [13]Jeremy had missed baseball and dinner at my house last week. [14]And he seemed thoughtful—he hadn't flashed his crinkly grin in days.

E [15]We found our seats as the Master of Ceremonies began. [16]After a few warmup jokes, he introduced The Dipsy Doodle Talking Poodles. [17]They were only mildly funny. [18]But by the time the Door Jams finished, we were rolling on the floor! [19]Time for mystery and drama: the Magic Moment act was about to commence…

F [20]I looked around anxiously, hoping Jeremy had finally made it, because this act looked like it would be really big.

G [21]KaBoom! [22]There was a bright glow, then a figure in black arose out of a mist. [23]His back was to us, and I caught a reflection of light off his glossy heels. [24]He slowly turned, one hand on the brim of his top hat, as his face crinkled into a grin…

DIRECTIONS: Choose or write the best answer to each of the following questions using the evidence presented in the passage. When required, list specific sentence numbers or paragraph letters from the story to support your answer.

1. Who is Sid's best friend?

   _____

   Give the number of the sentence that best supports your answer. ____

2. What was Sid's conflict with Jeremy in paragraphs A and B? Sid was trying to

   A. convince him to go to a show.
   B. make up with him after fighting.
   C. get him to go to the library.
   D. ask him to come to dinner.

   Give the number of the sentence in paragraph A that best supports your answer. ____

3. What persons are meant by "We" in sentence 15?

   _____

   _____

4. Sid uses the phrase "rolling on the floor" to show that they

   A. thought the act was very funny.
   B. were tired of sitting.
   C. were too bored to watch.
   D. had been scared.

5. What does the word *commence* mean as used in sentence 19?

   A. bomb
   B. cancel
   C. begin
   D. end

6. Give two clues from paragraph G that support the idea that Jeremy was the magician in the show.

   _____

   _____

   _____

   _____

   Give the number of the sentence that best supports each clue. ____, ____

7. Assuming that Jeremy was the magician, when do you think he found time to practice his magic act?

   _____

   _____

   _____

   _____

   Give the number of the sentence that best supports your answer. ____

26. Truth or Dare
by Carrie Beckwith

A   [1]Ann approached the house timidly. [2]Her first instinct was to run back to the safety of the tree house where Neve and Drew were waiting for her. [3]But this was a dare for her membership test, and that meant serious business.

B   [4]"The house has been abandoned for over a hundred years," Ann remembered Neve telling her.

C   [5]"The McWilliams family just picked up and left. [6]People said there was something strange about the way it all happened. [7]Since then, no one has set foot in the house," Drew had explained.

D   [8]Ann held her breath and placed one foot on the paint-chipped steps of the front porch. [9]Every step closer to the front door made her heart pound faster and louder. [10]Her cold, sweaty hand clenched and twisted the knob. [11]The door swung open with unexpected ease. [12]"Maybe it was the wind," Ann tried to reason.

E   [13]Her steps were cautious as she entered the dining room. [14]She stopped, her eyes darting wildly around the room. [15]Old, worn linens hung over the cherry wood tables and chairs. [16]Behind the cabinets, long-stemmed wine goblets were neatly arranged in rows, like little glass armies.

F   [17]Ann crept towards the winding, red-carpeted staircase. [18]*Were those pictures of the McWilliams family lining the walls of the hallway upstairs?* [19]Her curiosity was piqued. [20]She walked upstairs and gazed at the yellowed portraits of a family long gone. [21]Just down the hallway, an open door with a stream of light caught her attention. [22]The wood floors creaked as she walked down the hall. [23]The words came ringing back to her, "The McWilliams family just picked up and left. [24]People said there was something strange about the way it all happened."

G   [25]Ann couldn't take it anymore. [26]She raced down the stairs, out the back door, and straight to the tree house. [27]Nearly out of breath, she hollered, "Drew, Neve, I'm back! [28]I made it!" [29]The girls tried to hold back their amusement, but couldn't.

H   [30]"You're right. [31]You did make it, Ann. [32]Welcome to our Tree House Club! [33]And if it makes you feel any better, that old house isn't really abandoned. [34]It's going to be part of the new town museum called Village of Our Past!"

DIRECTIONS: Choose or write the best answer to each of the following questions using the evidence presented in the passage. When required, list specific sentence numbers or paragraph letters from the story to support your answer.

1. Which two sentences in paragraph A best support the idea that Ann was nervous about going into the house?

   Sentences ____, ____

2. Which sentence in paragraph E uses a simile to describe something? Write the sentence.

   _____

   _____

   _____

   _____

3. In paragraph F, Ann decided to go upstairs because she noticed
   A. the portraits of the McWilliams family.
   B. the long-stemmed wine goblets.
   C. the stream of light just down the hallway.
   D. the worn linens.

   List the numbers of the 2 sentences that best support your answer. ____,

   ____

4. The word *piqued*, as used in sentence 19, means
   A. controlled.
   B. stopped.
   C. mistaken.
   D. excited.

5. Put the following events in the order they happened in the story.

   ____ Ann goes upstairs.

   ____ Ann is dared.

   ____ Ann runs out the back door.

   ____ The front door swings open.

6. Using paragraphs E and F, list the numbers of the two sentences that best show that Ann was careful.

   Sentences ____, ____

7. Which two paragraphs best describe the way the house looks inside?
   A. Paragraphs F and G
   B. Paragraphs A and E
   C. Paragraphs E and F
   D. Paragraphs F and H

8. Which of the following can you conclude about Neve and Drew? (Choose all that apply.)
   A. They were relieved to see Ann come back.
   B. They knew what was going on all along.
   C. They have asked Ann to tell the truth about something.
   D. They are members of the Tree House Club.

   List the numbers of the 2 sentences that best support your answer. ____,

   ____

27. Case of the Missing Diamond
   by David White

[1]No one spoke in the small, hot room. [2]They all knew each other too well.

[3]Inspector Graham questioned each person in turn, making notes on a thin, white pad.

[4]The man in the striped trousers shifted in his chair, gripping his briefcase tightly. [5]The teenaged boy in the blue blazer leaned against the bookcase, trying to look bored.

[6]The woman in the red dress stood up and stretched. [7]Realizing she was being watched, she sat back down quickly and wrapped her hands around her purse. [8]When she was sure no one was looking, she opened the purse. [9]She looked inside, smiled, and snapped the purse shut.

[10]The man seated on the couch wiped his sweaty hands on his handkerchief. [11]He tapped his hearing aid in response to a question from the inspector. [12]When the question was repeated more loudly, he nodded his head. [13]His wife was sitting straight up at the end of the couch. [14]She stared at the wall and barely responded to the inspector's questions. [15]Her heavy earrings jingled over her knees.

[16]The antique clock struck two. [17]Everyone jumped. [18]The silence returned.

[19]"It's all clear to me now," the inspector said loudly. [20]"Mrs. Page's diamond has been missing for eighteen hours. [21]You have all remained here in this house. [22]One of you has that diamond right now."

[23]The suspects looked quickly at one another, then back at the inspector.

[24]The teen was the first to speak. [25]"When can I get out of here?" he said loudly, putting his hands back in his pockets. [26]"I have a date tonight."

[27]The woman in the red dress turned pale. [28]"You don't think it's me, do you?" she said softly. [29]Her hands were pale as she clutched her purse.

[30]The man in the striped trousers stood up angrily. [31]"You're mad, Graham," he said. [32]"I'm leaving."

[33]"This is an outrage!" the woman on the couch said, standing up suddenly. [34]Her left earring fell off and hit the floor, shattering into a dozen pieces. [35]The room was suddenly abuzz.

[36]"Good thing it's a fake," Inspector Graham whispered.

[37]"It is not a fake!" the man on the couch roared. [38]"We paid good money for those earrings!"

[39]"So," the inspector said with a smile, "you don't need the hearing aid after all. [40]In fact, the missing diamond is about that size."

DIRECTIONS: Choose or write the best answer to each of the following questions using the evidence presented in the passage. When required, list specific sentence numbers or paragraph letters from the story to support your answer.

1. Where do you predict the diamond will be found?

   A. in a purse
   B. in the clock
   C. in a briefcase
   D. in the hearing aid

   List the numbers of the 2 sentences that best support your answer. ____,

   ____

2. In sentence 17, why did everyone jump when the clock struck two?

   _____

   _____

   _____

   _____

3. What caused the earring to fall off?

   _____

   _____

   List the numbers of the 2 sentences that best support your answer. ____,

   ____

4. Which is true of *all* the suspects?

   A. They are all sitting down.
   B. They are all holding something.
   C. They all know one another.
   D. They all work for Mrs. Page.

   Give the number of the sentence that best supports your answer. ____

5. How did the setting, as described in sentence 1, affect the suspects?

   _____

   _____

   _____

   _____

6. Give one example of how the man in striped trousers revealed his nervousness through his actions.

   _____

   _____

   _____

   _____

   Give the number of the sentence that best supports the example. ____

7. Give two examples of how the woman in the red dress acts suspicious of other people.

   _____

   _____

   _____

   _____

   _____

   List the numbers of the 2 sentences that best support your answer. ____,

   ____

28. Buttered Up
by Margaret Hockett

A [1]It was a very hot day, and Pa and I were weary after driving Uncle Charlie to the train station in our new Model T Ford. [2]On the way back home, Pa pulled into the gravel drive by Sickle Tree. [3]The sprawling oak had got that name because of the rusty old sickle* trapped within its trunk. [4]A farmer had hung it on the tree before heading off to the Civil War, from which he had never returned.

B [5]As we neared the stout woman minding a churn,** I could see what Pa had in mind. [6]There was nothing he loved better than a big old glass of buttermilk on a good hot day.

C [7]"I'll give ya five cents for a glass of that," he told her. [8]But the good-hearted woman offered us both buttermilk in exchange for gossip, as she "didn't get to town much."

D [9]We sat under the tree and enjoyed our cool, rich drinks while the woman churned. [10]She and Pa chatted pleasantly about the weather, farming, and life in general. [11]I was the first to notice the mangy looking yellow cat sneaking up to the churn as the woman removed the churn lid.

E [12]I was too fascinated to make a sound as the cat jumped up on the edge of the churn and promptly fell in.

F [13]When Pa and I realized how that dirty old cat would affect the woman's wonderful buttermilk, we felt sorry for her. [14]But the woman didn't seem too disturbed. [15]She just pulled out the cat, held him up with one hand, and wrung him out into the churn. [16]"You fool cat!" she scolded. [17]"That's the third time you've been in there today!"

G [18]We left shortly after that. [19]Pa thanked the woman politely, but I noticed that it was the first time he had ever left a glass of buttermilk unfinished.

* sickle: a tool used for cutting grain

**churn: (1) a container in which milk is made into butter by stirring, (2) the act of stirring milk until it becomes butter

DIRECTIONS: Choose or write the best answer to each of the following questions using the evidence presented in the passage. When required, list specific sentence numbers or paragraph letters from the story to support your answer.

1. The story most likely takes place
   A. in the present time.
   B. just after the Civil War.
   C. in the early 20th century.
   D. in the future.

   List the numbers of the 2 sentences that best support your answer. ____, ____

2. As used in sentence 5, what does the word *minding* mean?
   A. tending
   B. baby-sitting
   C. being bothered by
   D. guarding against theft

3. Why does the narrator call the woman "good-hearted" in paragraph C?

   _____

   _____

   _____

   Give the number of the sentence that best supports your answer. ____

4. Why do you think the farmer never removed the sickle from the oak tree described in paragraph A?

   _____

   _____

   _____

5. As used in sentence 11, the word *mangy* is used to imply that the cat is
   A. groomed.
   B. bright.
   C. mean.
   D. unclean.

6. Pa probably left his glass unfinished because he realized that
   A. he was too full.
   B. they would be too late getting home.
   C. he didn't like cats.
   D. the cat had probably been in his milk.

   Give the number of the sentence that best supports your answer. ____

7. Do you think Pa will stop for buttermilk at Sickle Tree again? Why or why not?

   _____

   _____

   _____

   _____

   List the numbers of the 2 sentences that best support your answer. ____, ____

8. The woman seems most concerned about
   A. cleanliness.
   B. losing buttermilk from the churn.
   C. keeping the cat from drowning.
   D. health.

   Give the number of the sentence that best supports your answer. ____

29. It's All Downhill
by David White

[1]"Slow down, Brad, you're blowing dirt in my face!"

[2]"Hey, if you were ahead of me like you're supposed to be, you wouldn't even see this dirt," Brad yelled back, bracing himself as he skidded through more dirt.

[3]"Well, I'm not the one screaming around curves, nearly wiping out every minute."

[4]"Eric, those girls are ahead of us. [5]It's time to catch up."

[6]They zigzagged down a narrow stretch of trail, their eyes focused on the rocks and roots beneath them.

[7]"Maybe if you hadn't had that flat at the top—"

[8]"We fixed it in no time, didn't we? [9]Besides, it's not like we're racing them."

[10]"Yeah, but we will be soon," Eric said as he braked and turned the handlebars to avoid another rock. [11]"This is a training ride. [12]That race is in two weeks."

[13]"That's exactly why I want to go fast down this hill."

[14]Brad shifted into a higher gear and zoomed ahead, managing to keep one foot on the pedals as he swerved around another curve. [15]Eric carefully kept close behind. [16]Like a yo-yo, he soon caught up.

[17]"What are you, some kind of stuntman? [18]You're out of control, Brad. [19]I'm right behind you, and I'm in control. [20]You've got maybe 2 or 3 seconds on me at the most."

[21]They pedaled through grassland and across a shallow stream and then back into the trees. [22]Brad let out a whoop and zoomed ahead. [23]Bending to avoid hitting his head on a low branch, he came up too late to see a big rock in the middle of the trail. [24]He hit the rock, and bike and rider went airborne. [25]Fortunately, no branches hung low on the downward side. [26]The landing jolted him hard, but Brad stayed aboard. [27]He stopped to catch his breath. [28]Eric stopped right behind him.

[29]"Don't you remember that rock from the trip up?" Eric said. [30]His face was a mixture of laughter and concern. [31]"Who are you trying to impress? [32]The girls are way ahead of us now. [33]Be careful."

[34]"I didn't wipe out, did I? [35]Besides, it was a big rock."

[36]"Yeah, well, I'm not picking you up if you fall down. [37]See you at the bottom."

[38]"See you there!"

DIRECTIONS: Choose or write the best answer to each of the following questions using the evidence presented in the passage. When required, list specific sentence numbers or paragraph letters from the story to support your answer.

1. Which quote from the passage best sums up the main idea?

   A. "Be careful."
   B. "See you there!"
   C. "It's time to catch up."
   D. "This is a training ride."

   Give the number of the sentence that best supports your answer. ____

2. Which is the correct order for the following events? Choose A, B, C, or D.

   1. Brad has a flat tire.
   2. Brad shifts into a higher gear.
   3. Brad blows dirt in Eric's face.
   4. Brad goes airborne after hitting a rock.
       A. 1, 2, 3, 4
       B. 1, 3, 2, 4
       C. 4, 1, 3, 2
       D. 4, 3, 2, 1

3. Why did dirt blow in Eric's face?

   A. He was riding behind Brad.
   B. He was riding carefully.
   C. He stopped right behind Brad.
   D. He turned his handlebars to avoid a rock.

4. Based on the conversation the cyclists have, do you think Eric will stop to help Brad if Brad falls down? Explain your answer.

   _____

   _____

   _____

   _____

   Give the number of the sentence that best supports your answer. ____

5. Contrast the way the two riders go down the hill. To support your answer, list three sentences for each rider.

   _____

   _____

   _____

   _____

   _____

   _____

   Brad: ____, ____, ____

   Eric: ____, ____, ____

6. Which of these is the best reason why Brad wanted to go fast?

   A. He had a flat tire.
   B. He shifted into a higher gear.
   C. He was trying to show off in front of Eric.
   D. He knew his friends were ahead.

   List the numbers of the 2 sentences that best support your answer. ____, ____

7. Sentence 16 contains which kind of figure of speech?

   _____

8. Which of these quotes from the story is an opinion?

   A. "That race is in two weeks."
   B. "Besides, it was a big rock."
   C. "You're out of control, Brad."
   D. "Eric, those girls are ahead of us."

30. Teacher Turns Eleven
by Margaret Hockett

A [1]Ms. Henson thought she was getting too old. [2]She was annoyed that she couldn't see without her bifocals—"Those are for old 'folkles,'" she'd say—and that she had trouble bending to pick up papers. [3]"I'm just going to have to start getting younger," she finally said.

B [4]First, we noticed a new sparkle in her eye. [5]A couple of days later, it looked as if someone had erased her mouth wrinkles. [6]Her walk seemed bouncier, and she started wearing teenagers' clothes. [7]It was all pretty odd, but when she got shorter and started talking funny it got scary.

C [8]We could barely see her over the books on her desk. [9]A high-pitched voice would pierce the room with "Time for social studies, class." [10]The sight of this small creature acting like a teacher was even stranger than the voice. [11]It would have been funny except for that no-nonsense attitude in her voice and manner. [12]We got used to the changes, and class was pretty much "business as usual."

D [13]Ms. Henson showed her usual talent for problem solving. [14]When she couldn't reach the top of the blackboard, she declared "We'll just have to lower it." [15]After we helped her do that, she proceeded to fill it entirely with chalk marks. [16]Math, social studies, reading assignments—all appeared under her childish yet capable fingers.

E [17]Things went well until Genie Pix came to school. [18]On Genie's first day, we had a substitute for the morning since Ms. Henson was at the dentist and

wouldn't be back until recess. [19]It was obvious that Genie was a "do righter." [20]She scolded Won and me for passing notes. [21]She gave threatening looks to the girls who were making faces in class. [22]Anyway, during recess, Genie came in to the classroom to get her sweater. [23]She found Ms. Henson taking the field trip money out of her special locked drawer. [24]Well, when Genie found what appeared to be a student thief, she got all bent out of shape. [25]She yelled and tried to grab the money bag. [26]Ms. Henson held on tight, but when Genie gave a second yank, Ms. Henson went flying backward! [27]She ended up with four stitches and a whole bunch of bruises. [28]That's when she decided that being eleven was too dangerous.

F [29]Before long, Ms. Henson's head appeared higher and higher behind her desk. [30]A familiar quality came back to her voice. [31]The childish clothes and smooth skin went away. [32]But one thing that never did go away was that mischievous gleam in her eye.

DIRECTIONS: Choose or write the best answer to each of the following questions using the evidence presented in the passage. When required, list specific sentence numbers or paragraph letters from the story to support your answer.

1. Choose the main idea of the passage.
   A. The teacher learns a lesson.
   B. The teacher gets hurt.
   C. The class learns to cope.
   D. The new student takes a stand.

   Give the number of the sentence in paragraph E that best supports your answer. ____

2. From sentence 5, which of the following is reasonable to conclude?
   A. A sketch of Ms. H had been changed.
   B. Ms. H's wrinkles were disappearing.
   C. Some of Ms. H's makeup was removed.
   D. Ms. H had just gotten into a fistfight.

   Explain your answer.

   _____

   _____

   _____

3. Put the features of Ms. Henson in the order they appear in the story.
   ____   Short height

   ____   Sparkle in her eye

   ____   Bounce in her step

   ____   Bruises

4. What was the one change that remained with Ms. Henson at the end of the story?

   _____

   List the numbers of the 2 sentences that best support your answer. ____, ____

5. Based on her actions from the story, what do you think Genie Pix would do if she found someone cheating on a test?
   A. Talk them out of it.
   B. Point it out.
   C. Wait until after class to discuss it.
   D. Ignore it.

   Give the letter of the paragraph that best supports your answer. ____

6. As a result of Genie's letting go of the money bag, Ms. Henson
   A. yelled loudly.
   B. held on tight.
   C. knocked Genie over.
   D. lost her balance.

7. The narrator is
   A. a student in Ms. Henson's class.
   B. a teacher in Ms. Henson's school.
   C. the new student.
   D. an observer outside the class.

   Give the number of the sentence in paragraph E that best supports your answer. ____

8. Which could be the theme of this story?
   A. New students imagine things.
   B. Being young makes things better.
   C. Getting old is worse than anything.
   D. With change comes knowledge.

   Give the number of the sentence that best supports your answer. ____

nonfiction

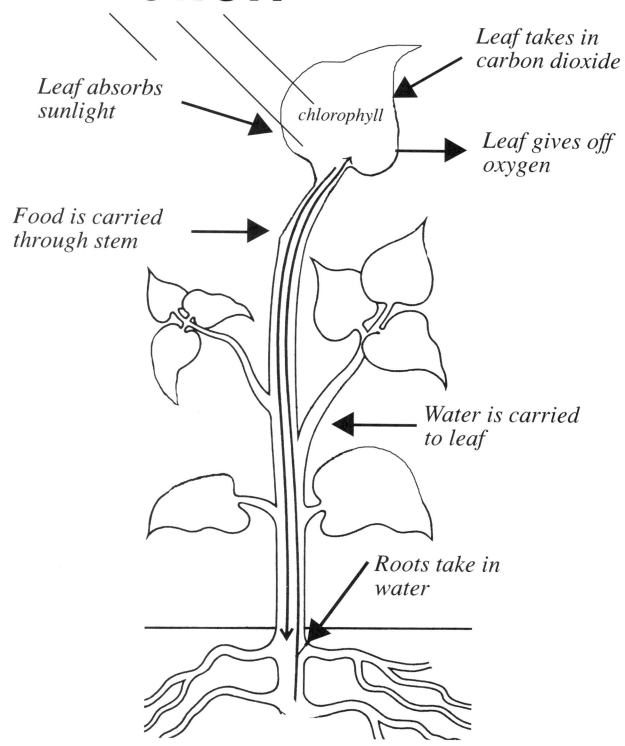

Leaf absorbs sunlight

Leaf takes in carbon dioxide

chlorophyll

Leaf gives off oxygen

Food is carried through stem

Water is carried to leaf

Roots take in water

31. "Pokey-pines"
by Margaret Hockett

A [1]Do you like getting stuck with thorns? [2]Then you probably won't enjoy getting too close to the "thorn pig," or porcupine.

B [3]The word porcupine comes from two Latin words, *porcus* and *spina*. [4]*Porcus* means pig, though the porcupine is not a pig. [5]*Spina* means thorn, though the porcupine has no real thorns. [6]Porcupines are slow and clumsy, and they can't see well. [7]How then does a porcupine protect itself?

C [8]The answer lies in the weapons on its body. [9]The porcupine carries about 30,000 little "darts," ready to pierce an enemy. [10]These darts are really stiff hairs called quills. [11]Quills grow out of the back, sides, and tail of the porcupine. [12]A porcupine cannot shoot quills. [13]Instead, it whirls around and flicks its tail back and forth. [14]Anyone coming too close to the rear end of the porcupine will be stuck with quills. [15]A quill can't be pulled out easily because its barbs point backwards. [16]Because of these quills, many animals have learned to stay far away from the porcupine!

DIRECTIONS: Choose or write the best answer to each of the following questions using the evidence presented in the passage. When required, list specific sentence numbers or paragraph letters from the story to support your answer.

1. Why do you think the Latin word *spina* was used in naming the porcupine?

   _____

   _____

   _____

   _____

   Give the number of the sentence in paragraph B that best supports your answer. ____

2. Which sentence best sums up the reasons a porcupine needs the protection of quills?

   Sentence ____

3. In sentence 9, the word *pierce* means to

   A. stab.
   B. tickle.
   C. protect.
   D. stroke.

4. How does an enemy get stuck with quills?

   A. The enemy gets shot by quills.
   B. The enemy moves away.
   C. The enemy gets near the porcupine's rear.
   D. The enemy stands in front of the porcupine.

   Give the number of the sentence that best supports your answer. ____

5. Explain why a quill can be painful to remove.

   _____

   _____

   _____

   _____

   Give the number of the sentence that best supports your answer. ____

6. The main idea of the passage is to describe how the porcupine can

   A. get food.
   B. protect itself.
   C. move around.
   D. grow quills.

32. Making "Sense" Out of Poetry
by Carrie Beckwith

A   [1]Writing a poem that uses your senses is a great way to express your feelings and ideas to the reader. [2]Not only does it let the reader see what you're talking about, it also lets him or her smell, touch, taste, and hear it! [3]Just follow these easy steps, and you'll be on your way to writing your own unique poem for the senses.

B   [4]First, pick something you are familiar with to write about. [5]For example, you may want to write about your favorite sport, your little sister, or chocolate chip cookies! [6]Next, describe your chosen subject using some or all of your senses: taste, touch, sight, hearing, and smell. [7]You don't have to use all five senses in your poem—using two or three is fine. [8]The important thing is to be specific in your choice of details. [9]For example, if you were to write about baseball, you could describe the sound of the bat hitting the ball as a "loud crack." [10]Or you might say that the air in the field smelled "like it was thick with dirt."

C   [11]Here is one example from 5th grade student Juan Gonzalez:

SOCCER
[12]People in the stands. [13]Black and white balls flying through the air. [14]Kids charging at me.
[15]People shouting "Move the ball upfield!" [16]Kids saying "Pass the ball!"
[17]Coach yelling plays.
[18]Feel the ball banging against my feet as I move it upfield.
[19]Taste the dirt as I hit the ground.
[20]Taste the salty sweat that rolls down my face.
[21]Smell the victory as my team shoots the goal for the winning point!

DIRECTIONS: Choose or write the best answer to each of the following questions using the evidence presented in the passage. When required, list specific sentence numbers or paragraph letters from the story to support your answer.

1. The purpose of the passage is to show you how to
   A. describe something you want to write a poem about.
   B. write a poem using your senses.
   C. use your sense of smell and taste to describe cookies.
   D. get started on a poem.

   Give the letter of the paragraph that best supports your answer. ____

2. What is the first step in writing a sense poem?
   A. Be specific with your details.
   B. Choose a subject.
   C. Use your senses.
   D. Write an example of a poem.

   Give the number of the sentence that best supports your answer. ____

3. Why is it a good idea to write about something you know well?

   _____

   _____

   _____

   _____

   List the numbers of the 2 sentences that best support your answer. ____, ____

4. In general, poems using the senses
   A. describe sight and hearing only.
   B. make comparisons.
   C. describe chocolate chip cookies.
   D. make words come to life.

   List the numbers of the 2 sentences that best support your answer. ____, ____

5. Fill each blank with the letter of the line from the poem (given below) that best describes the sense. The first one has been done for you.

   _e_   smell

   ____   touch

   ____   sight

   ____   hearing

   ____   taste

   a. Taste the dirt as I hit the ground.
   b. Feel the ball banging against my feet as I move it upfield.
   c. Black and white balls flying through the air.
   d. Kids saying "Pass the ball!"
   e. Smell the victory as my team shoots the goal for the winning point!

6. What three sentences, or lines, from the poem support Juan's idea that soccer is a loud sport?

   Sentences ____, ____, ____

33. Defining Geometry
by David White

[1]Geometry is a branch of mathematics that focuses on shapes. [2]A large part of geometry is the study of the lines, points, and angles used to form these shapes. [3]A line is a set of points that extend forever in two directions. [4]A line segment can be thought of as a part of a line joining two end points. [5]If two lines join at one point, they form an angle. [6]An angle is two rays* that extend from the same point. [7]Two rays that intersect at a right angle (90-degree) are called **perpendicular**.

[8]Lines can be joined to form geometric figures. [9]A three-sided figure is a **triangle**. [10]There are several different types of triangles, which vary according to the length and angles of the lines that form them. [11]Here are some definitions.

> [12]**Equilateral triangle:** a triangle with three equal sides
> [13]**Isosceles triangle:** a triangle with two equal sides
> [14]**Scalene triangle:** a triangle with no equal sides

[15]A four-sided figure is called a **quadrilateral**, which is four points joined by four lines to produce four sides. [16]The following are definitions of specific types of quadrilaterals:

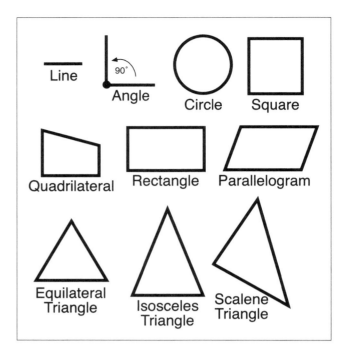

> [17]**Parallelogram:** a quadrilateral that has opposite sides that are parallel and equal in length
> [18]**Rectangle:** a parallelogram that has four right angles
> [19]**Square:** a rectangle that has four equal sides

[20]The last basic geometric figure to define is the **circle**, a perfectly round enclosed shape made by a curved line. [21]All points on the line are the same distance (equidistant) from a fixed point in the center of the circle.

*ray: a half line that extends forever in one direction from a point

DIRECTIONS: Choose or write the best answer to each of the following questions using the evidence presented in the passage. When required, list specific sentence numbers or paragraph letters from the story to support your answer.

1. According to the diagram, which of the following figures has the most right angles?

   A. circle
   B. square
   C. parallelogram
   D. scalene triangle

2. Using the diagram, choose the figure listed below that does NOT contain perpendicular lines.

   A. angle
   B. square
   C. rectangle
   D. parallelogram

3. Choose the statement that is accurate.

   A. All circles have sides.
   B. All squares are rectangles.
   C. All triangles are equilateral.
   D. All quadrilaterals have right angles.

   Give the number of the sentence that best supports your answer. ____

4. How does an equilateral triangle differ from a scalene triangle?

   _____

   _____

   _____

   _____

5. "A rhombus has four equal sides but no right angles." In which section of the passage would this sentence best fit?

   A. sentences 1–6
   B. sentences 7–11
   C. sentences 12–15
   D. sentences 16–21

6. Which of these best describes the purpose of the passage?

   A. to show similar things
   B. to match pictures to words
   C. to define triangles and circles
   D. to describe geometric shapes

34. Cesar Chavez: A Biography
by Carrie Beckwith

A [1]Cesar Chavez was a very important leader to Mexican and Mexican-American farm workers. [2]He had been a farm worker himself, and he knew firsthand the unfair treatment they faced. [3]Chavez led protests and strikes against farm owners for higher wages. [4]He also boycotted companies that did not treat their workers fairly.

B [5]Chavez began his political career working for a group that helped Mexican-Americans in California. [6]Chavez helped people sign up to vote and talked to them about their rights. [7]Chavez strongly believed that farm workers needed a union,* so he started the United Farm Workers Union and got many people to join.

C [8]Chavez's first strike with the union was against owners of grape farms in California. [9]The strike was a protest against the low pay farm workers received. [10]Chavez's strike kept union workers out of the fields, and many of the crops rotted. [11]The farm owners lost a lot of money. [12]Some farm workers were beaten for going on strike. [13]When people found out about the strike and the beatings, they decided to do something. [14]Buyers, shipping companies, and store owners boycotted the grape growers by refusing to buy, ship, or carry grapes. [15]Finally, after five years of bargaining with the union, farm owners raised the farm workers' pay. [16]It was a great victory for the workers and the union.

D [17]Chavez led many strikes and marches before his death in 1993. [18]He traveled all over the world, talking about the rights of farm workers. [19]The message that was first delivered in California spread throughout the entire world. [20]To this day, Cesar Chavez's life continues to have a powerful effect on the well-being of the farm worker.

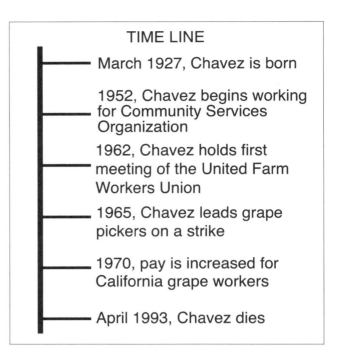

TIME LINE

— March 1927, Chavez is born

— 1952, Chavez begins working for Community Services Organization

— 1962, Chavez holds first meeting of the United Farm Workers Union

— 1965, Chavez leads grape pickers on a strike

— 1970, pay is increased for California grape workers

— April 1993, Chavez dies

*union: an organization that brings workers together to improve working conditions and wages

DIRECTIONS: Choose or write the best answer to each of the following questions using the evidence presented in the passage. When required, list specific sentence numbers or paragraph letters from the story to support your answer.

1. Which of the following sentences gives the main idea of the passage?
   A. Chavez helped people sign up to vote.
   B. Chavez traveled the world to speak about farm workers' rights.
   C. Chavez accomplished much for farm workers.
   D. Chavez organized a successful strike in California.

   List the letters of the 2 paragraphs that best support your answer. ____, ____

2. As used in paragraph C, the word *strike* means
   A. stopping of payment.
   B. notice of leaving.
   C. stopping of work.
   D. firing of a worker.

3. What was the final result of the strike against owners of grape farms in California?

   _____

   _____

   _____

   Give the number of the sentence that best supports your answer. ____

4. How long did it take before grape farm owners came to an agreement with the union?

   _____

5. How old was Chavez when he died?

   _____

   _____

6. Why did many people refuse to buy, ship, or carry grapes?

   _____

   _____

   _____

   _____

   List the numbers of the 2 sentences that best support your answer. ____, ____

7. List two sentences in paragraph D that support the fact that Chavez was an active union leader.

   Sentences ____, ____

35. How to Make Dough Ornaments
by Carrie Beckwith

A   [1]Making ornaments couldn't be easier! [2]Just follow these quick and easy directions for dough-making fun.

B   [3]Before you begin, you will need the following ingredients:

> 1 cup salt
> 1 1/2 cups hot tap water
> 4 cups flour

C   [4]Combine salt and hot water in a large bowl. [5]Stir the mixture until the salt dissolves into the water. [6]Then add flour to the salt water mixture and stir thoroughly. [7]Next, knead the flour and salt water until it becomes a soft and spongy dough. [8]Place your dough in a plastic bag and let it rest for several hours so that it can thicken. [9]After letting it rest, take the dough out of the bag.

D   [10]Preheat your oven to 300° Fahrenheit. [11]You can then roll out the dough and use cookie cutters to make shapes, or you can use your own two hands to make whatever you like. [12]Be careful not to make your dough ornaments too thick (no more than 1/2"), or they won't cook properly. [13]Once you are done crafting your ornaments, place them on a cookie sheet and bake them in the oven for about one hour to harden them. [14]Let them cool for at least another hour.

E   [15]The last part of making ornaments is the best. [16]Now it's time to get your watercolors out and paint your ornaments. [17]When the paint has dried, you can glue buttons, flowers, or glitter onto the ornaments. [18]You can also glue ornaments together, attach ribbons, or even glue a magnet to the back. [19]Be as creative as you like, and, most important, have fun!

DIRECTIONS: Choose or write the best answer to each of the following questions using the evidence presented in the passage. When required, list specific sentence numbers or paragraph letters from the story to support your answer.

1. The purpose of the article is to
   A. explain all the different things you can add to your ornament.
   B. explain how fun and easy it is to make ornaments.
   C. explain how to make the dough.
   D. explain how to decorate your home.

   Give the letter of the paragraph that best supports your answer. ____

2. What warning does the article give?

   _____

   _____

   Give the number of the sentence that best supports your answer. ____

3. What would happen if you didn't preheat the oven before putting in the dough ornaments?

   _____

   _____

   _____

   _____

4. What do you think causes the dough to get soft and spongy?

   _____

   _____

   Give the number of the sentence that best supports your number. ____

5. Is the following sentence a fact or an opinion? "The last part of making ornaments is the best."

   _____

6. In what order does the author present the information?
   A. by importance
   B. randomly
   C. step-by-step
   D. by difficulty

7. What must you do just after your mixture has become a dough?
   A. Preheat the oven.
   B. Place the dough in a bag and let it rest.
   C. Roll out the dough and begin making ornaments.
   D. Stir the mixture thoroughly.

   Give the number of the sentence that best supports your answer. ____

36. All Around the Sun
by David White

A [1]One way to study the planets in our solar system is by their distance from the Sun. [2]Mercury is closest to the Sun, with Venus not far behind. [3]Earth is the third planet out from the Sun. [4]From there outward, it's Mars, Jupiter, Saturn, Uranus, Neptune, and Pluto. [5]Pluto is farthest, more than 3 billion miles from the Sun.

B [6]A planet's distance from the Sun influences its surface temperature and atmosphere. [7]The closer a planet is to the Sun, the hotter that planet is. [8]Earth's average temperature is 57 degrees Fahrenheit. [9]Mercury can get as hot as 625 degrees. [10]Faraway Pluto, on the other hand, has an average temperature of 300 degrees below zero.

C [11]The number of moons a planet has also seems to be related to its distance from the Sun. [12]Generally, the closer a planet is to the Sun, the fewer moons it has. [13]Mercury and Venus, which are closest to the Sun, have no moons. [14]Earth has only one moon. [15]Saturn, which is much farther from the Sun, is believed to have 18 moons. [16]The only exception to the rule is Pluto, which has just one moon.

D [17]The closer a planet is to the Sun, the fewer days (or years) it takes for that planet to orbit (go once around) the Sun. [18]Earth's orbit is 365 days, or one year. [19]Mercury's orbit is only 88 days. [20]The largest planet, Jupiter, takes 11.86 Earth years to complete one orbit. [21]It's not just the large planets that have long orbits, though. [22]Tiny Pluto takes about 248 years to go once around the Sun.

The Nine Planets

Planet	Miles from Sun
Mercury	36 million
Venus	67 million
Earth	93 million
Mars	142 million
Jupiter	484 million
Saturn	888 million
Uranus	1.78 billion
Neptune	2.79 billion
Pluto	3.66 billion

DIRECTIONS: Choose or write the best answer to each of the following questions using the evidence presented in the passage. When required, list specific sentence numbers or paragraph letters from the story to support your answer.

1. List the six planets closest to the Sun in order from nearest to farthest.

   _____

   _____

   _____

   _____

2. Which sentence in paragraph A best supports the idea that the solar system is huge?

   Sentence ____

3. Name two things that are related to a planet's distance from the Sun.

   _____

   _____

   _____

   Give the number of the sentence that best supports each thing. ____, ____

4. Which of these planets is closest to Earth?
   A. Mars
   B. Venus
   C. Mercury
   D. Jupiter

5. If scientists discovered a tenth planet 1.1 billion miles away from the Sun, to which two planets would it be closest?
   A. Uranus and Neptune
   B. Saturn and Uranus
   C. Neptune and Pluto
   D. Jupiter and Saturn

6. Give two examples from paragraphs C and D that show how Mercury and Earth are different.

   _____

   _____

   _____

   _____

   _____

   _____

   List the numbers of the 2 sentences that best support each example.
   1. ____, ____ 2. ____, ____

7. The closer a planet is to the Sun,
   A. the smaller it is.
   B. the more moons it has.
   C. the thicker its atmosphere is.
   D. the hotter it is.

   Give the number of the sentence that best supports your answer. ____

37. What Do Owls Eat?
by Cheryl Block

A   [1]Owls are carnivores, animals that eat other animals. [2]In the wild, their diet is mainly small mammals such as mice and squirrels, and birds. [3]You can look at an owl's actual diet by studying an owl pellet. [4]An owl pellet is food that an owl has eaten but could not digest. [5]An owl usually coughs up one pellet a day. [6]The owl forms the pellet in its stomach and then coughs it up, similar to a cat's coughing up a hairball after grooming itself. [7]These pellets are usually found below the owl's roosting place.

B   [8]Dissecting a pellet will tell you what an owl has eaten. [9]Begin by placing the pellet in a bowl and adding a small amount of water to make it easier to remove the outer coating. [10]You should use forceps or tweezers to make it easier to remove the outer coating. [11]This coating is made up of the fur and feathers of animals the owl has eaten.

C   [12]Now carefully begin to break the pellet open. [13]Inside you will find bits and pieces of animal bones. [14]You may even find a tiny rat skull. [15]Place these skeletal parts on a sheet of paper or cardboard. [16]You might want to try to piece the bones together to determine what kind of animal the owl ate. [17]Parts of several animals may be found inside one pellet.

D   [18]When you are done dissecting the owl pellet, record the types of bones you found (leg bone, jawbone, etc.) and what kind of animal you think they belonged to. [19]You now have a record of an owl's diet.

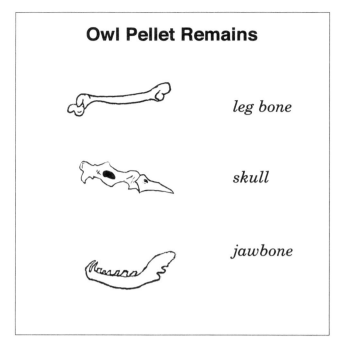

Owl Pellet Remains

leg bone

skull

jawbone

DIRECTIONS: Choose or write the best answer to each of the following questions using the evidence presented in the passage. When required, list specific sentence numbers or paragraph letters from the story to support your answer.

1. What coats the outside of an owl pellet?

   _____

   _____

   _____

   Give the number of the sentence that best supports your answer. ____

2. According to paragraph A, why does an owl cough up a pellet?

   _____

   _____

   _____

   Give the number of the sentence that best supports your answer.____

3. Looking at the skull pictured in the diagram, how might you determine that it belongs to a bird?

   _____

   _____

4. Why would it be helpful to identify what kind of body parts are in the pellet? (as shown on the diagram)

   _____

   _____

   _____

   _____

5. How does a cat's hairball compare to an owl pellet?

   _____

   _____

   _____

   _____

   List the numbers of the 2 sentences that best support your answer. ____, ____

6. As used in sentences 8 and 18, what does the word *dissecting* most closely mean?
   A. giving an estimate
   B. putting together
   C. separating into pieces
   D. cleaning thoroughly

7. Why do you think owl pellets are commonly found beneath an owl's roosting place?
   A. This is the place an owl rests and sleeps during the day.
   B. The pellets are used to make the owls' nests.
   C. Owls toss them out when they clean their nests.
   D. The pellets are used to attract prey.

38. Comanche Horsemen
by Carrie Beckwith

[1]The North American tribe called the Comanche were known for their outstanding skill with horses. [2]As early as age four or five, Comanche children—boys and girls—were given ponies. [3]Young boys, in particular, were trained for war. [4]They were taught how to pick up objects from the ground while riding their ponies at full speed. [5]Gradually, the objects increased in size until the rider was able to pick up another man! [6]This skill was necessary in battle when a rider would have to rescue an injured tribe member.

[7]The Comanche also learned how to ride alongside the horse's flank. [8]The rider was able to ride this way by hooking his heel over one side of the horse and resting his elbow in a rope looped round the horse's neck. [9]This position protected him from enemy arrows. [10]The rider was still able to shoot his own arrows from either above the horse's back or underneath its neck.

[11]Part of the Comanche's success with horses was due to their skill at horse-breeding. [12]Their horses came from the half-Andalusian, half-Arab horses that the Spaniards brought over in the 16th century. [13]After many years of breeding only their finest stallions, the Comanche produced what is now known as the Indian pony, a very strong and responsive horse.

horse's flank

[14]In addition to being skilled riders and breeders, many of the Comanche were also skilled horse thieves! [15]For the Comanche, wealth was measured by the number of horses they had, and no other tribe owned more horses than the Comanche. [16]One Comanche band of 2000 owned close to 15,000 horses!

[17]The Comanche's skill in horse riding, horse breeding, and even horse stealing helped them to become one of the most successful tribes of the Plains.

DIRECTIONS: Choose or write the best answer to each of the following questions using the evidence presented in the passage. When required, list specific sentence numbers or paragraph letters from the story to support your answer.

1. What is the main idea of the passage?
   A. The Comanche were skilled at horse stealing.
   B. The Comanche were skilled with horses.
   C. The Comanche were trained to ride horses.
   D. The Comanche children were trained for war.

   Give the number of the sentence that best supports your answer. _____

2. Which detail from the story best supports the idea that the Comanche were talented horse riders?
   A. Comanche children were given ponies at an early age.
   B. The Comanche measured wealth by the number of horses they had.
   C. The Comanche learned how to ride alongside a horse's flank.
   D. The Comanche helped develop the Indian pony.

3. Why was it necessary for riders to learn how to pick up objects from the ground?

   _____

   _____

   _____

   _____

   Give the number of the sentence that best supports your answer. _____

4. Why was it helpful to be able to ride alongside the horse's flank?

   _____

   _____

   _____

   _____

   List the numbers of the 2 sentences that best support your answer. _____, _____

5. "One Comanche band of 2000 owned close to 15,000 horses!" According to the passage, what can you conclude about this band?
   A. The band was wealthy.
   B. The band stole the horses.
   C. The band had the same number of horses as other tribes.
   D. The band trained all 15,000 of the horses.

   Give the number of the sentence that best supports your answer. _____

6. What can you conclude about the Comanche's horses?
   A. They required little care.
   B. They were hard to train.
   C. They were dressed and painted for war.
   D. They were important to the tribe.

   Give the number of the sentence that best supports your answer. _____

39. Blowing Hot and Cold
by David White

A   [1]Differences in air temperature can tell us which way the wind blows. [2]Hot air is lighter than cold air. [3]So, the colder the air is, the heavier it is. [4]The heavier it is, the more pressure it has (and the more it pushes downward).

B   [5]A difference in air pressure, created by differences in air temperature, causes wind. [6]Air in a high-pressure area (cold air) will move to a low-pressure area (hot air). [7]So, if a large pocket of cold air is east of a large pocket of hot air, the wind will blow west.

C   [8]Also, the greater the difference between the temperatures of the two pockets of air, the faster the wind blows. [9]If the cold air is biting cold and the hot air is blazing hot, then the wind will blow at a high rate of speed between those two pockets of air.

D   [10]Wind is especially noticeable near the oceans. [11]In the daytime, the temperature of seawater is usually lower than the temperature of land at the seashore, so people on the coast almost always feel a sea breeze coming inland. [12]At night, the temperature of the land may become cooler than the water (ocean). [13]The breeze then switches directions and blows from land to ocean—a land breeze.

E   [14]Wind, the movement of air around us, is caused by differences in air temperature and pressure.

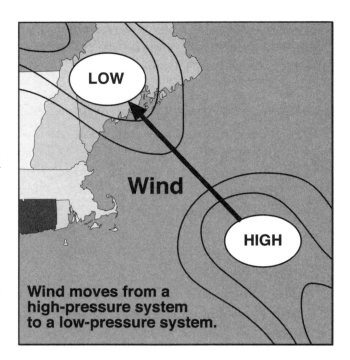

Wind moves from a high-pressure system to a low-pressure system.

DIRECTIONS: Choose or write the best answer to each of the following questions using the evidence presented in the passage. When required, list specific sentence numbers or paragraph letters from the story to support your answer.

1. What causes wind?

_____

_____

Give the number of the sentence that best supports your answer. ____

2. What is the main idea of the passage?
   A. to describe how wind blows
   B. to compare hot air and cold air
   C. to describe how temperature and air pressure affect wind
   D. to describe the range of air temperatures throughout the day

3. Why does the wind along the seashore change direction at night?

_____

_____

_____

List the numbers of the 2 sentences that best support your answer. ____,
____

4. If the wind is blowing south toward you, what does that suggest about the air pressure to the north of you?

_____

_____

_____

Give the number of the sentence that best supports your answer. ____

5. Look at the diagram below. Between which two points is the wind blowing more quickly?

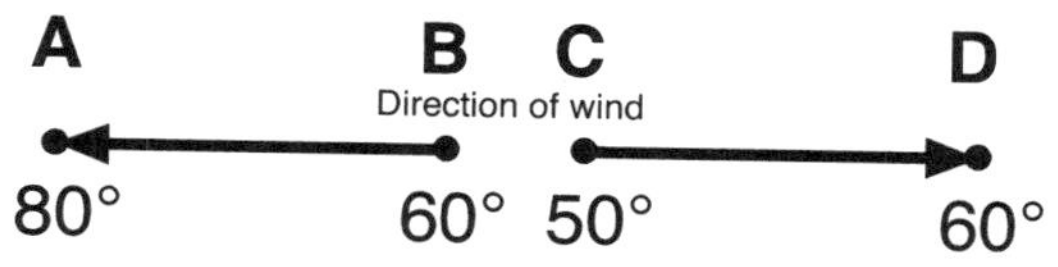

A   **B** **C**   **D**
        Direction of wind
80°   60° 50°   60°

_____

_____

Give the number of the sentence that best supports your answer. ____

6. In the diagram above, the air above Point B is colder than the air above Point A. What two other comparisons can be made about the air above Point B and Point A?

_____

_____

_____

List the numbers of the 2 sentences in paragraph A that best support your answer. ____, ____

7. How do the words "biting" and "blazing" in sentence 9 help to describe how the air might feel?

_____

_____

_____

_____

40. The Challenger Disaster
by Carrie Beckwith

[1]On January 28, 1986, the space shuttle *Challenger* was getting ready to blast off into space. [2]Inside the shuttle were seven astronauts, one of whom was a school teacher, Christa McAuliffe. [3]Christa was the first private citizen in the entire history of space travel to be chosen for a space flight. [4]She was chosen from more than 11,000 teachers. [5]NASA officials felt that Christa would be able to capture the experience of space travel and put it into words for students all over the world. [6]While aboard the *Challenger*, McAuliffe's duties were to include presenting two "live" lessons: one on the roles and duties of all the astronauts aboard the *Challenger* and the second on the purpose of space exploration.

[7]Students and faculty members from McAuliffe's school were watching the event on television. [8]They held big signs that said "We're with U Christa." [9]It was a dangerous mission and the astronauts understood that, but they were confident and excited. [10]McAuliffe hoped students would get excited about space exploration as a result of seeing her, an "ordinary person," in space.

[11]The countdown began: "T minus 10, 9, 8, 7, 6, we have main engine start, 4, 3, 2, 1, and lift-off." [12]Shouts and happy cheers rang out from the auditorium of McAuliffe's Concord, New Hampshire, elementary school. [13]Seventy-three seconds later, an explosion lit up the sky. [14]Someone yelled to quiet the cheering.

The Space Shuttle *Challenger*
January 28, 1986

[15]"The vehicle has exploded," the voice from the television said. [16]Some people cried; others stared at the television in disbelief. [17]The excited cheers and happy faces of McAuliffe's students and coworkers quickly disappeared.

[18]Afterwards, many national leaders spoke about the event. [19]In a memorial service for the astronauts, President Reagan remembered Christa McAuliffe, who he said had "captured the imagination of the entire nation."

[20]The next six months were spent investigating the cause of the disaster. [21]As a result of the investigation, several changes were made to ensure a safer, more reliable space shuttle. [22]Since then, NASA has launched many successful shuttles into space.

DIRECTIONS: Choose or write the best answer to each of the following questions using the evidence presented in the passage. When required, list specific sentence numbers or paragraph letters from the story to support your answer.

1. What was the author's main purpose in writing this article?
   A. to describe the *Challenger* disaster and the members of the crew
   B. to explain how the shuttle exploded
   C. to describe the *Challenger* disaster and Christa McAuliffe's role in the mission
   D. to call attention to the importance of space exploration

2. Give two examples of how Christa McAuliffe was different from the other astronauts.

   _____

   _____

   _____

3. List the numbers of the two sentences that best support the idea that the people watching were excited about the *Challenger* mission.

   Sentences ____, ____

4. What was going to be one of McAuliffe's duties while aboard the *Challenger?*

   _____

   _____

   _____

   _____

   Give the number of the sentence that best supports your answer. ____

5. What did McAuliffe hope would get students excited about space exploration?

   _____

   _____

   _____

   _____

6. From the last paragraph of the article, you can conclude that the space program
   A. is in danger of being done away with.
   B. has had several disasters.
   C. is safer than it was.
   D. is larger than it once was.

   Give the number of the sentence that best supports your answer. ____

41. Little Green Food Factories
by Cheryl Block

[1]Humans and animals must eat plants or other animals to get energy. [2]They cannot make their own food. [3]Plants are able to make their own food through a process called photosynthesis. [4]Most of this process takes place in the plant's leaves.

[5]A plant is like a little green food factory. [6]Just as a factory uses raw materials to make a product, a plant uses raw materials to make its food. [7]These raw materials are carbon dioxide and water. [8]Leaves take in carbon dioxide from the air through their pores (tiny openings in the surface). [9]Roots take in water from the soil; the water passes up through the stem to the leaves. [10]The plant leaves will convert, or change, these raw materials into food.

[11]Both a factory and a plant need energy to convert raw materials. [12]The energy for photosynthesis comes from sunlight. [13]Chlorophyll, the pigment that gives plants their green color, absorbs the sunlight and then changes it into chemical energy.

[14]Using this chemical energy, the plant combines water and carbon dioxide to make sugar. [15]At the same time, the plant gives off oxygen we need to breathe.

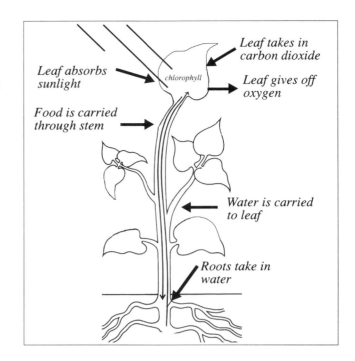

Leaf absorbs sunlight

Leaf takes in carbon dioxide

chlorophyll

Leaf gives off oxygen

Food is carried through stem

Water is carried to leaf

Roots take in water

[16]Sugar is the food that a plant needs to survive. [17]The sugar is carried from the leaves to other parts of the plant and stored. [18]During winter, plants that lose their leaves must rely on this stored food until they regrow their leaves in the spring.

[19]Green plants are the only living things that are able to make their own food. [20]Even animals who eat only other animals depend on plant-eating animals for food. [21]Humans and animals could not survive if the little green food factories stopped producing food.

DIRECTIONS: Choose or write the best answer to each of the following questions using the evidence presented in the passage. When required, list specific sentence numbers or paragraph letters from the story to support your answer.

1. Besides providing food, what is another way that plants help us?

_____

_____

_____

_____

Give the number of the sentence that best supports your answer. ____

2. Which of the following occurs first after chlorophyll converts sunlight to chemical energy?

A. The plant absorbs water through its roots.

B. The plant combines water and carbon dioxide.

C. The chemical energy turns leaves green.

D. Sugar is transported throughout the plant.

Give the number of the sentence that best supports your answer. ____

3. What is the meaning of the word *pigment* in sentence 13?

A. A kind of chemical used on plants.

B. A kind of sugar produced by the plant.

C. A substance that produces color.

D. A kind of energy.

4. Where is most of the chlorophyll in a plant located?

_____

_____

5. Which of the following gives the main idea of the passage?

A. Both a factory and a plant use energy to convert raw materials.

B. Humans and animals must eat plants or other animals.

C. Plants make their own food through a process called photosynthesis.

D. Chlorophyll absorbs sunlight and then changes it into chemical energy.

6. The article compares a plant to a factory. Give two examples that show how they are alike.

_____

_____

_____

_____

List the numbers of the 2 sentences that best support your answer. ____,
____

42. Ancient Egyptian Hieroglyphs
by Cheryl Block

A   [1]The writing system of the early Egyptians was tied to their religious beliefs. [2]Ancient Egyptians used a form of picture writing called hieroglyphs. [3]In early hieroglyphic writing, a picture symbol stood for the object shown. [4]A picture of an owl meant an owl.

B   [5]Eventually, the Egyptians began to develop an alphabet. [6]The picture symbol came to stand for the sound of the letter the word began with, rather than the object itself. [7]For instance, the symbol of an owl came to represent the sound of the letter *m*, with which the Egyptian word for owl begins. [8]Symbols could now be combined to represent more complex words and ideas.

C   [9]Hieroglyphic writing was an important part of the Egyptians' belief in life after death. [10]Egyptians believed that written words had magical powers that captured the spirit of a person or object. [11]If a person's name was written or carved, the person's spirit would remain within that writing forever after death. [12]They also believed that if they wrote an object's name on the object itself and on the walls of the tomb, they would have that object in their next life. [13]Names were also written on the walls in case the actual objects were removed by robbers. [14]As a result, there are examples of

EGYPTIAN HIEROGLYPHS		
Symbol	Object	Letter
	a foot	B as in bat
	a snake	F as in fat
	an owl	M as in mummy

hieroglyphic writing on the walls of tombs and temples, on statues, and on ordinary items such as mirrors.

D   [15]Because of their magical powers, hieroglyphs were also considered a powerful weapon. [16]Removing a person's name from the tomb erased not only all memory of the person, but also his or her chance for an eternal life. [17]When Queen Hatshepsut died in 1470 B.C., her stepson Tuthmosis II, who had always hated her, took his revenge by having her name and pictures removed from all her temples. [18]To him and other Egyptians, it was as if she had never existed.

DIRECTIONS: Choose or write the best answer to each of the following questions using the evidence presented in the passage. When required, list specific sentence numbers or paragraph letters from the story to support your answer.

1. How was early hieroglyphic writing different from later hieroglyphic writing?

   _____

   _____

   _____

   _____

   List the numbers of the 2 sentences that best support your answer. ____,

   ____

2. In paragraph B, how did the development of an alphabet help the Egyptians?

   _____

   _____

   _____

   _____

   Give the number of the sentence that best supports your answer. ____

3. Egyptian alphabet symbols represented
   A. the sound of the first letter in a word.
   B. the sound of the vowel in a word.
   C. the sound of the last letter in a word.
   D. the first syllable in the word.

   Give the number of the sentence that best supports your answer. ____

4. What did Egyptians think would happen if a person's written name were erased?
   A. The gods could not find that person.
   B. The person would die sooner.
   C. The person's spirit would be erased.
   D. The person would live eternally.

   Give the number of the sentence that best supports your answer. ____

5. How did writing an object's name on the wall allow the person to have that object in the next life?

   _____

   _____

   _____

   _____

   Give the number of the sentence that best supports your answer. ____

6. The main idea of the passage is that hieroglyphic writing was
   A. commonly used in the Egyptians' daily lives.
   B. found on the walls of tombs.
   C. important to the Egyptians' belief in the afterlife.
   D. used mainly to decorate homes.

43. Almonds for Sale
by Margaret Hockett

A [1]DELICIOUS...and so <u>NUTRITIOUS</u>!
[2]Buy Heart Almonds—They Have It All.

B   **Bone-Building Calcium**:
[3]Maintain strong bones, teeth, and nails—almonds have about twice the calcium of milk!

C   **Tasty Treat**: [4]Each nut rewards you with a delicate flavor you won't forget!

D   **Convenient Snack**: [5]Grab a handful on your way out the door each morning. [6]They pack a big nutritional punch but are small enough to take anywhere.

E   **Choice of Blanched or Unblanched**: [7]Blanched almonds cost a little more, but you'll be sure of a tasty, nutritional snack that has no prussic acid.* ([8]If you choose almonds that have not been blanched, we recommend that you remove the skins yourself—see below for instructions.)

F   [9]To remove the skins from a handful of almonds, start by boiling a cup of water. [10]Drop almonds carefully into the water and soak them for 20 to 30 seconds. [11]Drain and rinse with cold water. [12]Finally, squeeze each almond between your thumb and finger. [13]Be careful—the slippery almonds may try to escape by shooting out in any direction! [14]But they can't escape giving you plenty of calcium for healthy bones, teeth, and nails.

*prussic acid: another name for hydrocyanic acid, a poisonous chemical

DIRECTIONS: Choose or write the best answer to each of the following questions using the evidence presented in the passage. When required, list specific sentence numbers or paragraph letters from the story to support your answer.

1. Why is the word *nutritious* shown as it is in paragraph A?

   _____

   _____

   _____

   _____

2. From paragraph B, you CANNOT conclude that

   A. calcium builds strong bones.
   B. milk contains calcium.
   C. almonds have more vitamins than milk.
   D. milk has less calcium than almonds.

3. Based on the information in the passage, you can conclude that prussic acid

   A. is a nutrient.
   B. is good for the stomach.
   C. is in milk.
   D. is in the almond skin.

   List the numbers of the 2 sentences that best support your answer. ____,

   ____

4. If you are "careful" as it warns in sentence 13, you will most likely

   A. avoid the hot water.
   B. hold a knife correctly.
   C. keep the almond skin out of your food.
   D. prevent the nut from escaping.

   Give the number of the sentence that best supports your answer. ____

5. In section F, you are told to do five different things to the almonds after boiling the water. List these five actions in the correct order.

   1. _____

   2. _____

   3. _____

   4. _____

   5. _____

6. The author's main purpose is to

   A. educate you about health.
   B. convince you to buy almonds.
   C. describe how to remove skins.
   D. entertain you with descriptions.

   Give the number of the sentence that best supports your answer. ____

7. In general, you could say that almonds are

   A. good for you.
   B. difficult to eat.
   C. inexpensive.
   D. full of iron.

44. The Food Chain
by Cheryl Block

A [1]What is a food chain? [2]All organisms are connected by their need for food. [3]Food provides energy. [4]A food chain shows how the living things in a community are connected by who eats what. [5]Each link in the chain represents an organism in the community. [6]Energy is transferred through the chain as one organism feeds on another.

B [7]All food chains begin with the producers, which are the plants. [8]Plants are able to produce their own food. [9]The animals in a community are called consumers. [10]There are two types of consumers, primary and secondary. [11]Primary consumers are animals that eat only plants. [12]Secondary consumers are animals that eat smaller animals or both plants and animals. [13]Consumers cannot make their own food; they must rely on plants and other animals for energy.

C [14]Let's look at a woodland community as an example. [15]In the woodland, grass, trees, and other plants are the producers. [16]Rabbits are primary consumers; they eat the grass and plants. [17]Foxes are secondary consumers; they eat the rabbits. [18]This is how a food chain is linked together. [19]One organism feeds on another.

D [20]At the end of each food chain are the decomposers. [21]All living things die. [22]The decomposers feed on waste products and dead matter, both plant and animal. [23]Fungi and bacteria are the main decomposers. [24]As they break down dead material, they add nutrients* to the soil. [25]These nutrients help the plants to grow, and the chain continues.

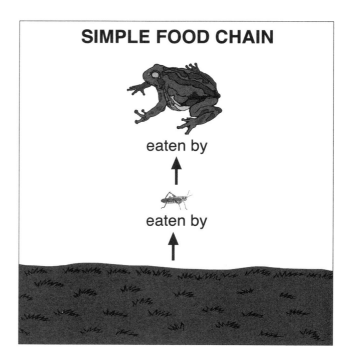

SIMPLE FOOD CHAIN

eaten by

eaten by

*nutrient: a substance, such as a mineral or vitamin, that is found in a food and needed for health

DIRECTIONS: Choose or write the best answer to each of the following questions using the evidence presented in the passage. When required, list specific sentence numbers or paragraph letters from the story to support your answer.

1. How is a primary consumer different from a secondary consumer?

   _____

   _____

   _____

   _____

   List the numbers of the 2 sentences that best support your answer. ____, ____

2. You can conclude that plants are self-supporting because they
   A. produce food for animals.
   B. produce their own food.
   C. get energy from the Sun.
   D. feed on dead matter.

   Give the number of the sentence that best supports your answer. ____

3. Which of the following is the correct sequence in a food chain?
   A. A secondary consumer is eaten by a primary consumer.
   B. A secondary consumer is eaten by a producer.
   C. A decomposer is eaten by a producer.
   D. A producer is eaten by a primary consumer.

   List the numbers of the 2 sentences that best support your answer. ____, ____

4. Which animal shown in the diagram is a primary consumer?

   _____

5. How are all organisms in a community connected?

   _____

   _____

   Give the number of the sentence that best supports your answer. ____

6. In an ocean community, which of the following would be a producer?
   A. whale
   B. tuna fish
   C. clam
   D. seaweed

   Give the number of the sentence that best supports your answer. ____

7. What might happen if the rabbits disappeared from the woodland community?
   A. The grass would stop growing.
   B. The foxes would have to eat grass.
   C. The foxes would have to find other food.
   D. There would be too many foxes.

   Give the letter of the paragraph that best supports your answer. ____

8. Part of a decomposer's role in the food chain is to
   A. add nutrients to the soil.
   B. produce its own food.
   C. eat plants.
   D. feed other animals.

   List the numbers of the 2 sentences that best support your answer. ____, ____

45. Who Was Benjamin Banneker?
by David White

[1]In the 18th century, when most African-Americans were considered second-class citizens or property, Benjamin Banneker was making a name for himself.

[2]Born a free man in 1731, Banneker showed an early interest and skill in math and science. [3]He was also good at designing and building things. [4]Seeing a pocket watch for the first time when he was 19, Banneker decided to build a clock of his own. [5]This remarkable hand-carved clock was made entirely of wood, and it kept accurate time for more than 40 years.

[6]Banneker also developed a strong interest and skill in astronomy. [7]In fact, he correctly predicted a solar eclipse for April 14, 1789, proving wrong many well-known astronomers. [8]His successful prediction made him famous.

[9]Banneker's scientific ability and new-found fame led to his publishing an annual almanac, beginning in 1791. [10]Each year, people of all races would read the almanac for its information on medicine, weather, moon phases, and times for sunrise and sunset.

[11]The almanac's accuracy and its wide audience disproved a common belief of the day—that African-Americans were inferior to European-Americans. [12]When Thomas Jefferson publicly made racist remarks, Banneker sent a strongly worded response to Jefferson along with a copy of his almanac. [13]Jefferson was so impressed with Banneker's scientific accuracy that he sent the almanac to

European scientists. [14]Thus, Banneker's fame spread to Europe.

[15]From such widespread recognition came the opportunity for Benjamin Banneker to make his most lasting impression. [16]In 1791, President George Washington appointed Banneker to the engineering group that was designing the city of Washington, D.C. [17]Banneker thus became the first African-American to receive a presidential appointment. [18]Pierre Charles L'Enfant, the head of the group, quit in 1792 after a disagreement and took his plans back to France. [19]Banneker reproduced those plans from memory, and the new capital was born.

[20]Benjamin Banneker published his almanac until 1802, when he was physically unable to continue. [21]He died four years later, a famous and well-respected African-American.

DIRECTIONS: Choose or write the best answer to each of the following questions using the evidence presented in the passage. When required, list specific sentence numbers or paragraph letters from the story to support your answer.

1. What were the gears of Benjamin Banneker's clock made of?

   _____

   Give the number of the sentence that best supports your answer. ____

2. What is the main idea of the passage?
   A. to show how hard work can pay off
   B. to tell how to predict a solar eclipse
   C. to show the problems that African-Americans faced
   D. to describe a remarkable African-American's accomplishments

3. Put these accomplishments by Benjamin Banneker in their correct time order.

   ____ creates clock

   ____ publishes first almanac

   ____ reproduces Washington, D.C., plans

   ____ writes letter to Thomas Jefferson

   ____ predicts solar eclipse

4. How often did Benjamin Banneker publish his almanac?
   A. once a day
   B. once a week
   C. once a month
   D. once a year

   Give the number of the sentence that best supports your answer. ____

5. Which of these would Benjamin Banneker NOT have witnessed in his lifetime?
   A. The Revolutionary War (1775–1783)
   B. The Louisiana Purchase (1803)
   C. The completion of Washington, D.C. (1800)
   D. The War of 1812 (1812–1814)

   List the numbers of the 2 sentences that best support your answer. ____, ____

6. List one accomplishment of Benjamin Banneker in each of the following fields:

   Astronomy _____

   _____

   Architecture _____

   _____

   Writing _____

   _____

7. Why did Thomas Jefferson send Benjamin Banneker's almanac to European scientists even though he knew the book was written by an African-American?

   _____

   _____

   Give the number of the sentence that best supports your answer. ____

46. The Land Down Under
by Cheryl Block

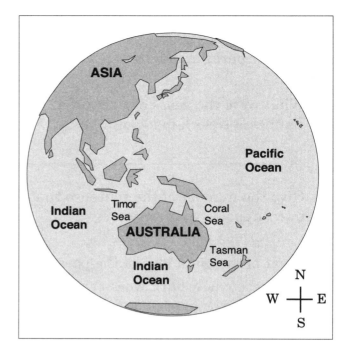

[1]The smallest of the seven continents and the only continent that is an island, Australia is unique in many ways. [2]Located between the Indian Ocean and the Pacific Ocean, Australia is sometimes called the land "Down Under" because of its location in the Southern Hemisphere. [3]In fact, the name Australia comes from a Latin word meaning "southern."

[4]While Australia has rain forests, plains, and mountains, nearly a third of Australia is desert. [5]It has a larger percentage of desert land for its size than any other continent and is also the driest, except for Antarctica. [6]The largest desert in Australia is called the Outback. [7]In over two-thirds of the country, the average annual rainfall is less than twenty inches.

[8]Australia is also the flattest continent. [9]This is the result of millions of years of erosion by wind, rain, and heat.

[10]The world's largest coral reef, the Great Barrier Reef, is located in the Coral Sea off the coast of Australia. [11]It measures about 1250 miles (2,025 km) in length.

[12]Because Australia was geographically isolated for millions of years, unique varieties of animals have developed there. [13]Australia has pouched mammals (marsupials) such as the kangaroo and the wallaby, and egg-laying mammals like the duck-billed platypus. [14]Only in the last two hundred years have new animal species been introduced by settlers from Europe and Asia.

[15]Given all of its unusual features, Australia would be a fascinating place to visit.

DIRECTIONS: Choose or write the best answer to each of the following questions using the evidence presented in the passage. When required, list specific sentence numbers or paragraph letters from the story to support your answer.

1. Which two statements support the idea that Australia is unique compared to other continents?
   A. Australia is flattest.
   B. Australia is in the Southern Hemisphere.
   C. Australia is an island.
   D. Australia has rain forests.

   Give the number of the sentence that best supports each answer. ____, ____

2. Which of the following was the greatest influence in the development of Australia's unusual animal population?
   A. Australia lies in the Southern Hemisphere.
   B. Australia was isolated for millions of years.
   C. Australia has a large percentage of desert.
   D. Australia has the world's largest coral reef.

   Give the number of the sentence that best supports your answer. ____

3. Where does the name Australia come from?

   _____

   _____

   _____

   _____

   Give the number of the sentence that best supports your answer. ____

4. Which of the following statements from the passage is an opinion?
   A. While Australia has rain forests, plains, and mountains, nearly a third of Australia is desert.
   B. Australia is also the flattest continent.
   C. Only in the last two hundred years have new animal species been introduced by settlers from Europe and Asia.
   D. Given all of its unusual features, Australia would be a fascinating place to visit.

5. The author's main purpose in writing this article is to
   A. show how geographic isolation has affected Australia in many ways.
   B. describe how Australia is different compared to other continents.
   C. show that Australia is the smallest of the continents.
   D. describe how unique Australia's animal life is.

   List the numbers of the 3 sentences that best support your answer. ____, ____, ____

6. Which sea is located to the northeast of Australia?
   A. Timor Sea
   B. Coral Sea
   C. Tasman Sea
   D. Pacific Ocean

47. Dress Like an Egyptian
by Margaret Hockett

A   [1]Early Egyptians dressed according to their wealth and their role in society. [2]Those who did common work wore what was practical, and those who were rich wore what was beautiful.

B   [3]The clothing of servants and laborers was simple and inexpensive. [4]It was usually white in color and rough in quality. [5]Not only was simple dress cheaper, it was easier to work in. [6]Men wore a cloth like a Scottish kilt. [7]Women wore long skirts with plain shawls or dresses without sleeves, and no jewelry. [8]Children often wore nothing at all. [9]Even their scalps were bare because they were shaved to prevent lice.

C   [10]Wealthy people dressed differently. [11]They wore colorful clothing, though fabric dye was expensive (the vibrant colors, such as gold and yellow were especially costly). [12]They could afford delicate linens of fine quality (so fine that some were as transparent as a screened window.) [13]The rich sometimes wore pleated and loosely flowing robes that would have ruled out hard work. [14]The rich also wore wigs, eye makeup, perfume, and jewelry. [15]Even children wore jewels about the neck.

D   [16]Yes, the dress of the poor was practical for labor while the decorations of the rich were not. [17]However, these rich decorations did serve at least two purposes. [18]They made the wearer feel beautiful. [19]They also reminded the working-class Egyptians of the rank and majesty of those who were wealthy.

DIRECTIONS: Choose or write the best answer to each of the following questions using the evidence presented in the passage. When required, list specific sentence numbers or paragraph letters from the story to support your answer.

1. Choose the ending that completes the main idea of the passage: Early Egyptian dress style was

   A. based on wealth.
   B. too expensive.
   C. beautifully displayed.
   D. often simple and rough.

   Give the number of the sentence that best supports your answer. _____

2. Why do you think the lower class wore mostly white clothing?

   A. White was a symbol of innocence.
   B. Colored cloth was not permitted.
   C. Rough cloth came in white only.
   D. Fabric dyes were too expensive.

   Give the number of the sentence in paragraph B that best supports your answer. _____

3. As used in sentence 11, the word *vibrant* means

   A. bright.
   B. dull.
   C. many.
   D. dark.

4. The very wealthy Egyptians dressed splendidly for several reasons. Which of the following was NOT a reason for their style of dress?

   A. It made them feel beautiful.
   B. It showed their majesty.
   C. They could buy it cheaply.
   D. They did not have to work hard.

5. You can tell from sentence 12 that transparent clothing is easy to

   A. recognize.
   B. clean up.
   C. do work in.
   D. see through.

6. Why might it have been difficult for a servant to work in clothing like that of the wealthy?

   _____

   _____

   _____

   _____

7. Why do you think a pharaoh (ruler) might dress even more elaborately than the wealthy class?

   _____

   _____

   _____

   _____

48. Natural Rhythm
by Margaret Hockett

A   [1]Many of us think of rhythm as the regular patterns of sound in music. [2]But where did rhythm come from? [3]Rhythm has been around since there have been ears and minds to appreciate it. [4]For example, within our bodies, our hearts beat with a regular tha-thump, tha-thump. [5]From the world around us come the flap-flap of bird wings and the steady pelting of rain accented by the baBOOM of thunder. [6]These patterns of sound fascinate us humans. [7]We create various rhythms with our voice, with our hands, and with objects.

B   [8]Early rhythm was primitive. [9]The first planned rhythms were probably made by clapping hands and pounding sticks on logs. [10]The pattern would have been simple, with one hit as hard as the next and equal time between hits: whack-whack-whack-whack. [11]Before long, other objects would have been added and the patterns would have grown more complex: da-da WHACK adeedle, da-da WHACK adeedle.

C   [12]Humans have developed the "logs" into hundreds of percussion* instruments from bongos to snares. [13]Modern recording artists use a number of complex rhythms within a single work of music. [14]These days, most of us are content to listen to their recordings instead of playing instruments of our own.

D   [15]Does this mean we have left our own natural rhythm-making ability behind? [16]Can we no longer relate to our rhythmical roots? [17]Let's try a test and see:

[18]1) Play a recording of your favorite music.
[19]2) Close your eyes as you listen to the rhythm.
[20]3) Check your body.

E   [21]Chances are, you're tapping your feet and swaying back and forth! [22]Yes, you've picked out a simple, regular pattern in that music—and you've still got that natural human rhythm.

*percussion: hit or struck to make sound

DIRECTIONS: Choose or write the best answer to each of the following questions using the evidence presented in the passage. When required, list specific sentence numbers or paragraph letters from the story to support your answer.

1. Describe how the cymbal in an orchestra could be compared to thunder.

   _____

   _____

   _____

   _____

2. The author uses the made-up word "baBOOM" in sentence 5. From paragraph B, give another example of a made-up word.

   _____

   _____

   Explain why you think these "words" are used.

   _____

   _____

   _____

3. As used in sentence 8, *primitive* means
   A. simple.
   B. loud.
   C. grunted.
   D. early.

4. The "logs" mentioned in sentence 12 refer to what kind of instruments?
   A. wind instruments
   B. drums
   C. organs
   D. brass instruments

   Give the letter of the paragraph that best supports your answer. _____

5. In sentence 15, why does the author ask whether we have left our rhythm-making ability behind? Choose all of the following that apply.
   A. She doesn't know the answer.
   B. She wants to introduce a test.
   C. She wants to make us think.
   D. She stresses an earlier question.

6. The purpose of paragraph B is to describe how
   A. rhythm became more complicated.
   B. objects were used to make rhythm.
   C. rhythm could make us healthy.
   D. particular patterns were created.

7. Paragraph A gives an example of rhythm that occurs in our bodies. What is that example?

   _____

   _____

   _____

   _____

49. Jackie Robinson, All-star
by Margaret Hockett

A   [1]Jackie Robinson was a superb baseball player. [2]However, in the 1940s, a black man had little hope of playing in the major leagues. [3]Little hope, that is, until Branch Rickey came along.

B   [4]Branch Rickey was general manager for the Brooklyn Dodgers. [5]After World War II, the Dodgers needed to rebuild their team. [6]Rickey decided to tap a new source of talent and hire the Dodgers' first black player. [7]He found Jackie Robinson.

C   [8]Rickey knew that many people would object to Jackie's presence and would try to get him to quit. [9]He told Robinson he'd need "guts enough not to fight back" when people said or did mean things to him. [10]He would be accepted only if he were *more* of a gentleman than anyone else in baseball.

D   [11]Robinson understood. [12]He knew it would be hard, but he agreed to take the taunts without fighting back.

E   [13]At first, some of his own teammates were against him. [14]Restaurants refused to serve him. [15]Both fans and players called him names. [16]Some opposing players even tried to "spike" Jackie at first base by stepping on his foot. [17]But when Jackie wanted to fight back, he remembered his promise. [18]He remained silent.

F   [19]Jackie Robinson concentrated on playing ball. [20]He was bold and speedy, and he stole more bases than anyone else. [21]His teammates came to like and respect him. [22]His daring moves brought excitement to the games. [23]Fans came especially to watch Jackie. [24]He played so well, in fact, that by the end of his first season he was named Rookie of the Year. [25]Robinson went on to play nine more seasons for the Dodgers.

G   [26]It was largely because of his self-control that Jackie Robinson was accepted in major league baseball. [27]In fact, he paved the way for many black athletes whose skill and sportsmanship we admire today.

DIRECTIONS: Choose or write the best answer to each of the following questions using the evidence presented in the passage. When required, list specific sentence numbers or paragraph letters from the story to support your answer.

1. From paragraph A, you can tell that Jackie Robinson probably started playing for the Dodgers during what decade?

   _____

   List the numbers of the 2 sentences that best support your answer. ____,

   ____

2. As used in sentence 12, what could the word *taunts* mean?

   A. pitches
   B. jobs
   C. insults
   D. offers

   Give the letter of the paragraph that best supports your answer.____

3. Which of the following was probably NOT an important ingredient of Jackie Robinson's success?

   A. strong self-control
   B. ability to steal bases
   C. ability to fight back
   D. advice from Rickey

4. By "having guts enough *not* to fight back," Rickey probably meant that Jackie would have to

   A. claim rights.
   B. remain calm.
   C. lecture others.
   D. argue back.

   Give the number of the sentence that best supports your answer. ____

5. Number the following events in the order they occur in the passage.

   ____ **A.** Jackie is Rookie of the Year.

   ____ **B.** Fans are impressed with Jackie's skill.

   ____ **C.** World War II ends.

   ____ **D.** Jackie is told to be gentlemanly.

   ____ **E.** Jackie's self-control is challenged.

6. Why did Branch Rickey look for a black baseball player for the Dodgers?

   _____

   _____

   _____

   _____

   List the numbers of the 2 sentences that best support your answer. ____,

   ____

7. What caused Jackie to remain silent when players tried to "spike" him?

   _____

   _____

   _____

   _____

   List the numbers of the 2 sentences that best support your answer. ____,

   ____

50. Magellan's Voyage Around the World by David White

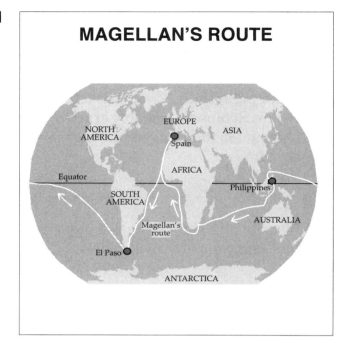

MAGELLAN'S ROUTE

[1]Ferdinand Magellan was the first explorer to lead a voyage that circled the globe. [2]In doing so, he helped prove once and for all that the world was round.

[3]Magellan was 12 when Christopher Columbus first landed in the New World in 1492. [4]Magellan went to school to learn how to be a page—an assistant at the royal court of Portugal. [5]While in school, he learned celestial navigation, which is how to find your way in uncharted water or open seas by following the stars. [6]His studies created in him a lifelong desire to explore. [7]After several years as a page, he left the Portuguese court for a life at sea.

[8]Magellan wanted to lead his own voyage and tried unsuccessfully to persuade the king of Portugal to finance it. [9]He finally won financial support from the king of Spain. [10]In 1519, Magellan set off as captain of a five-ship Spanish expedition. [11]The goal was to find a way to Asia by going west.

[12]Legends told of El Paso—a water passage that went through the newly discovered American continents. [13]A year into the voyage, Magellan found this passage. [14]It was at the southern tip of South America.

[15]The sailors were not happy with Magellan because the water and winds were very cold. [16]Still, they sailed on. [17]After making it through the passage, Magellan and his men sailed 98 days across the Pacific Ocean without once seeing land. [18](Maps at the time showed the ocean to be small.)

[19]Finally, Magellan reached Guam. [20]It was 1521—two years after the voyage had begun. [21]Their food supply had long since run out, and the sailors were famished. [22]The people of Guam gave the sailors lots of exotic foods and fresh water. [23]They rested for a few days. [24]Some would have been happy to stay, but Magellan wanted to go on. [25]Nine days later, they reached the Philippines.

[26]While there, Magellan tried to spread his religion to anyone who would listen. [27]He was successful in converting the natives of one island, but he was killed by natives on another island. [28]The voyage continued without him, though. [29]Only one ship was left in the end. [30]The *Victoria* returned to Spain in 1522. [31]The voyage around the world was complete.

[32]Even though Magellan himself did not survive the voyage, his discovery did. [33]The world was indeed round.

DIRECTIONS: Choose or write the best answer to each of the following questions using the evidence presented in the passage. When required, list specific sentence numbers or paragraph letters from the story to support your answer.

1. How long did the voyage last?

   _____

   List the numbers of the 2 sentences that best support your answer. ____, ____

2. According to the passage, which of these was NOT a part of Magellan's many travels?
   A. sailing the seas
   B. exploring the world
   C. spreading religion
   D. conquering countries

3. Why did Magellan ask the king of Spain to send him on a voyage?

   _____

   _____

   Give the number of the sentence that best supports your answer. ____

4. Number these events in correct time order as performed by Magellan.
   ____   lands in Philippines

   ____   finds El Paso

   ____   reaches Guam

   ____   studies to be a page

   ____   sails into the Pacific Ocean

5. What is Magellan's voyage famous for?

   _____

   _____

   List the numbers of the 2 sentences that best support your answer. ____, ____

6. What could have convinced Magellan to continue sailing the Pacific Ocean even though the crew had gone for days without seeing land?

   _____

   _____

   _____

   _____

   Give the number of the sentence that best supports your answer. ____

7. Which of these words is closest in meaning to *famished,* as used in sentence 21?
   A. lost
   B. sore
   C. tired
   D. hungry

8. Explain why celestial navigation, as described in sentence 5, was useful to sailors.

   _____

   _____

   _____

   _____

posttests

FICTION POSTTEST—Half Dozen to Go

A [1]"We'll just take six small ones," Jon said as he crouched under the window. [2]He was persuading me to "borrow" the neighbor's roses for Mom's birthday. [3]He'd spent our savings on a stupid video.

B [4]"Mom won't know the difference, Ben, and absentminded Chump will never miss them," Jon said. [5]I had a funny feeling but went along. [6]After all, Jon was older.

C [7]"Stay down so Chump can't see us," Jon instructed as he cut three roses and pointed out three for me to cut. [8]"The trick is to spread out the holes so it looks even."

D [9]We put the roses in a vase and set them by Mom's chair. [10]She was thrilled.

E [11]"For me? [12]You boys didn't have to spend all that money!" [13]Jon was as smug as if he got the Best-Son award. [14]But when Dad told us we were great, I cracked. [15]"We took them from Mr. Chump's garden," I blurted.

F [16]Dad and Mom looked at me blankly, but Jon's look sent me a million poison darts. [17]It's a good thing Mr. Chump barged in, or Jon might have killed me.

G [18]"Has anyone seen my prize—oh, there they are! [19]I must have cut them and left them with you for safekeeping! [20]Well, thanks so much," he swooped over, collected the vase, and was gone.

H [21]Mom and Dad came back to life. [22]"What were you saying, Ben?" [23]Dad asked. [24]I had to save Jon's skin *and* make myself look good. [25]Thinking quickly, I said, "Uhh…Jon wanted to buy you something, but I thought we'd do some clipping for Mr. Chump and let you enjoy his roses before he took them to the show."

I [26]"Isn't that clever!" said Mom. [27]"That's thrifty *and* neighborly," said Dad.

J [28]Jon looked at me with new respect.

K [29]Since the rose incident, I use my head and think about the consequences before acting. [30]Once in awhile, *Jon* even listens to *me*.

DIRECTIONS: Choose or write the best answer to each of the following questions using the evidence presented in the passage. When required, list specific sentence numbers or paragraph letters from the story to support your answer.

1. Why couldn't the boys afford to buy roses?

   _____

   _____

   _____

   Give the number of the sentence that best supports your answer. ____

2. Number the following according to the order of events in the passage.

   ____ The neighbor takes his roses back.

   ____ The boys cut flowers.

   ____ Jon respects Ben.

   ____ Mom gets roses.

   ____ Ben lies.

3. In sentence 8, what did Jon mean by "spread out the holes"?

   _____

   _____

   _____

4. Sentence 12 in paragraph E suggests that Mom thought the boys

   A. shouldn't have bought the video.
   B. got the flowers for free.
   C. had gone out and bought flowers.
   D. had done their neighbor a favor.

5. What might have caused Ben to tell where the flowers came from?

   _____

   _____

   _____

6. By the end of paragraph G, who did Chump think cut his flowers?

   _____

   _____

   Give the number of the sentence that best supports your answer. ____

7. By the words "came back to life" (sentence 21), we can tell that Mom and Dad had been

   A. dead.
   B. frozen.
   C. showing no reaction.
   D. numb from excitement.

8. From where did the boys steal the flowers?

_____

_____

_____

9. In sentence 5, Ben goes along because Jon is older. How do you think Ben's view has changed by the end of the story?

_____

_____

_____

_____

10. Which is probably true most of the time?

A. Mr. Chump is forgetful.
B. Dad is forgiving.
C. Jon goes along with Ben.
D. Mom is thrilled.

List the numbers of the 2 sentences that best support your answer. ____,

____

NONFICTION POSTTEST—The Good in Forest Fires

A [1]Wildfires are thought to be bad for a forest because they burn out of control, destroying the forest. [2]However, a fire can actually be good for a forest.

B [3]Tree leaves, bark, and branches fall naturally to the forest floor. [4]This forest "litter" can become a huge fire danger because it is so dry and brittle. [5]Also, there are pests living in this litter that can threaten the lives of plants and trees. [6]To keep too much of this litter from building up, firefighters sometimes set a controlled fire that burns the forest floor in only one area. [7]When the litter has burned away, firefighters put the fire out. [8]A controlled forest floor fire protects the trees by destroying litter and pests, but sparing the grown trees.

C [9]Fires, both wild and controlled, have other benefits for the forest. [10]Wood smoke stops the growth of fungi* that harm some trees. [11]Fire keeps trees from growing too close together by thinning out the small seedlings. [12]Fire also controls the growth of fir trees. [13]Fir trees grow quickly and can take over a forest when fire does not control their growth. [14]When these trees become too large and dense, they keep sunlight from reaching the forest floor. [15]As a result, the low-growing plants that elk, deer, and other animals depend on as a major food source have difficulty growing.

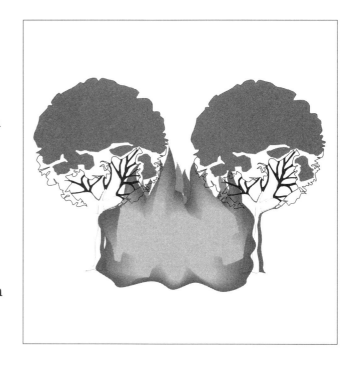

D [16]Some plants and trees grow quickly after a fire. [17]After a fire, the soil more quickly releases such important nutrients** as protein and calcium. [18]This enriched soil encourages plant growth.

E [19]It is not always the best idea to put out a forest fire. [20]Fire has been a part of the life of the forest for many, many years. [21]Trees, plants, and animals are used to fire and have found ways to live with it. [22]If we as humans take away such a big part of this life cycle, we may find that we have done more harm than good.

*fungi: plants with no leaves or flowers, such as mushrooms

**nutrient: a substance, such as a vitamin or mineral, that is found in a food and needed for health

DIRECTIONS: Choose or write the best answer to each of the following questions using the evidence presented in the passage. When required, list specific sentence numbers or paragraph letters from the story to support your answer.

1. Which of these words is closest in meaning to the word *enriched* in sentence 18?
   A. larger
   B. polluted
   C. newer
   D. improved

2. In what two ways does a controlled fire help a forest?

   _____

   _____

   _____

   _____

   Give the number of the sentence that best supports your answer. ____

3. What can happen to elk and deer if a forest does not have a fire for a long time?

   _____

   _____

   _____

   _____

   Give the number of the sentence that best supports your answer. ____

4. Which of the following statements could you make about all forest fires?
   A. They help fungi to grow.
   B. They destroy only the forest litter.
   C. They can help the forest.
   D. They are started by people.

5. Which of these is probably NOT a pest like the ones mentioned in sentence 5?
   A. woodpecker
   B. beetle
   C. termite
   D. ant

6. Give a reason why some plants grow more quickly after a fire.

   _____

   _____

   _____

   _____

   List the numbers of the 2 sentences that best support your answer. ____,
   ____

7. How is a controlled fire different from a wildfire?

_____

_____

_____

_____

List the numbers of the 2 sentences that best support your answer. ____,

____

8. Which of these statements from the story best describes the main idea?

A. Tree leaves, bark, and branches fall naturally to the forest floor.

B. Some trees and plants grow faster as a result of fire.

C. However, a fire can actually be good for a forest.

D. Fire has been a part of the life of the forest for many, many years.

Give the letter of the paragraph that best supports your answer. ____

9. Which of the following statements is an opinion?

A. Fire also controls the growth of fir trees.

B. It is not always the best idea to put out a forest fire.

C. Tree leaves, bark, and branches fall naturally to the forest floor.

D. This enriched soil encourages plant growth.

ANSWER KEYS

The answer key provides the following information: a copy of the student passage with superscripted numbers, questions with the reading skill in parentheses, the correct answer given in bolded text, the numbers or letters of the evidence sentences or paragraphs, and an explanation of the answer (when necessary).

Although we give a recommended answer choice for each question, teachers should discuss any different responses with students to clarify their reasoning. If the teacher feels a student has made a good case for a response, based on the evidence in the passage, the teacher may want to accept the student's answer, also.

For the short answer questions, students do not have to follow the suggested wording exactly as long as they include the key information needed to answer the question. The literature and fiction stories, in particular, are open to greater interpretation than the nonfiction as to author meaning. The primary focus of this program is to get students to think about what they read and to improve their understanding of the material. You may find your students involved in a lively debate as to which is the best answer to a question. By all means, encourage this!

PRE- AND POSTTESTS
FICTION PRETEST: A "Dog-gone" Day

A [1]It was no fun staying behind the fence of my person's backyard while she was at school. [2]Just beyond those wood boards was a whole world of activity. [3]There were squirrels to be chased, dogs to be sniffed, fire hydrants to be marked, cats to be had! [4]What else could I do? [5]It was the call of the wild, so I jumped the fence!

B [6]I headed for the park first. [7]The squirrels didn't even see me coming! [8]I

chased them from rock to rock and hole to hole. [9]I heard a few people yell, "Get that dog on a leash!" so I decided I had better get going before I got caught. [10]My next stop was down the street from the park, where my good friend Lucky lives. [11]We greeted each other with all the proper sniffings.

C [12]"Lucky," I said, "you can jump this gate. [13]It's only three feet high." [14]But Lucky wouldn't do it. [15]She had been a stray and wanted nothing to do with getting out of the yard.

D [16]"You'll get lost, Blazer," she warned with a bark, but I didn't listen. [17]Instead, I kept going and going and going until nothing looked familiar. [18]I was really on my own. [19]At first, I panicked. [20]Then, being the intelligent dog that I am, I decided to play the "helpless animal routine." [21]I found a sweet young girl walking along the street and looked up at her with my big brown eyes. [22]I played shy to gain her sympathy, then moved in a little closer. [23]Licking and tail wagging followed. [24]I ended up in her car. [25]A short time later, I was right back where I started.

E [26]My person was not thrilled with me. [27]I was forced to use the "please forgive me routine." [28]My sad eyes and wagging tail worked like a charm. [29]Once again, everything was okay. [30]I was at home, at least until the next call of the wild!

1. What is the theme of the story? (theme)

  A. Getting lost is fun.
  B. Live life adventurously.
  C. Don't depend on people.
  D. Tame your wild instincts.

1 best evidence paragraph: **A**

B is the best answer because we see Blazer living adventurously throughout the story (jumping the fence, chasing squirrels, etc.) A is incorrect because Blazer panicked when she realized she was lost, and then quickly figured out a way to get back home (19, 24). C is incorrect because Blazer did depend on a person (21). D is incorrect because Blazer will jump the fence again when she hears the next call of the wild (30).

2. Where does the story begin? (setting)

    A. at the park
    B. in the backyard
    C. on the street
    D. at Lucky's house

    1 best evidence sentence: **1**

3. Compare Lucky's view of getting out of the yard to Blazer's view. (compare/contrast, point of view)

    Lucky doesn't want to get out of the yard. Blazer does like to get out of the yard.

    2 best evidence sentences: **15, 5** (Also acceptable: **1**)

4. In general, Blazer (generalization)

    A. likes to sleep during the day.
    B. knows how to get what she wants.
    C. is a little out of shape.
    D. listens to advice.

    1 best evidence sentence from paragraph D: **20**

    B is the best answer because Blazer went about her day the way she wanted. She also knew how to get what she wanted from people, as seen with the young girl who found her and took her home. There is no evidence to support A. Blazer is probably not out of shape given her activities during the day, so C is unlikely. D is unlikely

because Blazer didn't listen to the advice of her friend Lucky.

5. Put the following events in their correct time order. (sequence)

    1 Blazer jumps the fence.
    4 Blazer makes it home.
    2 Blazer goes to the park.
    3 Blazer gets lost.

6. In sentence 28, what does Blazer mean when she says the routine "worked like a charm"? (figurative language)

    A charm is an action or saying that may have magical powers. Blazer's comment means that her routine worked like magic.

7. How did some people at the park feel about Blazer's running loose? (inference)

    They yelled, "Get that dog on a leash," so they probably didn't like Blazer running loose.

    1 best evidence sentence: **9**

8. Give one example of what Blazer did when she needed the help of people. (reading for detail).

    (Accept any one of the three.)

    1. She looked up at them with her big brown eyes. 2. She played shy to gain their sympathy, then moved in a little closer. 3. She licked them and wagged her tail.

    1 best evidence sentence: **21, 22,** or **23**

9. What resulted from Blazer's meeting the young girl? (conclusion)

    A. Blazer was taken to the pound.
    B. Blazer was given a bath.
    C. Blazer was taken home.

D. Blazer was punished.

1 best evidence sentence: **25**

C is correct because Blazer found her way home once she figured out how to ask the young girl for help. There is no evidence to support A, B, or D.

10. Do you think Blazer will jump the fence again? Explain your answer. (prediction)

Yes. The last line of the story states that Blazer will listen to the next call of the wild, meaning she will jump the fence again.

1 best evidence sentence: **30**

NONFICTION PRETEST: Quartz: Our Most Common Mineral

[1]Quartz is the most common mineral on earth. [2]You can find different kinds of quartz almost everywhere.

[3]Most of the sand on beaches and deserts is actually tiny pieces of quartz. [4]Through a process called weathering,* rocks gradually break down into pebbles, then gravel, and finally become sand. [5]Quartz does not dissolve or wear away like most other rock materials. [6]So when rocks that contain quartz are weathered, only little bits of quartz are left. [7]In fact, there are few minerals harder than quartz. [8]Take a close look at some grains of sand. [9]The many different colors and shapes you see show the rocks the grains originally came from.

[10]There are many kinds of quartz. [11]Some of the best known are the quartz crystals used in watches and jewelry. [12]Most people are familiar with the clear quartz known as rock crystal. [13]Amethyst is a deep purple gemstone that is actually purple quartz. [14]The color comes from impurities** in the quartz.

[15]Flint is another common type of quartz. [16]Nearly half a million years ago, cavemen in the early Stone Age used flint to make cutting tools and weapons. [17]Although quartz is hard, it is also brittle, so it breaks easily. [18]Small pieces of the flint could be chipped away to shape a tool. [19]This shaping left a sharp edge good for cutting. [20]Examples of these flint tools have survived to the present day.

[21]There are many kinds and forms of quartz, from large crystals to tiny grains of sand. [22]It is a mineral that withstands both weather and time.

*weathering: gradually wearing down by heat, wind, and rain

**impurities: things mixed in that don't belong to the original object

1. Why does the quartz remain when a rock becomes weathered? (conclusion)

   Quartz does not wear away or dissolve.

   1 best evidence sentence: **5**

2. Why is there such variety in sand particles? (supporting detail)

   Grains of sand are pieces of different kinds of rocks.

   1 best evidence sentence: **9**

3. Why do you think flint was useful for tools and weapons? (inference)

   Flint could be shaped to create a sharp tool.

   2 best evidence sentences: **18, 19**

4. How does amethyst get its purple color? (reading for detail)

   The color comes from impurities in the quartz.

1 best evidence sentence: **14**

5. What is the main idea of this passage? (main idea)

   A. Sand comes from many different rocks.
   B. Quartz is the hardest mineral.
   C. People have used quartz for centuries.
   D. There are many kinds of quartz found worldwide.

   A and C are details about quartz. B is incorrect; there are some minerals harder than quartz.

6. How is rock crystal different from amethyst? (compare/contrast)

   Rock crystal is clear, and amethyst is purple.

   2 best evidence sentences: **12, 13**

7. Which of the following statements can you make about quartz in general? (generalization)

   A. Quartz crystals are colorless.
   B. Quartz is made from sand.
   C. Quartz is hard to find.
   D. Quartz lasts a long time.

   2 best evidence sentences: **16, 20** (Also acceptable: **5, 20**)

   D is the best answer because there are quartz pieces that date back nearly half a million years ago (16, 20). The passage also states that quartz does not dissolve or wear away (5). A is incorrect; not all quartz is colorless (13). B is incorrect; sand is made from quartz (3). C is incorrect; quartz is the most common mineral on earth (1).

8. As a rock breaks down, what stages does it go through? (sequence)

   A. Rock, gravel, sand, pebble

   B. Rock, sand, pebble, gravel
   C. Rock, gravel, pebble, sand
   D. Rock, pebble, gravel, sand

   1 best evidence sentence: **4**

9. How do rocks become sand? (cause/effect)

   They are gradually worn down by weathering.

   1 best evidence sentence: **4**

FICTION POSTTEST: Half Dozen to Go

A [1]"We'll just take six small ones," Jon said as he crouched under the window. [2]He was persuading me to "borrow" the neighbor's roses for Mom's birthday. [3]He'd spent our savings on a stupid video.
B [4]"Mom won't know the difference, Ben, and absentminded Chump will never miss them," Jon said. [5]I had a funny feeling but went along. [6]After all, Jon was older.
C [7]"Stay down so Chump can't see us," Jon instructed as he cut three roses and pointed out three for me to cut. [8]"The trick is to spread out the holes so it looks even."
D [9]We put the roses in a vase and set them by Mom's chair. [10]She was thrilled.
E [11]"For me? [12]You boys didn't have to spend all that money!" [13]Jon was as smug as if he got the Best-Son award. [14]But when Dad told us we were great, I cracked. [15]"We took them from Mr. Chump's garden," I blurted.
F [16]Dad and Mom looked at me blankly, but Jon's look sent me a million poison darts. [17]It's a good thing Mr. Chump barged in, or Jon might have killed me.
G [18]"Has anyone seen my prize—oh, there they are! [19]I must have cut them and left them with you for safekeeping! [20]Well, thanks so much," he swooped over, collected the vase, and was gone.
H [21]Mom and Dad came back to life. [22]"What were you saying, Ben?" [23]Dad

asked. ²⁴I had to save Jon's skin *and* make myself look good. ²⁵Thinking quickly, I said, "Uhh…Jon wanted to buy you something, but I thought we'd do some clipping for Mr. Chump and let you enjoy his roses before he took them to the show."

I ²⁶"Isn't that clever!" said Mom.

²⁷"That's thrifty *and* neighborly," said Dad.

J ²⁸Jon looked at me with new respect.

K ²⁹Since the rose incident, I use my head and think about the consequences before acting. ³⁰Once in awhile, *Jon* even listens to *me*.

1. Why couldn't the boys afford to buy roses? (supporting detail)

   Jon spent their savings on a video.

   1 best evidence sentence: **3**

2. Number the following according to the order of events in the passage. (sequence)

   3 The neighbor takes his roses back.
   1 The boys cut flowers.
   5 Jon respects Ben.
   2 Mom gets roses.
   4 Ben lies.

3. In sentence 8, what did Jon mean by "spread out the holes"? (inference)

   He meant not to cut all the roses from the same place.

   Jon did this so Chump would not be able to tell some were missing.

4. Sentence 12 in paragraph E suggests that Mom thought the boys (inference)

   A. shouldn't have bought the video.
   B. got the flowers for free.
   C. had gone out and bought flowers.
   D. had done their neighbor a favor.

Sentence 12 implies that she thought they spent money on the roses.

5. What might have caused Ben to tell where the flowers came from? (cause/effect)

   Since Ben "cracked" when Dad told them they were great, he probably felt that what he had done was wrong.

6. By the end of paragraph G, who did Chump think cut his flowers? (reading for detail)

   He thought he himself had cut the roses.

   1 best evidence sentence: **19**

7. By the words "came back to life" (sentence 21), we can tell that Mom and Dad had been (figurative language)

   A. dead.
   B. frozen.
   C. showing no reaction.
   D. numb from excitement.

   In sentence 16, the parents were looking blank (as if they couldn't reconcile what they believed with what they were hearing). Therefore, C is the best answer. There is no evidence for choice A, B or D.

8. From where did the boys steal the flowers? (setting)

   They took the roses from the neighbor's garden, under his window.

   Sentences 1, 2, and 15 indicate the location.

9. In sentence 5, Ben goes along because Jon is older. How do you think Ben's view has changed by the end of the story? (point of view)

Ben would no longer go along with what Jon suggests just because Jon is older. He now uses his head before following Jon.

10. Which is probably true most of the time? (generalization)

    A. Mr. Chump is forgetful.
    B. Dad is forgiving.
    C. Jon goes along with Ben.
    D. Mom is thrilled.

    2 best evidence sentences: **4, 19**

    Chump is called absentminded (sentence 4), so he has probably shown forgetfulness before. In addition he demonstrates forgetfulness in sentence 19. Therefore, there is more evidence for choice A than any other choice. There is no evidence for B (in the story, Dad has no need to forgive since he never knew of any wrongdoing). Mom was thrilled once (sentence 10) in the passage, but there is nothing to show that she is usually thrilled. There is no evidence that Jon has ever followed Ben.

NONFICTION POSTTEST: The Good in Forest Fires

A [1]Wildfires are thought to be bad for a forest because they burn out of control, destroying the forest. [2]However, a fire can actually be good for a forest.
B [3]Tree leaves, bark, and branches fall naturally to the forest floor. [4]This forest "litter" can become a huge fire danger because it is so dry and brittle. [5]Also, there are pests living in this litter that can threaten the lives of plants and trees. [6]To keep too much of this litter from building up, firefighters sometimes set a controlled fire that burns the forest floor in only one area. [7]When the litter has burned away, firefighters put the fire out. [8]A controlled forest floor fire protects the trees by destroying litter and pests, but sparing the grown trees.
C [9]Fires, both wild and controlled, have other benefits for the forest. [10]Wood smoke stops the growth of fungi* that harm some trees. [11]Fire keeps trees from growing too close together by thinning out the small seedlings. [12]Fire also controls the growth of fir trees. [13]Fir trees grow quickly and can take over a forest when fire does not control their growth. [14]When these trees become too large and dense, they keep sunlight from reaching the forest floor. [15]As a result, the low-growing plants that elk, deer, and other animals depend on as a major food source have difficulty growing.
D [16]Some plants and trees grow quickly after a fire. [17]After a fire, the soil more quickly releases such important nutrients** as protein and calcium. [18]This enriched soil encourages plant growth.
E [19]It is not always the best idea to put out a forest fire. [20]Fire has been a part of the life of the forest for many, many years. [21]Trees, plants, and animals are used to fire and have found ways to live with it. [22]If we as humans take away such a big part of this life cycle, we may find that we have done more harm than good.

*fungi: plants with no leaves or flowers, such as mushrooms

**nutrient: a substance, such as a vitamin or mineral, that is found in a food and needed for health

1. Which of these words is closest in meaning to the word *enriched* in sentence 18? (vocabulary)

    A. larger
    B. polluted
    C. newer
    D. improved

D is suggested by the context because the enriched soil encourages plant growth. There is no evidence for A, B, or C.

2. In what two ways does a controlled fire help a forest? (cause/effect)

It gets rid of dry leaves, bark, and branches. It also destroys pests that harm trees.

2 best evidence sentences: **4**, **5** (Also acceptable: **8**)

3. What can happen to elk and deer if a forest does not have a fire for a long time? (conclusion)

The elk and deer might have a hard time finding enough food in the forest.

1 best evidence sentence: **15**

4. Which of the following statements could you make about all forest fires? (generalization)
   A. They help fungi to grow.
   B. They destroy only the forest litter.
   C. They can help the forest.
   D. They are started by people.

C is supported by the third paragraph. A is contradicted by Sentence 10. B and D are true of controlled fires only.

5. Which of these is probably NOT a pest like the ones mentioned in sentence 5? (inference)
   A. woodpecker
   B. beetle
   C. termite
   D. ant

The pests referred to in Sentence 5 live on the forest floor; of the choices above, only the woodpecker does not live on the forest floor.

6. Give a reason why some plants grow more quickly after a fire. (supporting detail)

Some plants grow quickly after a fire because the soil becomes enriched.

2 best evidence sentences: **17**, **18**

7. How is a controlled fire different from a wildfire? (compare/contrast)

A controlled fire is set by firefighters to burn only one area. A wildfire burns out of control.

2 best evidence sentences: **1**, **6** (Also acceptable: **8**)

8. Which of these statements from the story best describes the main idea? (main idea)
   A. Tree leaves, bark, and branches fall naturally to the forest floor.
   B. Some trees and plants grow faster as a result of fire.
   C. However, a fire can actually be good for a forest.
   D. Fire has been a part of the life of the forest for many, many years.

1 best evidence paragraph: **C**

A and B are details. D is also true, but most of the passage lists the benefits of fire.

9. Which of the following statements is an opinion? (fact/opinion)
   A. Fire also controls the growth of fir trees.
   B. It is not always the best idea to put out a forest fire.
   C. Tree leaves, bark, and branches fall naturally to the forest floor.
   D. This enriched soil encourages plant growth.

1 best evidence paragraph: **E**

While the passage points out the many benefits of fire, it is still the writer's opinion that some forest fires should be allowed to burn. A, C, and D are facts supported by the passage.

LITERATURE

1. *Fudge•a•mania* by Judy Blume (Excerpt)

[1]"Guess what, Pete?" my brother, Fudge, said. [2]"I'm getting married tomorrow."

[3]I looked up from my baseball cards. [4]"Isn't this kind of sudden?" I asked, since Fudge is only five.

[5]"No," he said.

[6]"Well...who's the lucky bride?"

[7]"Sheila Tubman," Fudge said.

[8]I hit the floor, pretending to have fainted dead away. [9]I did a good job of it because Fudge started shaking me and shouting, "Get up, Pete!"

[10]*What's this* Pete *business?* I thought. [11]*Ever since he could talk, he's called me* Pee-tah.

[12]Then Tootsie, my sister, who's just a year and a half, danced around me singing, "Up, Pee...up."

[13]Next, Mom was beside me saying, "Peter...what happened? [14]Are you all right?"

[15]"I told him I was getting married," Fudge said. [16]"And he just fell over."

[17]"I fell over when you told me *who* you were marrying," I said.

[18]"Who are you marrying, Fudge?" Mom asked, as if we were seriously discussing his wedding.

[19]"Sheila Tubman," Fudge said.

[20]"Don't say that name around me," I told him, "or I'll faint again."

[21]"Speaking of Sheila Tubman..." Mom began.

[22]But I didn't wait for her to finish. [23]"You're making me feel very sick..." I warned.

[24]"Really, Peter..." Mom said. [25]"Aren't you overdoing it?"

[26]I clutched my stomach and moaned but Mom went right on talking.

1. Which of the following statements gives the main idea of the passage? (main idea)
   A. Fudge is worried that something is wrong with Peter.
   B. Peter clutches his stomach and pretends to be sick when he hears the name Sheila Tubman.
   C. Peter reacts strongly to the mention of Sheila Tubman's name.
   D. Fudge talks about marrying Sheila Tubman.

   C is supported by sentences 8, 17, and 20. A, B, and D are incorrect because they are details of the passage.

2. Peter notices a change in the way his little brother speaks to him. Explain the change. (supporting detail)

   Peter notices that his brother is calling him "Pete" and not "Pee-tah."

3. Which of these words best describes Peter? (character trait/generalization)
   A. dramatic
   B. mean
   C. worried
   D. tired

   4 best evidence sentences: **8, 20, 23, 26**

   A is the best answer because Peter pretends to faint (8, 20) and to be sick to his stomach (23, 26). His overreactions are done for drama. There is no evidence for B or D. Peter is more flippant about the situation than worried (8–9, 20, 26), so C is incorrect.

4. What caused Peter to fall to the ground? (cause/effect)

   A. Fudge told him he was getting married.
   B. He had a bad stomachache.
   C. Fudge told him he was marrying Sheila Tubman.
   D. He saw Sheila Tubman walk in.

1 best evidence sentence: **17**

A is incorrect because Peter didn't fall to the ground right after Fudge told him he was getting married. B is incorrect because we know that Peter is just being dramatic when he clutches his stomach. There is no evidence for D.

5. Put the following events in their correct order. (sequence)

   3 Mom enters the scene.
   4 Mom says Sheila Tubman's name, and Peter holds his stomach and moans.
   2 Peter falls to the ground, pretending to have fainted.
   1 Fudge tells Peter he is getting married.

6. How do you think Fudge and Tootsie will react if Peter faints again? (prediction)

   A. They will think he's very sick.
   B. They will be afraid and very worried.
   C. They will know he's pretending.
   D. They will play a trick on him.

Explain your answer.

Fudge and Tootsie have already seen Peter faint and then get back up again. Their mother doesn't seem worried about Peter, so they will probably know that Peter is pretending if he faints again.

7. Which sentence from the passage makes you think that Fudge is not actually getting married? (inference)

   A. I hit the floor, pretending to have fainted dead away.
   B. "Isn't this kind of sudden?" I asked, since Fudge is only five.
   C. "Well...who's the lucky bride?"
   D. "Speaking of Sheila Tubman..." Mom began.

B is correct since 5 year olds can't marry. A, C, and D are incorrect because they do not indicate that Fudge is not actually getting married.

2. *Mr. Popper's Penguins* by Richard Atwater (Excerpt)

A [1]The penguins all loved to climb the stairs that led up to the kitchen, and never knew when to stop unless they found the kitchen door closed. [2]Then, of course, they would turn around and toboggan down the steps again. [3]This made rather a curious noise sometimes, when Mrs. Popper was working in the kitchen, but she got used to it, as she had got used to so many other strange things this winter.
B [4]The freezing plant that Mr. Popper had got for the penguins downstairs was a large and good one. [5]It made very large blocks of ice, instead of small ice cubes, so that soon Mr. Popper had made a sort of ice castle down there for the twelve penguins to live in and climb over.
C [6]Mr. Popper also dug a large hole in the cellar floor and made a swimming and diving pool for the birds. [7]From time to time he would throw live fish into the pool for the penguins to dive for. [8]They found this very refreshing, because, to tell the truth, they had got a little tired of canned

shrimps. [9]The live fish were specially ordered and were brought all the way from the coast in tank cars and glass boxes to 432 Proudfoot Avenue. [10]Unfortunately, they were quite expensive.

D [11]It was nice that there were so many penguins because when two of them (usually Nelson and Columbus) got into a fight, and began to spar at each other with their flippers, the ten other penguins would all crowd around to watch the fight and make encouraging remarks. [12]This made a very interesting little scene.

E [13]Mr. Popper also flooded a part of the cellar floor for an ice rink, and here the penguins often drilled like a sort of small army, in fantastic marching movements and parades around the ice. [14]The penguin Louisa seemed especially fond of leading these marching drills. [15]It was quite a sight to see them, after Mr. Popper had the idea of training Louisa to hold a small American flag in her beak while she proudly led the solemn parades.

1. This story could best be classified as a (theme)

   A. mystery.
   B. comedy.
   C. adventure.
   D. science fiction.

   The penguins are having an adventure in their surroundings, but the main focus of the story is on the penguins' humorous antics, so B is the best choice. There is no evidence for A or D.

2. In sentence 13, how did the author use figurative language to describe the penguins? (figurative language/ simile)

   He compared them to a small army.

3. In sentence 11, what does the word *spar* mean? (vocabulary)

   A. to wave
   B. to swim
   C. to box
   D. to argue

   The other penguins watch them fight with their flippers, so A and B are incorrect. Since the penguins use their flippers to spar, D is incorrect.

4. Which of the following statements can you make about penguins in general? (generalization)

   A. Penguins like to be alone.
   B. Penguins will eat anything.
   C. Penguins are easily trained.
   D. Penguins like a cold environment.

   D is the best choice because the entire cellar was cooled by a freezing plant and filled with ice. A is incorrect because the 12 penguins did things together. B is incorrect because the penguins ate only seafood. C is incorrect because Mr. Popper did not train the penguins; they did most things, such as marching, on their own. The fact that Mr. Popper trained one penguin to carry a flag is insufficient evidence that all penguins are easily trained.

5. What did Mr. Popper feed the penguins? (reading for detail)

   He fed them canned shrimp and live fish.

6. Which of the following actions of the penguins supports the idea that their behavior was unusual? (inference)

   A. The penguins would dive for live fish.
   B. The penguins liked to climb over the blocks of ice.
   C. The penguin Louisa liked to lead the marching drills.

D. The penguins liked to climb up the stairs and toboggan down them.

1 best evidence sentence: **14**

Penguins like to slide in the wild, so it would not be unusual for them to slide down the stairs. Marching in formation seems more unusual behavior, so C is a better choice than D. Penguins dive for fish and live on ice in the wild, so A and B are incorrect.

7. From paragraphs B and C, give three examples that support the conclusion that the penguins were expensive to care for. (conclusion)

1. Mr. Popper had to buy a freezing plant. 2. Mr. Popper made a swimming pool. 3. Mr. Popper bought live fish, which were expensive.

1 best evidence sentence for each example: **4, 6, 10**

3. *Maniac Magee*
by Jerry Spinelli (Excerpt)

A [1]"Where you goin'?" he said. [2]Candy bar flakes flew from his mouth.
B [3]"I'm looking for Sycamore Street," said Maniac. [4]"Do you know where it is?"
C [5]"Yeah, I know where it is."
D [6]Maniac waited, but the kid said nothing more.
E [7]"Well, uh, do you think you could tell me where it is?"
F [8]Stone was softer than the kid's glare.
G [9]"No."
H [10]Maniac looked around. [11]Other kids had stopped playing, were staring.
I [12]Someone called: "Do 'im, Mars!"
J [13]Someone else: "Waste 'im!"
K [14]The kid, as you probably guessed by now, was none other than Mars Bar

Thompson. [15]Mars Bar heard the calls, and the stone got harder. [16]Then suddenly he stopped glaring, suddenly he was smiling. [17]He held up the candy bar, an inch from Maniac's lips. [18]"Wanna bite?"
L [19]Maniac couldn't figure. [20]"You sure?"
M [21]"Yeah, go ahead. [22]Take a bite."
N [23]Maniac shrugged, took the Mars Bar, bit off a chunk, and handed it back. [24]"Thanks."
O [25]Dead silence along the street. [26]The kid had done the unthinkable, he had chomped on one of Mars's own bars. [27]Not only that, but white kids just didn't put their mouths where black kids had had theirs, be it soda bottles, spoons, or candy bars. [28]And the kid hadn't even gone for the unused end; he had chomped right over Mars Bar's own bite marks.
P [29]Mars Bar was confused. [30]Who *was* this kid? [31]*What* was this kid?

1. List two sentences from the passage that best support the idea that Maniac was not welcome in the neighborhood. (supporting detail)

Sentences **12, 13**

2. What does the author mean when he states "Stone was softer than the kid's glare"? (figurative language)
   A. Stone *is* actually softer than the glare of an angry kid.
   B. The kid's glaring eyes were gray like stone.
   C. **The kid's glare was really intense.**
   D. The kid's glare was beginning to soften.

   The author is comparing the intensity and hardness of the kid's glare to stone.

3. What does the author mean when he writes "Mars Bar heard the calls, <u>and the stone got harder</u>"? (figurative language)

The author means that Mars Bar's glare is becoming even stronger.

4. Why was Maniac confused when Mars Bar quit glaring at him and then offered him a bite of his candy bar? (conclusion)

Until now, he had been unfriendly to Maniac.

5. What was a key event in the story? (key event)
   A. **Maniac bit Mars Bar's candy bar.**
   B. The kids stopped playing.
   C. Mars Bar glared at Maniac.
   D. Mars Bar didn't answer Maniac.

   B, C, and D are details in the story, but not main events.

6. What do you think Mars Bar was doing when he offered his candy bar to Maniac? (inference)
   A. He was trying to get rid of his candy bar.
   B. He wanted to share his candy bar with Maniac.
   C. **He was testing Maniac to see what he'd do.**
   D. He wanted to prove he didn't mind a white kid eating his candy bar.

   1 best evidence paragraph: **O**

   C is the best answer. Mars Bars was being unfriendly to Maniac as evidenced by his not telling Maniac where Sycamore Street is and then glaring at him. Mars Bar probably did not want to get rid of or share his candy bar, especially not to a kid who he didn't seem to like (A, B). This would point to another motive. Therefore, he was probably testing or tormenting Maniac. There is no evidence for D.

7. What two things caused Mars Bar to become confused? (cause/effect)

   1. Maniac took a bite of his candy bar. 2. He also put his mouth right where Mars Bar's mouth had been on the candy bar, something white kids just didn't do.

   1 best evidence sentence for each example: **26, 27**

4. *Owls in the Family*
   by Farley Mowat (Excerpt)

A [1]Mother and Dad and I were having dinner. [2]The dining room windows were open because it had been such a hot day. [3]All of a sudden there was a great *swoooooosh* of wings—and there, on the window sill, sat Wol. [4]Before any of us had time to move, he gave a leap and landed on the floor beside my chair. [5]And he hadn't come empty-handed. [6]Clutched in his talons was an enormous skunk. [7]The skunk was dead, but that didn't help matters much because, before he died, he had managed to soak himself and Wol with his own special brand of perfume.
B [8]"Hoo-hoohoohoo-HOO!" Wol said proudly.
C [9]Which probably meant: "Mind if I join you? [10]I've brought my supper with me."
D [11]Nobody stopped to answer. [12]We three people were already stampeding through the door of the dining room, coughing and choking. [13]Wol had to eat his dinner by himself.
E [14]It was two weeks before we could use the dining room again, and when Mother sent the rug and drapes to the cleaners, the man who owned the shop phoned her right back and wanted to know if she was trying to ruin him.
F [15]Wol didn't smell so sweet either, but he couldn't understand why he was so unpopular all of a sudden. [16]His feelings

must have been hurt by the way everybody kept trying to avoid him. ¹⁷After two or three days, when even I wouldn't go near him, or let him come near me, he became very unhappy. ¹⁸Then an idea must have come into his funny head. ¹⁹He must have decided we were mad at him because he hadn't shared his skunk with us! ²⁰So one day he went down to the riverbank and caught a second skunk, and brought it home for us.

G ²¹By this time he was so soaked in skunk oil that you could smell him a block away. ²²Some of our neighbors complained about it, and so finally my father had to give Wol a bath in about a gallon of tomato juice. ²³Tomato juice is the only thing that will wash away the smell of skunk.

H ²⁴Poor Wol! ²⁵By the time Dad was through with him he looked like a rag mop that had been dipped in ketchup. ²⁶But he got the idea, and he never again brought his skunks home to us.

1. Why did the cleaner think Mother was trying to ruin him? (inference)

   The smell was so strong the cleaner probably thought it would drive away customers.

   1 best evidence sentence: **14**

2. Which of the following sentences best describes the family's reaction to Wol's arrival with the skunk? (inference)
   A. They were thrilled.
   B. They were angry with Wol.
   C. They thought it was funny.
   D. They were surprised.

   3 best evidence sentences: **4, 11, 12**

   Sentence 4 mentions that they didn't have time to move before he landed with the skunk. After that, they ran

from the room. There is no evidence for choices A, B, or C.

3. Which of the following explains why the family was unable to use the dining room for two weeks? (inference, cause/effect)
   A. Wol's supper was still lying there.
   B. The room still smelled of skunk.
   C. It was too hot to eat in there.
   D. Mother wanted to wait for the rug and drapes.

   We know from sentence 12 that the smell was quite strong, so B is the best answer. Common sense dictates they would remove the dead skunk, so A is incorrect. There is no evidence for C or D.

4. In sentence 3, why is it more effective for the author to use *swoooooosh* to describe Wol's arrival than to simply say he flew in the window? (figurative language)

   The word sounds like a bird flying.

   You can almost hear his wings and feel the rush of air as he flies in the window.

5. Which of the following is the most likely reason that Wol never brought a skunk home again? (cause/effect)
   A. He didn't want the neighbors to get mad at him.
   B. He decided to bring home squirrels instead.
   C. He didn't want another tomato juice bath.
   D. He didn't want to mess up the house.

   1 best evidence sentence: **26**

It was right after the tomato juice bath that Wol stopped bringing his skunks home. There is no evidence for A, B, or D.

6. Based on his behavior, you can conclude that Wol (conclusion)

   A. did not like getting dirty.
   B. wanted to please the family.
   C. was afraid of people.
   D. did not like to share.

   3 best evidence sentences: **19, 20, 26**

   There is no evidence for A, especially since it was the humans who decided to clean him up. C is contradicted by the fact that Wol wanted to be with people (4, 17). D is contradicted by the fact that Wol brought home his skunks twice (6, 20).

7. In paragraph F, the narrator presents Wol's point of view in human terms. Give one example of how the narrator thought Wol was feeling. (point of view, reading for detail)

   In sentence 15, the narrator said Wol *felt unpopular*. In sentence 16, he said Wol's *feelings were probably hurt*. In sentence 19, he said Wol *thought we were mad at him for not sharing* his skunk.

   1 best evidence sentence: **15, 16, or 19**

5. "Rikki-tikki Tavi" from *The Jungle Book* by Rudyard Kipling (Excerpt)

[1]One day, a high summer flood washed him out of the burrow where he lived with his father and mother, and carried him, kicking and clucking, down a roadside ditch. [2]He found a little wisp of grass floating there, and clung to it till he lost his senses. [3]When he revived, he was lying in the hot sun on the middle of a garden path, very draggled indeed, and a small boy was saying, "Here's a dead mongoose. [4]Let's have a funeral."

[5]"No," said his mother, "let's take him in and dry him. [6]Perhaps he isn't really dead."

[7]They took him into the house, and a big man picked him up between his finger and thumb and said he was not dead but half choked. [8]So they wrapped him in cotton wool, and warmed him over a little fire, and he opened his eyes and sneezed.

[9]"Now," said the big man (he was an Englishman who had just moved into the bungalow), "don't frighten him, and we'll see what he'll do."

[10]It is the hardest thing in the world to frighten a mongoose, because he is eaten up from nose to tail with curiosity. [11]The motto of all the mongoose family is "Run and find out," and Rikki-tikki was a true mongoose. [12]He looked at the cotton wool, decided that it was not good to eat, ran all around the table, sat up and put his fur in order, scratched himself, and jumped on the small boy's shoulder.

[13]"Don't be frightened, Teddy," said his father. [14]"That's his way of making friends."

[15]"Ouch! He's tickling under my chin," said Teddy.

[16]Rikki-tikki looked down between the boy's collar and neck, snuffed at his ear, and climbed down to the floor, where he sat rubbing his nose.

[17]"Good gracious," said Teddy's mother, "and that's a wild creature! [18]I suppose he's so tame because we've been kind to him."

[19]"All mongooses are like that," said her husband. [20]"If Teddy doesn't pick him up by the tail, or try to put him in a cage, he'll run in and out of the house all day long. [21]Let's give him something to eat."

[22]They gave him a little piece of raw meat. [23]Rikki-tikki liked it immensely,

and when it was finished he went out into the veranda and sat in the sunshine and fluffed up his fur to make it dry to the roots. [24]Then he felt better.

1. Why do you think the boy thought the mongoose was dead? (inference)

   He was lying in the path, probably not moving.

   1 best evidence sentence: **3**

2. What do you think the author means in sentence 10 when he says a mongoose is "eaten up from nose to tail with curiosity"? (figurative language)

   A. He is interested in everything.
   B. He is afraid of people.
   C. He is always looking for food.
   D. He is full of fleas.

   The phrase means that a mongoose is full of curiosity; his curiosity consumes him. He has to explore everything. A is supported by the motto "run and find out" in sentence 11 and by Rikki-tikki's behavior. There is no evidence for B, C, or D.

3. What did Teddy's father think Rikki-tikki was trying to do when he jumped on Teddy's shoulders? (reading for detail)

   He thought Rikki-tikki was trying to make friends with Teddy.

   1 best evidence sentence: **14**

4. What did Rikki-tikki do that made Teddy's mother think he was tame? (inference)

   He wasn't afraid of them. He climbed up on Teddy.

   2 best evidence sentences: **12, 16**

5. In sentence 2, the author says that Rikki-tikki "lost his senses." What does this mean? (figurative language)

   A. He lost his way.
   B. He fell asleep.
   C. He was unconscious.
   D. He went crazy.

   1 best evidence sentence: **3**

   There is some evidence for A, since losing your senses could include losing your sense of direction, but C is supported by sentence 3. He revived, or regained consciousness, *after* he lost his senses. There is no evidence for choices B or D.

6. Why do you think Rikki-tikki felt better after he fluffed up his fur? (conclusion)

   Once he fluffed his fur, it would dry completely. He felt better now that he was drying out.

   1 best evidence sentence: **23**

6. *Where the Red Fern Grows* by Wilson Rawls (Excerpt)

A [1]Mr. Kyle and I were told to go to one end of the table. [2]Our dogs were placed at the other end. [3]Mr. Kyle snapped his fingers and called to his dog.
B [4]The big hound started walking toward his master. [5]What a beautiful sight it was. [6]He walked like a king. [7]His body was stiff and straight, his head high in the air, his large muscles quivered and jerked under his glossy coat, but something went wrong. [8]Just before he reached the end, he broke his stride, turned, and jumped down from the table.
C [9]A low murmur ran through the crowd.
D [10]It was my turn. [11]Three times I tried to call to Little Ann. [12]Words just wouldn't come out. [13]My throat was too dry. [14]The

vocal cords refused to work, but I could snap my fingers. [15]That was all I needed. [16]She started toward me. [17]I held my breath. [18]There was silence all around me.

E [19]As graceful as any queen, with her head high in the air, and her long red tail arched in a perfect rainbow, my little dog walked down the table. [20]With her warm gray eyes staring straight at me, on she came. [21]Walking up to me, she laid her head on my shoulder. [22]As I put my arms around her, the crowd exploded.

F [23]During the commotion I felt hands slapping me on the back, and heard the word congratulations time after time. [24]The head judge came over and made a speech. [25]Handing me a small silver cup, he said, "Congratulations, son. [26]It was justly won."

1. In sentence 19, the author uses a simile and a metaphor to describe Little Ann. Write one of these below and identify which kind of figurative language it is. (figurative language)

   "As graceful as any queen" is a simile and "tail arched in a perfect rainbow" is a metaphor.

2. Choose the two sentences that best show how the crowd supported the boy and his dog. (supporting detail)

   A. During the commotion I felt hands slapping me on the back...
   B. There was silence all around me.
   C. As I put my arms around her, the crowd exploded.
   D. A low murmur ran through the crowd.

   In B, you might think that the crowd was silent because they didn't want to distract the dog, but this is not directly stated.

3. Which word best describes the main

feeling the author is trying to create? (author's purpose/mood)

   A. enthusiasm
   B. tension
   C. indifference
   D. sadness

   B is the best answer because the story takes place in the midst of a contest. The reader is not sure what will happen until the end of the passage. There is no evidence for C or D. There is some evidence to support that the characters are enthusiastic when Little Ann wins, but this comes at the end of the passage, so A is incorrect.

4. What causes Little Ann to start walking across the table? (cause/effect)

   A. The crowd murmurs quietly.
   B. The boy snaps his fingers.
   C. The boy calls to her.
   D. The big hound barks.

   1 best evidence sentence: **14**

   There is no evidence that A affects the dog. C is incorrect because in sentences 12 and 14 the boy is unable to call her. There is no evidence for D.

5. Compare the big hound's performance to Little Ann's. (compare/contrast)

   The hound walked like a king and Little Ann walked like a queen. They both held their heads up high. Also acceptable: **The big hound jumped down; Little Ann kept on.**

   3 best evidence sentences: **6, 7, 19**

6. Give two examples from paragraph D that suggest the boy might be nervous. (inference/character trait)

   1. The boy could not speak to call his dog. 2. He held his breath as Little Ann started toward him.

1 best evidence sentence for each example: **12 (or 14), 17**

7. In sentence 23, what does the word *commotion* mean? (vocabulary)

   A. excitement
   B. calm
   C. contest
   D. discussion

In sentence 22, the crowd explodes in excitement when Little Ann wins. They probably clapped and cheered. The scene is definitely not calm, so B is incorrect. The contest is over, so C is incorrect. There is no evidence for D.

7. *Island of the Blue Dolphins* by Scott O'Dell (Excerpt)

A ¹That night they came back to the headland. ²I had buried what was left of my supper, but they dug it up, snarling and fighting among themselves over the scraps. ³Then they began to pace back and forth at the foot of the rock, sniffing the air, for they could smell my tracks and knew that I was somewhere near.
B ⁴For a long time I lay on the rock while they trotted around below me. ⁵The rock was high and they could not climb it, but I was still fearful. ⁶As I lay there I wondered what would happen to me if I went against the law of our tribe which forbade the making of weapons by women—if I did not think of it at all and made those things which I must have to protect myself.
C ⁷Would the four winds blow in from the four directions of the world and smother me as I made the weapons? ⁸Or would the earth tremble, as many said, and bury me beneath its falling rocks? ⁹Or, as others said, would the sea rise over the island in a terrible flood? ¹⁰Would the weapons break in my hands at the moment when

my life was in danger, which is what my father had said?
D ¹¹I thought about these things for two days and on the third night when the wild dogs returned to the rock, I made up my mind that no matter what befell me I would make the weapons. ¹²In the morning I set about it, though I felt very fearful.

1. Which of the following statements best shows the main conflict in the passage? (conflict)

   A. They snarl and fight among themselves over the scraps.
   B. She wonders what will happen if she goes against the laws.
   C. She decides to make weapons.
   D. She wonders how she will find food.

The main conflict is an inner one between the woman's knowledge of her tribe's laws and her need to survive now that they cannot protect her. This is supported by paragraphs B and D. A is a detail of the passage, not the main conflict. C does not explain the woman's inner conflict; the decision she makes is not part of the conflict, it is the resolution to the conflict. There is no evidence to support D.

2. In paragraph A, who do you think are "they"? (inference)

the wild dogs

1 best evidence sentence: **11**

Paragraph A states that *they* snarled and fought over scraps, then sniffed the air for the woman's scent. This is most likely something a wild animal would do. However, it is not until sentence 11 that *they* is identified as wild dogs.

3. The woman decides to make the weapons because she probably believes (inference)

   A. defending herself is more important than her tribe's laws.
   B. she is above her tribe's laws.
   C. her tribe would understand if they found out.
   D. her tribe will never find out.

   1 best evidence sentence: **11**

   A is the best answer because the woman has decided that no matter what may happen, she will make weapons. Since this decision is made while she is being threatened by wild dogs, it is very likely that she will be making the weapons to defend herself. We know that B is incorrect because the woman is very concerned about going against her tribe's laws. There is no evidence that the woman believes her tribe would understand her decision if they knew her circumstances, so C is incorrect. There is no evidence for D.

4. Give two examples from paragraph C that explain why the woman was afraid to make weapons. (supporting detail) Accept any 2 examples:

   1. The four winds would blow and smother her. 2. The earth would tremble and then bury her. 3. The island would be flooded by the sea. 4. The weapons would break in her hands.

5. Why was the woman fearful in paragraph A? (inference)

   The dogs had fought over her food. They were also pacing at the foot of the rock and sniffing her scent.

2 best evidence sentences: **2, 3**

6. What does the rock provide for the woman? (setting)

   The rock provides protection from the wild dogs below.

   1 evidence paragraph: **B**

7. What can you tell about the tribe based on the woman's concerns? (conclusion)

   A. The tribe believes the earth is flat.
   B. The tribe believes man has power over a woman's ability to make weapons.
   C. The tribe is watching what the woman is doing.
   D. The tribe believes in forces that respond to human misbehavior.

   1 evidence paragraph: **C**

   There is no evidence for choices A, B, or C.

8. What does the woman's decision tell you about her character? (character trait)

   A. She is unconcerned.
   B. She is brave, but fearful.
   C. She is unsure of herself.
   D. She is fearless.

   2 evidence sentences: **11, 12**

   The woman is concerned about her fate, so A is incorrect. The woman does make a decision, so C is incorrect. Although she does take a risk by deciding to make weapons, she is not fearless, so D is incorrect.

8. *Blue Willow*
   by Doris Gates (Excerpt)

A ¹"Hello buddy," he called jauntily as

Mr. Larkin rose and started toward the open door. ²"When did you move in?"

B ³It was still broad daylight and Janey had plenty of opportunity to study their visitor. ⁴And what she saw she did not like. ⁵She couldn't decide exactly what there was about him to make her feel distrust. ⁶"It must be his eyes," she concluded. ⁷They moved shiftily about, never seeming able to rivet themselves on any one thing for more than a second. ⁸Moreover, his attitude seemed to indicate plainly that he held the destiny of the Larkins in the hollow of his very dirty right hand. ⁹The manner with which he stalked boldly into the house and looked casually about couldn't have made it any plainer. ¹⁰Janey had the feeling, even, that if there were anything in sight which he considered worthy of his interest it would become his on the spot. ¹¹For once, she was extremely thankful that the blue willow plate was safely out of sight.

C ¹²"Something I can do for you?" ¹³Janey could tell that Dad was indignant. ¹⁴His voice was hard and even. ¹⁵Evidently he felt exactly as she did toward this intruder.

D ¹⁶"I'll say there is," returned the stranger. ¹⁷"You can just hand over five dollars a month rent for this shack. ¹⁸Rent starting from the day you moved in, whenever that was."

E ¹⁹"We've been here a week," said Mr. Larkin.

F ²⁰The man narrowed his eyes for an instant while he thought rapidly. ²¹"Yeh," he finally said, "I guess that's about right. ²²The last time I was out this way, there wasn't nobody here."

G ²³Mr. Larkin, ignoring this remark, walked away to speak in low tones to his wife, who had remained at the stove, her back to the room. ²⁴Now he faced that man again and said, reaching into his pocket and drawing forth a buckskin bag:

H ²⁵"Here's your money, and I'll take a receipt."

I ²⁶For just a second the man hesitated, then ²⁷"That ain't necessary, buddy. ²⁸I'm Bounce Reyburn, everybody knows me around here."

J ²⁹"Just the same," said Mr. Larkin quietly, but drawing up the strings of the buckskin bag, "I'll take a receipt from you, or you won't take any money from me."

K ³⁰An ugly light came into Bounce's eyes, and Janey, catching it, felt a queer little shiver run along her spine. ³¹The glint remained for the merest instant and then Bounce shrugged and grinned, a little too broadly, Janey thought.

L ³²"O.K.," he said, "give me a scrap of paper, somebody, and I'll put my John Henry* on it."

1. In sentence 7, what does the word *rivet* mean? (vocabulary)

   A. find
   B. stay put
   C. balance
   D. move about

   The visitor's eyes were constantly moving. They never seemed able to stay on one thing for more than a second. There is no evidence for A, C, or D.

2. From Janey's description of the visitor in paragraph B, how do you think the visitor felt towards the family? (inference)

   A. He felt friendly towards them.
   B. He felt threatened by them.
   C. He felt power over them.
   D. He felt sorry for them.

   3 best evidence sentences: **8, 9, 10**

   C is the best answer because the passage indicates that the visitor felt he held the destiny of the Larkin's family in his hand (8). A is incorrect because Janey felt that even though Bounce acted friendly at first, he didn't mean it (4, 5). There is no evidence for B or D.

3. In sentence 30, what do you think is the "ugly light" Janey sees in Bounce's eyes? (inference)

The ugly light appeared in Bounce's eyes when Mr. Larkin wouldn't just hand over the money. The light could mean anger towards Mr. Larkin.

4. In sentence 29, why do you think Mr. Larkin wanted a receipt for the money? (inference)

A. He did not trust Bounce.
B. He always kept receipts.
C. He wanted to make Bounce angry.
D. He needed Bounce's signature.

1 best evidence sentence: **15**

Mr. Larkin had never met Bounce before, and he did not know if he could trust him. Sentence 15 says that Mr. Larkin felt the same as Janey about Bounce. There is no evidence for B, C, or D.

5. What was it about the visitor's eyes that made Janey distrust him? (supporting detail)

A. He seemed to be looking for something.
B. He squinted a lot.
C. He never looked at anything for very long.
D. He stared at her.

1 best evidence sentence: **7**

6. What might have made Bounce finally agree to give Mr. Larkin a receipt? (conclusion)

A. He planned to sign a different name.
B. He didn't really mind giving Mr. Larkin a receipt.
C. He agreed with Mr. Larkin that a receipt was important.
D. He thought that Mr. Larkin wouldn't change his mind.

1 best evidence sentence: **29**

There is no evidence for A; to "put your John Henry" on something means to sign it. B and C are both contradicted by sentences 27 and 28 when Bounce says a receipt isn't necessary.

7. In sentence 11, why do you think Janey was glad that the blue willow plate was hidden? (inference)

Janey felt that Bounce would take anything of theirs that he wanted.

1 best evidence sentence: **10**

9. *The Witch of Blackbird Pond* by Elizabeth George Speare (Excerpt)

A [1]"After the keen still days of September, the October sun filled the world with mellow warmth. [2]Before Kit's eyes a miracle took place, for which she was totally unprepared. [3]She stood in the doorway of her uncle's house and held her breath with wonder. [4]The maple tree in front of the doorstep burned like a gigantic red torch. [5]The oaks along the roadway glowed yellow and bronze. [6]The fields stretched like a carpet of jewels, emerald and topaz and garnet. [7]Everywhere she walked the color shouted and sang around her. [8]The dried brown leaves crackled beneath her feet and gave off a delicious smoky fragrance. [9]No one had ever told her about autumn in New England. [10]The excitement of it beat in her blood. [11]Every morning she woke with a new confidence and buoyancy she could not explain. [12]In October any wonderful unexpected thing might be possible.

B [13]"As the days grew shorter and colder, this new sense of expectancy increased and her heightened awareness seemed to give new significance to every common thing around her. [14]Otherwise she might have overlooked a small scene that, once noticed, she would never entirely forget. [15]Going through the shed door one morning, with her arms full of linens to spread on the grass, Kit halted, wary as always, at the sight of her uncle. [16]He was standing not far from the house, looking out toward the river, his face half turned from her. [17]He did not notice her. [18]He simply stood, idle for one rare moment, staring at the golden fields. [19]The flaming color was dimmed now. [20]Great masses of curled brown leaves lay tangled in the dried grass, and the branches that thrust against the graying sky were almost bare. [21]As Kit watched, her uncle bent slowly and scooped up a handful of brown dirt from the garden patch at his feet, and stood holding it with a curious reverence, as though it were some priceless substance. [22]As it crumbled through his fingers his hand convulsed in a sudden passionate gesture. [23]Kit backed through the door and closed it softly. [24]She felt as though she had eavesdropped. [25]When she had hated and feared her uncle for so long, why did it suddenly hurt to think of that lonely defiant figure in the garden?"

1. What do you think Kit's uncle is doing when she sees him? (supporting detail)
   A. crying
   B. playing
   C. working
   D. thinking

1 best evidence sentence: **21**

There is no evidence for A. He stares at the handful of dirt for awhile, so both B and C are incorrect.

2. Which of the following does the author describe with a simile? (figurative language)
   A. the sun (sentence 1)
   B. maple tree (sentence 4)
   C. oak trees (sentence 5)
   D. brown leaves (sentence 8)

In sentence 4, the author says, "The maple tree…burned like a gigantic red torch."

3. Which of these sentences from the passage best expresses the main idea? (main idea)
   A. "She felt as though she had eavesdropped."
   B. "No one had ever told her about autumn in New England."
   C. "In October any wonderful unexpected thing might be possible."
   D. "Before Kit's eyes a miracle took place, for which she was totally unprepared."

Paragraph A describes Kit's surprise and pleasure at the unexpected changes taking place her surroundings. In paragraph B, her uncle's behavior was another unexpected event.

4. How had Kit felt about her uncle before she saw him in the garden? (reading for detail)
   A. She had been scared of him.
   B. She had been jealous of him.
   C. She had been grateful to him.
   D. She had been worried about him.

1 best evidence sentence: **25**

Sentence 25 says that she had feared him.

5. Which of these events happens first? (sequence)

   A. Kit sees her uncle.
   B. Kit closes the shed door.
   C. Kit gathers up linens.
   D. Kit stands in the doorway of the house.

   See Sentence 3.

6. How do you think Kit felt after watching her uncle scoop up the dirt and squeeze it with a passionate gesture? (inference)

   A. She hated and feared him.
   B. She was worried about him.
   C. She felt sympathy toward him.
   D. She wished she hadn't seen anything.

   1 best evidence sentence: **25**

   Sentence 25 illustrates that her feelings towards her uncle at the beginning of the passage were hate and fear. At the end of the passage, she is feeling differently. It "hurts" to think of that lonely figure, suggesting sympathy.

7. In paragraph A, which of the following is described as though it were human? (figurative language)

   A. leaves
   B. color
   C. maple tree
   D. fields

   1 best evidence sentence: **7**

   In sentence 8, the leaves "crackled," and in sentence 4, the maple tree "burned." These are not human traits, so A and C are incorrect. In sentence 6, the fields were "stretched" like a carpet, but they were not doing the

stretching so D is incorrect. Sentence 7 says the color "shouted" and "sang."

8. In paragraph A, what do you think was Kit's first reaction to the changes in her surroundings? (conclusion)

   A. amazement
   B. surprise
   C. concern
   D. fright

   2 best evidence sentences: **2, 3**

   Sentence 2 tells of a "miracle" for which she was "totally unprepared." Sentence 3 says she "held her breath with wonder." Both suggest amazement.

10. *Charlie's House* by Clyde Robert Bulla (Excerpt)

A [1]When he had his own farm, he would still be near the Chapmans, he thought. [2]He would always help them if they needed him.

B [3]Charlie came to know the neighbors. [4]He went to barn dances with other young people. [5]He listened to the fiddle music and watched the dancers and pretended he was dancing, too.

C [6]When the rivers and ponds froze over, he went to moonlight skating parties. [7]But almost every night he was at home with the Chapmans. [8]Mistress Chapman was teaching him to read and write.
                          ***
D [9]A visitor came—a man named Oliver Greer. [10]He was Master Chapman's cousin from Carolina. [11]He had come north on business.

E [12]He was slim and dark, with a neat, black mustache. [13]He dressed like a gentleman, and he seemed proud of the way he looked.

F [14]He thought the Chapmans were much too good to Charlie.

G [15]"That boy thinks he's one of the family," he said.

H [16]While Master Greer was there, Charlie never ate at the table with the others.

I [17]Master Greer gave him work to do, and he never called him by name. [18]"Boy," he would say, "shine my boots. [19]Boy, light my pipe."

J [20]"Do as he says, Charlie," said Mistress Chapman. [21]"It won't be for long."

K [22]But Master Greer stayed on and on. [23]Every night he and Master Chapman sat up, drinking and playing cards.

L [24]"I do wish he would go," said Mistress Chapman. [25]"Sometimes I'm so afraid—"

M [26]There was a change in Master Chapman. [27]He took to staying in his room all morning. [28]He looked ill. [29]He often stumbled when he walked.

N [30]Master Greer had been there almost a month when Mistress Chapman called Charlie into the kitchen. [31]She said, "Master Greer is leaving today."

O [32]He thought she would be glad. [33]Instead she began to cry.

P [34]Master Chapman came in. [35]His face was gray, and his hands shook. [36]"Charlie, I must talk to you."

Q [37]"Yes sir," said Charlie.

R [38]"My cousin is going home," said Master Chapman, "and you—you are going with him."

S [39]Charlie heard the words, but he did not believe them. [40]He waited.

T [41]"You are going with him," Master Chapman said again. [42]"I lost you. [43]I lost you in a game of cards."

U [44]"But you—" began Charlie.

V [45]Master Chapman turned away from him. [46]"I'm sorry."

W [47]"I came to work for *you*," said Charlie. [48]"*You* bought my bond."

X [49]"That's true, but Cousin Oliver won it from me. [50]The bond will be the same. [51]You'll still have your land when you've worked for it—only you'll work for him instead," Master Chapman said. [52]"Now go. [53]Cousin Oliver is waiting."

1. Which of the following supports the idea that Master Greer thought he was better than Charlie? (inference)
   A. He gave him work to do.
   B. He didn't call him by name.
   C. He dressed like a gentleman.
   D. He treated Charlie like family.

   2 best evidence sentences: **17, 18** (19 is also acceptable)

   Master Greer called him "Boy."

2. Give an example of how Master Chapman changed. (supporting detail)

   (Accept any one example below.)

   He stayed in his room. **He looked ill**. **He often stumbled**.

   1 best evidence sentence for each example: **27, 28, 29**

3. Which of the following caused Charlie's having to leave? (cause/effect)
   A. Master Chapman's gambling loss.
   B. Master Chapman's kindness to Charlie.
   C. Master Chapman's ill health.
   D. Master Chapman's apology to Charlie.

   2 best evidence sentences: **42, 43**

   There is no evidence that choices B and D caused Charlie's leaving. Master Chapman's gambling resulted in his losing Charlie to Master Greer.

His illness may have been indirectly related to the outcome, but there is no definite evidence.

4. Which was a key event in the story? (key event)

   A. Charlie came to know the neighbors.
   B. Charlie went moonlight skating.
   C. Master Greer came to visit.
   D. Master Greer bought Charlie's bond.

   1 best evidence sentence: **9**

   The first two choices are details in the story. D is incorrect; he won Charlie's bond. Life changed for Charlie after Master Greer arrived.

5. Compare Charlie's life before and after Master Greer came. (compare/contrast)

   Before Master Greer came, Charlie was treated much better by the family. After Master Greer arrived, Charlie was treated more like a servant.

   4 best evidence paragraphs: **B, C, H, I**

6. Charlie is a bonded servant. Which of the following statements can you make based on Charlie's experience? A bonded servant (conclusion)

   A. could make his or her own decisions.
   B. was controlled by whoever owned his or her bond.
   C. was always considered part of the family.
   D. was always dependable.

   There is no evidence for A or D. Although Charlie was treated as family at first, it didn't last, so C is incorrect. Charlie had no say over

where he was sent; he had to go with whoever owned his bond. (48, 49)

7. From the information given, which of the following is true about a bond? (reading for detail)

   A. You can buy land in exchange for working.
   B. You are given land after you work for it.
   C. You become a landowner right away.
   D. You remain a servant all your life.

   1 best evidence sentence: **51**

   Charlie would be given land once he had worked for it.

FICTION

11. Iggy by Cheryl Block

[1]Iggy, my pet garter snake, is a lot of fun, but he always seems to be getting into trouble. [2]I never know where I'm going to find him next. [3]He has his own special bed in my room. [4]It's a cardboard box with a towel on the bottom to keep him warm. [5]But Iggy is always climbing out of his box to explore.

[6]Iggy likes warm places. [7]He loves to lie beneath the window when the sun is shining. [8]One day, he discovered the clothes dryer. [9]Mom had just finished unloading some laundry, and the dryer was nice and warm. [10]Iggy wriggled inside and went to sleep. [11]His pleasant nap was quickly cut short, however. [12]Mom didn't see him curled up inside and proceeded to pile another load of clothes in the dryer and turn it on. [13]Poor Iggy! [14]He was tossed and tumbled all around. [15]When Mom opened the door, Iggy quickly slithered out. [16]I could hear Mom's scream clear out in the backyard. [17]Iggy seemed okay after his tumble in the dryer, but I did notice that he was going around in

circles more for the next few days. [18]He never did go in the dryer again.

1. What are two things that Iggy does that get him into trouble? (supporting detail)

   He is always climbing out of his box. He climbed into the dryer.

   2 best evidence sentences: **5, 10**

2. Why did Iggy climb inside the dryer? (inference)

   Iggy likes warm places, and the dryer was still warm from the last load of laundry.

   2 best evidence sentences: **6, 9**

3. In sentence 17, why do you think Iggy was going in circles more? (cause/effect)

   Iggy was still feeling the effects from being tossed around in the dryer.

4. Iggy's actions show that he is (character traits)

   A. shy.
   B. curious.
   C. friendly.
   D. noisy.

   2 best evidence sentences: **5, 8**

   There is no evidence for A, C, or D. Iggy climbs out of his box to explore.

5. What happened just before Mom turned on the dryer? (sequence)

   A. Iggy wriggled into the dryer.
   B. Mom piled in a load of clothes.
   C. Iggy went to sleep.
   D. Mom unloaded some laundry.

6. Why do you think Mom screamed when Iggy came out of the dryer? (inference)

A. She doesn't like snakes.
B. She was startled by Iggy.
C. She thought the clothes were ruined.
D. She had to redo the laundry.

1 best evidence sentence: **12**

There is no evidence for A. Mom may have thought that the clothes were soiled or needed to be redone, but that probably wouldn't cause her to scream out loud. So choices C and D seem unlikely. Choice B is the most likely because people often scream when they are surprised by something unexpected, such as a snake in the dryer. It is also supported by the fact that Mom did not see Iggy get into the dryer.

12. Caught White-Handed
by Cheryl Block

A [1]Police today reported the capture of the man who has been robbing doughnut shops in the area. [2]The robber would break in during the early morning hours while employees were getting ready to open shop. [3]He would tie up the workers, then empty the cash register and steal a bag of freshly made doughnuts. [4]By the time customers found the workers and called police, the robber was long gone.
B [5]There were still two stores in the area that the robber hadn't hit. [6]Police decided to set a trap for him. [7]They knew he always stole a bag of powdered sugar doughnuts. [8]Police coated several dollar bills with a special glue that left the surface slightly sticky. [9]When the robber touched the money with his sugarcoated fingers, the sugar would stick to the bills. [10]The trap was now ready.
C [11]Two days later, the robber struck again. [12]Police had told store owners in the area to be on the lookout for the sugary

bills. ¹³The next day, police caught their man at a local grocery store. ¹⁴He had paid for his groceries in cash, and the clerk had noticed white spots on all the bills.

D ¹⁵As he was led away, the robber said, "My mother always said sugar was bad for you."

1. What were the white spots on the bills? (inference)

   The white spots were powdered sugar from the doughnuts.

   1 best evidence sentence: **9**

2. What do you think the robber meant in sentence 15 when he quoted his mother? (inference)
   A. He was overweight from eating doughnuts.
   B. He became a robber because he liked doughnuts.
   C. He was unhealthy because he ate too much sugar.
   D. He got caught because his sugar-coated fingers left white spots on the doughnuts.

   2 best evidence sentences: **3**, **7**

   D is the best answer because the powdered sugar on the bills tipped off the clerk. There is no evidence for A or C. The robber did like to take doughnuts, but he was also robbing the shops for the money, so B is incorrect.

3. The police coated the money with glue so (cause/effect)
   A. the bills would stick to the robber's fingers.
   B. the robber would leave sugar on the bills.
   C. the robber would leave his fingerprints.

D. the robber wouldn't be able to pick up the bills.

1 best evidence sentence: **9**

There is no evidence for A or D. The police did not expect to get fingerprints on the bills, so C is incorrect. Since police knew the robber liked to eat powdered sugar doughnuts, they hoped some of the sugar would be left on the bills after he touched the money.

4. From the time they set up the trap, how long did it take the police to capture the robber? (sequence)

   Three days. He struck two days after the trap was ready, and they caught him the next day.

   2 best evidence sentences: **11, 13**

5. Which moral is best supported by the story? (theme)
   A. Crime doesn't pay.
   B. Life is short; eat dessert first.
   C. Life is full of sticky situations.
   D. Doughnuts are bad for you.

   2 best evidence paragraphs: **C, D**

   There is no evidence for B or D. You might make a case for C, but there's no evidence to support that life is full of sticky situations.

6. What did the thief do to make sure he wasn't caught while robbing? (reading for details)

   He broke in before the store opened and tied up the employees.

   2 best evidence sentences: **2, 3**

13. Letter from the Mother Lode by Carrie Beckwith

December 5, 1849

Dearest Lillian,

A [1]I have finally arrived in Gold Country after nearly eight months of sailing, three of which were spent on land in South America during poor weather. [2]I am now living in a makeshift tent in Sacramento along a vein of quartz known as the Mother Lode. [3]The gold is rich here, and I am finding almost $20 worth every day! [4]However, food and clothing are unreasonably high—nearly $10 for a dozen eggs and $40 for a shirt! [5]For some men, the costs are enough to break them, and they have gone home penniless. [6]For more successful miners, these costs are only a drop in the bucket.

B [7]I work every day but Sunday, from sunup to sundown. [8]Three of us sit by the river with what is called a cradle, a wooden box that is set on rockers. [9]On top of the box lies a tray with wooden slats. [10]One man shovels gravel from the river bed into the tray and another pours water over the gravel. [11]The large rocks are caught in the tray, and the rest flows down to the cradle. [12]It is my job to then shake the cradle until the dirt has washed away, and all that is left is the precious gold. [13]We do this all day, and it is exhausting.

C [14]When we are not working, we are playing cards or chess. [15]Other men prefer the fights—boxing, wrestling, even animal fights. [16]They are bloody, horrible things to watch, but it is wild here and so too are the games.

D [17]I hope it will not be long before I can afford to send for you and little Joe. [18]I look forward to seeing you again.

All my love,

Daniel

1. Give two examples of some of the hardships Daniel is *now* experiencing. (supporting details)

   (Accept any two of the following.)

   Daniel is living in a tent. His food and clothing are very expensive. He works six days a week. His work is tiring.

   1 best evidence sentence for each example given: **2**, **4**, **7**, or **13**

2. In paragraph B, what happens just after the men have put the gravel and water into the tray? (sequence)

   The large rocks are caught in the tray.

3. What has caused some miners to go home penniless? (cause/effect)

   The cost of food and clothing has caused some miners to go home penniless.

   1 best evidence sentence: **5**

4. In what region of the country is Daniel living? (map reading)
   A. North
   B. Midwest
   C. South
   D. West

   Daniel is living in California on the West coast of the United States.

5. During what period in American history is the writer of the letter living? (conclusion)
   A. The Revolutionary War
   B. The Civil War
   C. The Gold Rush
   D. The Dust Bowl

   3 best evidence sentences from paragraph A: **1, 2, 3**

Daniel is in the California Mother Lode, looking for gold. The date of the letter supports the conclusion that this is the California Gold Rush of 1849.

6. What can you say about Daniel? (generalization/character traits)

    A. He is rich.
    B. He is bored.
    C. He is frightened.
    D. He is hard working.

3 best evidence sentences: **7, 12, 13**

D is the best answer as illustrated by the difficulties of the work described in paragraph B. Although Daniel is finding gold every day, the cost of living is high and he cannot yet afford to send for his wife and child, so A is incorrect. There is no indication that Daniel is bored, so B is incorrect. There is no evidence to indicate Daniel is frightened, so C is incorrect.

7. In sentence 6, what does the phrase "a drop in the bucket" mean? (figurative language)

"A drop in the bucket" is something that it is so small that it may seem like only one drop of water in a bucket.

Metaphorically speaking, the bucket is the amount of money a successful miner has, and the drop is the amount of money it costs him in order to live. The word "only" helps define the phrase.

14. Bad Reputation by David White

A [1]"My name is Wolf, and I've been given a bad name. [2]I hope that when I am finished speaking to you today, you will see my side of the story.
B [3]"First off, Little Red Riding Hood and her grandmother are alive and well. [4]In fact, they're living in Australia right now. [5]They said they couldn't stand the cold and wanted to live in a warmer climate. [6]They also said they were tired of sneezing. [7]They had developed severe allergies from all those leaves. [8]Why they stayed in the forest for so long I don't know, but they have a nice little hut in the Outback now. [9]They love it—not a tree for miles.
C [10]"Secondly, that girl was a spoiled child. [11]Her grandmother gave her everything she wanted. [12]Sure, she was bringing food to 'dear old Granny.' [13]But what did Little Miss Riding Hood expect in return? [14]I'll tell you—she wanted a new set of clothes. [15]She was tired of the red outfit. [16]When I talked to her in the woods that day, she said she hoped her grandmother would have a nice new green outfit all ready for her. [17]The last time she visited, she brought a few small cakes and left with a big shiny bracelet. [18]She does nothing 'just because.'
D [19]"OK, let's get another thing straight—I'm not exactly big. [20]I'm not even four feet tall. [21]People just say that I'm big because they think I was a bully to an innocent girl. [22]I'm just an ordinary animal trying to get by on what nature allows me. [23]I don't eat people, I don't wear women's clothing, I don't even talk to people that often.
E [24]"Let me pause here. [25]Does anyone have any questions?
F [26]"Yes, I know it looks like I did all those terrible things, but that's because you're reading that from a book, aren't you? [27]And who published that book? [28]It wasn't Wolves and Coyotes Press, now was it? [29]You people are all alike. [30]You always take the people's point of view.
G [31]"All I ask is that you compare what you've been told all these years with what I've said today. [32]Make up your own

minds. ³³After all, those stories say I'm dead. ³⁴But I'm here talking to you now. ³⁵Isn't that enough to make you start to doubt?"

1. Which of these statements best describes the main idea of the story? (main idea)

   A. Wolf questions facts.
   B. Wolf wants revenge.
   C. Wolf makes his case.
   D. Wolf pleads for mercy.

   1 best evidence sentence: **2**

   There is no evidence for B. Wolf does not plead for mercy, so D is incorrect. Wolf *does* question the facts, but he also urges his audience to see him in a different light; this makes C a better choice than A.

2. Which of these conclusions is best supported? (conclusion)

   A. Wolf wants people to believe him.
   B. Wolf wants people to dislike Grandmother.
   C. Wolf wants to see his own book published.
   D. Wolf wants to see Little Red Riding Hood again.

   1 best evidence sentence: **2**

   There is no evidence for B, C, or D.

3. Give three examples of how Wolf tries to restore his good name. (supporting detail)

   1. He argues that he didn't harm Little Red Riding Hood.
   2. He tells us that he isn't really big.
   3. He says he doesn't eat people.

   3 best evidence sentences: **3, 19** (or 20), **23**

4. Whose viewpoint is Wolf trying to change? (point of view)

   A. his own
   B. Little Red Riding Hood's
   C. Grandma's
   D. the public's

   2 best evidence paragraphs: **A, G**

   Wolf is not trying to change his own mind, so A is incorrect. In paragraph B, he says that Little Red Riding Hood and her grandmother are in Australia. It is clear in the passage that Wolf is talking to an audience who is there with him, so B and C are incorrect.

5. In Sentence 18, Wolf says of Little Red Riding Hood, "She does nothing 'just because.'" Explain what this means. (figurative language)

   She brings food to her grandmother but expects something in return. She doesn't bring food without reason.

   1 evidence paragraph: **C**

6. Why did Little Red Riding Hood and her grandmother leave the forest? (cause/effect)

   They became allergic to the leaves on the trees and wanted to go somewhere where it was warm.

   2 best evidence sentences: **5, 7**

7. Which of these words best describes what Wolf thinks he is? (inference)

   A. heroic
   B. forgotten
   C. unrewarded
   D. misunderstood

   2 best evidence paragraphs: **A, G**

   He wants to present his side.

15. A Shot at Problem Solving
by David White

[1]"Catalina, leave your shoes here!" my brother called as he stopped dribbling the basketball.

[2]I was putting my sneakers back on so I could go home and fix dinner. [3]"Mom will be home soon," I said. [4]Sitting on the grass barefoot was OK, but I wasn't going home that way, not in this heat.

[5]"But we're using your shoes as the boundary line," my brother said, wiping his forehead with his shirt. [6]It was so hot that my brother and his friend kept stopping to wipe the sweat from their heads and hands.

[7]"You can use a big rock or something else instead," I said. [8]"You'll figure it out."

[9]Mom encouraged us to solve our own problems. [10]So it didn't surprise me that when my brother asked for a basketball hoop, she told him to invent his own. [11]That's right—a basketball hoop.

[12]See, Jose (that's my brother) and his friend Tyrone had found this old ball and then wanted their own hoop. [13]In a flash of brilliance, Jose had said, "What about that plastic trash can in the garage?" [14]Mom had then carved out the bottom and used wire to hang the can from a telephone pole down the street. [15]She had a big smile on her face the whole time.

[16]Today, they were playing Make It–Take It, this game where you get to keep control of the ball as long as you keep scoring. [17]Each basket was a point. [18]Jose was ahead 32–26. [19]The first player to score 50 won the game.

[20]I headed home. [21]An hour later, Jose came home—with Tyrone and another boy.

[22]"Can Tyrone and Masako stay for dinner?" Jose asked, grinning.

[23]"They can if you all wash up first," Mom said. [24]"Jose, let them go first."

[25]As the two others headed off, Mom said, "Jose, have I seen Masako before?"

[26]"No, Mom. [27]We said he could play if he gave us an out-of-bounds line. [28]So he took off his belt and we used that."

[29]"You made him play in jeans that were falling down?" Mom said, laughing.

[30]"Well, they weren't that loose," he said with a smile. [31]"Besides, we couldn't let him win the first time. [32]He's good!"

1. Who was winning when Catalina left? (reading for detail)
   A. Jose
   B. Tyrone
   C. Masako
   D. Catalina
   1 best evidence sentence: **18**

2. Give one reason why Masako took off his belt. (cause/effect)
   (Accept either) **Masako took off his belt so the boys could use it as a boundary line. He also took it off because he wanted to play.**
   1 best evidence sentence: **27** (or **28**)

3. Why do you think Mom was smiling, as described in Sentence 15? (inference)
   She was proud of her son's problem-solving skill.
   1 best evidence sentence: **9**

4. Which two details support the idea that it was a hot day? (supporting detail)
   Catalina said she wasn't going home barefoot in the heat. Both boys wiped the sweat from their heads and hands.
   2 best evidence sentences: **4, 6**

5. If the boys hadn't wiped the sweat

from their hands during the game, how would that have affected their ability to play basketball? (conclusion)

(Accept any reasonable answer.)

The basketball might have slipped out of their hands and they wouldn't have been able to play as well.

6. Show two ways in which Jose demonstrates his problem-solving skills. (supporting detail)

He uses a trash can for a basketball hoop. He also uses his sister's shoes and Masako's belt for a boundary line.

2 best evidence sentences: **13, 5 (or 28)**

7. According to the game description in sentence 16, what would happen if Jose missed a shot, Tyrone got the ball, and then Tyrone put the ball through the hoop? (conclusion)

Tyrone would get to keep control of the ball until he missed.

16. Capsized! by Cheryl Block

A ¹Fusako kept checking her helmet and life vest to make sure they were tight. ²It was her first time white-water rafting. ³Even though it was a cold day, her hands were sweating. ⁴The guide gave them instructions on handling the raft. ⁵Then they all climbed aboard and slid the raft into the water. ⁶The water was calm at first, but the raft soon began to pick up speed as the currents* became stronger. **B** ⁷As they rounded a bend, she saw them. ⁸Rapids! ⁹The swirling waves looked like a pot of boiling water. ¹⁰She felt her stomach churning the same way. ¹¹She took a deep breath and dug in her paddle as they plunged into the rapids.

C ¹²The raft rode up and down the waves like a roller coaster. ¹³Each time the waves lifted it a little higher out of the water until it was nearly upright. ¹⁴Fusako felt exhilarated. ¹⁵This was better than any ride at the amusement park. ¹⁶As the raft started to rise again, it suddenly slammed down hard and hit a large rock, making the boat flip over. ¹⁷Fusako was thrown into the rushing water. ¹⁸She was carried along, bobbing up and down like a cork. ¹⁹Waves threw her against rocks and logs. ²⁰Thank goodness she was wearing a helmet and life vest! ²¹Finally she came to a section of river where the water was calm. ²²Bruised and exhausted, she climbed onto the shore.

*current: water flowing in a definite direction

1. Which of the following sentences from the story best supports the idea that Fusako is nervous? (inference/character trait)
   A. It was Fusako's first time white-water rafting.
   B. The guide gave them instructions on handling the boat.
   C. Even though it was a cold day, her hands were sweating.
   D. She took a deep breath and dug in her oar as they plunged into the rapids.

Sweating hands are often an indication of nervousness, so C is the best answer. There is no evidence for B. Both A and D might indicate that Fusako was nervous, but she could also be excited or eager; there is no evidence to clearly support one feeling.

2. In paragraph C, how does the narrator describe the raft ride? (figurative language/simile)

She compares the raft ride to a roller coaster.

1 best evidence sentence: **12**

3. The raft flipped over because it (cause/effect)

   A. was gradually filling with water.
   B. rose up too high in the water.
   C. slammed down against a rock.
   D. was overloaded.

   1 best evidence sentence: **16**

   There is no evidence for A or D. B is incorrect; the raft was only starting to rise.

4. In sentence 14, what does the word *exhilarated* mean? (vocabulary)

   A. joyful
   B. frightened
   C. timid
   D. unhappy

   Since the raft is lifting out of the water, B seems possible. However, in sentence 15 Fusako thinks the ride is *better* than a roller coaster, so she must be enjoying it.

5. Choose the two sentences that best show how the author builds tension in the story. (key events)

   A. As they rounded the bend she saw them.
   B. Fusako felt exhilarated.
   C. Fusako was thrown into the rushing water.
   D. Then they all climbed aboard and slid the raft into the water.

   Both A and C are setting the reader up for more action. Neither B nor D really indicate that something exciting is about to happen.

6. How did the helmet and life vest help Fusako? (conclusion)

The life vest kept her afloat until she reached calm water. The vest and helmet protected her as she banged against the rocks.

2 best evidence sentences: **18, 19**

7. In paragraph B, what one thing does the author compare to both Fusako's stomach and the rapids? (figurative language)

a pot of boiling water

8. Which two of the following sentences support the idea that you can be hurt while white-water rafting? (supporting details)

   A. The raft rode up and down the waves like a roller coaster.
   B. The swirling waves looked like a pot of boiling water.
   C. Thank goodness she was wearing a helmet and life vest!
   D. Waves threw her against rocks and logs.

   A and B indicate that the ride was rough, but do not indicate actual injury to passengers. C emphasizes that protective gear is needed. D gives an example of how she was hurt.

17. A Uniform Approach
by Carrie Beckwith

A [1]"Having to wear school uniforms violates my right as an individual to express myself," fourteen-year-old Maya argued from her seat in the cafeteria. [2]"I attend a public school, and I don't think anyone should be able to tell me what to wear."

B [3]"Yes, Maya, but we've had *four* gang-related fights on campus because someone was wearing the 'wrong' color. [4]We need to make our school safe. [5]Not to mention the fact that it's hard for kids whose parents can't afford to buy them a closetful of nice clothes," Juan said.

C ⁶The group of Compton Middle School students had gathered to discuss a solution to the problem of lunchtime fights on campus. ⁷Some students thought school uniforms were the answer. ⁸Others, like Maya, disagreed.

D ⁹"But where do we draw the line, Juan? ¹⁰First you take away the right to wear what we want. ¹¹Next, you'll be telling us what we can and cannot read or say!"

E ¹²"Who's to say wearing uniforms is going to stop fights?" a usually quiet boy asked from the back of the room.

F ¹³"Yeah! How is a uniform going to end that?" Maya added.

G ¹⁴"It may not, Maya. ¹⁵But I think it's worth trying." ¹⁶The school's student body president turned to his classmates. ¹⁷"What if we wore school uniforms on a trial basis? ¹⁸If it ends fighting on campus, we'll wear school uniforms. ¹⁹If not, we'll meet again and work out another solution. ²⁰How does that sound?"

H ²¹Vi spoke up quickly. ²²"That sounds like a great idea, Adam. ²³We could try it out for a year and see how it works." ²⁴Nods of approval could be seen throughout the cafeteria. ²⁵Maya saw the positive response from her classmates.

I ²⁶"Wearing uniforms helped end fights at Central Elementary School and East Town High School, Maya," another boy added.

J ²⁷"All right, we can give it a try," Maya finally accepted. ²⁸"But don't expect me to wear plaid pants!" she finished with a grin. ²⁹Laughter broke the tension of the room. ³⁰A show of hands made the decision final: School uniforms would be worn on a trial basis for a year.

1. Give two reasons from paragraph B that support the argument for wearing school uniforms. (supporting details)

   1. Uniforms may stop gang-related fights.
   2. Some parents can't afford to buy their kids lots of nice clothing.

   2 best evidence sentences: **3, 5**

2. What does the comment the boy made in sentence 12 suggest? (inference)
   A. He is for school uniforms.
   B. He doesn't agree that every school needs rules.
   C. He is unconvinced that school uniforms are the solution.
   D. He doesn't understand the argument.

   C is the best answer because the question reveals that the boy is not convinced that school uniforms will stop fights. A is incorrect because he doubts whether school uniforms will stop fights. D is incorrect because he seems to understand the argument—his comment is relevant to the debate. There is no evidence for B.

3. What is the main conflict in the passage? (conflict)

   Students disagree over whether to wear school uniforms.

   2 best evidence sentences: **7, 8**

4. Which of the following traits best describes Maya? (character traits)
   A. outspoken
   B. shy
   C. agreeable
   D. confused

   2 best evidence paragraphs: **A, D, F, or J** (accept any two)

A is correct because Maya speaks more than any of the other students, as evidenced by paragraphs A and D. B is incorrect because Maya speaks up and asserts herself. Maya does agree to try school uniforms for a year, but one instance of agreeing does not make an agreeable trait; therefore, C is not the best answer. There is no evidence for D.

5. What caused students to call the meeting? (cause/effect)

Students called the meeting to discuss a solution to the problem of lunchtime fights.

1 best evidence sentence: **6**

6. Which of the following quotes from the passage is a fact? (fact/opinion)

   A. "That sounds like a great idea, Adam."
   B. "We've had four gang-related fights on campus."
   C. "I don't think anyone should be able to tell me what to wear."
   D. "Next, they may be telling us what we can and cannot read or say!"

B is correct because it is not a value statement, and it has been proven. A and D are incorrect because they are based on assumptions that have not been proven. C is incorrect because it is a value judgment.

7. What do you predict will happen to the campus as a result of wearing school uniforms? (predict outcome)

On-campus fighting will probably go down as it did at the other schools, especially since the fighting was related to dress.

2 best evidence sentences: **3, 26**

18. The Bear and the Bees: A Fable by David White

A [1]In the forest there lived a big bear. [2]The bear was often hungry but didn't want to work for his food. [3]"So much is available, why should I waste my energy?" the bear would say to any animal that listened.
B [4]The other animals were careful to guard their food as best they could, but the bear always seemed to find a way to discover where their food was hidden. [5]Since the bear was bigger than all the other animals in the forest, the bear got his way.
C [6]Not even the bees were free from the bear. [7]They learned the hard way that the place to build their hive was high up in a tall, thin tree that the bear couldn't climb. [8]The bees worked hard all summer long, taking nectar from flowers and making honey so they would have something to eat in the winter. [9]The bear, meanwhile, did nothing to prepare for winter.
D [10]As the days grew shorter and colder, the bees enjoyed their honey and didn't worry about running out. [11]Many other animals, such as the squirrels and the ants, had stored food as well. [12]Taking a tip from the bees, the squirrels and ants had stored their food in tall, thin trees. [13]Other animals had moved away. [14]It seemed that the bear was on his own.
E [15]Time went by, and the bear grew hungry. [16]He followed some bees to their home tree one day and tried and tried to climb to the top of the tree. [17]But he was too tired and weak from not eating to go more than a few feet up. [18]Seeing this, the bees buzzed with laughter.
F [19]"Please, share some of your food with me," the bear groaned. [20]"It's mighty cold out here, and I have nothing to eat. [21]I've tried hibernating, but I just can't stay asleep."

G ²²"You should have thought of that in the summer," an angry squirrel chattered in reply. ²³"You depended on stealing our food then. ²⁴You can't get it now. ²⁵No nuts for you!"

H ²⁶Knowing he was beaten, the bear hung his head and walked sadly out of the forest. ²⁷The bees, squirrels, and ants felt not a bit sorry for him.

> ²⁸Moral: Cheaters get what they deserve.

1. What is the main conflict in the story? (conflict)
   A. The bear can't stay asleep.
   B. The bees won't share their food with the squirrels.
   C. The bees argue over where to hide their food.
   D. The other animals object to the bear stealing their food.

   1 best evidence sentence: **4**

   A is not a conflict. There is no evidence for B or C.

2. Why did the bees laugh at the bear? (inference)
   A. He was cold.
   B. He was hungry.
   C. He was asking them for food.
   D. He was too weak to climb the tree.

   2 best evidence sentences: **17, 18**

3. Which of these sentences is an opinion? (fact/opinion)
   A. The bear was often hungry but didn't want to work for his food.
   B. Not even the bees were free from the bear.
   C. "You should have thought of that in the summer."
   D. "No nuts for you!"

   A and B are facts. D is a statement of

fact, not an opinion of the squirrel. C is something that a character (in this case the squirrels) thinks, feels, or believes and is, therefore, an opinion.

4. In the last half of the story, the author uses sounds to describe the animals' speech. Below, fill in the word used to describe the sound made by each animal. (figurative language)

   bear   **groaned** (19)
   bees   **buzzed** (18)
   squirrel **chattered** (22)

5. Tell how the bear's attitude is different from the bees' attitude. (compare/contrast)

   The bear was lazy and didn't prepare for winter. The bees worked hard so they would have food in the winter.

   4 best evidence sentences: **2, 3, 9** (bear), **8** (bees)

6. Based on what you know about the bees, ants, and squirrels, what do you think they might say if the bear came back a week later and asked for food? (prediction)

   Possible answer: **They probably would not give him any food because they would still be angry at him for taking their food. They had refused to give him food once already.**

   1 best evidence sentence: **27**

7. How does the story support the moral? (theme/supporting details)

   The bear cheated by stealing food from other animals. In the end, he had made enemies with the other animals, and they were not willing to help him.

3 best evidence paragraphs: **B, G, H**

19. My First Alien Sighting
by Cheryl Block

A [1]Carlos and I had been planning this campout all summer. [2]We didn't want to sleep in a tent in the fenced back yard, as Mom would have preferred. [3]We wanted "real" camping. [4]Mom finally agreed to let us spend the night in the woods behind our yard. [5]We were only a few yards from the house, but to us it seemed like another country.

B [6]We set up the tent and rolled out our sleeping bags. [7]Mom had packed us sandwiches for dinner. [8]It was getting dark, so we turned on the lantern. [9]We told stories and joked around for awhile, then we went to bed. [10]We left the lantern outside and turned on, just in case there were any wild animals around.

C [11]I don't know how late it was when I was awakened by someone talking in a high, squeaky voice. [12]I figured some of the guys were trying to scare us, so I woke up Carlos. [13]We decided to crawl out the back of the tent and surprise them.

D [14]As we came around the tent, we both got a shock. [15]A small, glowing green creature was standing next to the lantern. [16]All eight arms were waving and pointing wildly as he carried on in that high-pitched voice. [17]He seemed to be upset that the lantern wasn't responding. [18]Grabbing it, he shook the lantern.

E [19]He wouldn't have seen us if Carlos hadn't sneezed. [20]The alien creature slowly turned and stared directly at us. [21]The green glow came from a green globe attached to the end of his nose (or what we thought was his nose). [22]But we didn't have time to get a good look at him. [23]Whirling around, he squealed and disappeared into the trees, leaving a glowing green trail behind him.

F [24]Carlos wanted to follow him, but I wasn't so sure it was a good idea. [25]As we were arguing about it, we heard a roar and looked up just in time to see a shining silver disk rise from the woods into the dark sky. [26]It was gone in a flash. [27]Carlos and I ducked into the tent and hid in our sleeping bags until morning. [28]When we got up, there was no sign of the little creature or his slimy trail. [29]Luckily, Mom didn't notice the glowing green spots that had baked onto the lantern.

1. Why do you think Mom preferred that the boys sleep in the back yard? (inference)

   She probably thought the back yard was safer.

   1 best evidence sentence: **10**

   Sentence 10 mentions the possibility of wild animals.

2. In sentence 5, what did the narrator mean when he said "it seemed like another country"? (figurative language)

   Being in the woods made it seem like they were far away from home.

   2 best evidence sentences: **2, 4**

3. Why did the boys think that some of their friends were outside? (inference)

   It sounded like someone was talking in a high, squeaky voice.

   1 best evidence sentence: **11**

   They thought their friends were playing a trick on them.

4. What do you think happened to the little green creature? (predict outcome)

   A. He took off in the shining disk.

B. He went back to his home in the woods.

C. He was eaten by a wild animal.

D. He disappeared without leaving a trace.

1 best evidence sentence: **25**

There is no evidence in the story for B or C. D seems possible, but it is contradicted by the glowing trail in sentence 23 and the spots in sentence 29. Therefore, A is most likely since the disk appeared shortly after the alien left the campsite.

5. What probably caused the alien to disappear into the trees? (cause/effect)

A. He heard an animal in the woods.

B. He was startled by the boys.

C. The lantern wouldn't respond.

D. It was getting late.

3 best evidence sentences: **19, 20, 23**

There is no evidence for choices A, B, or C. When Carlos sneezed, the alien turned to look at the boys and then disappeared.

6. How do you think the green spots got on the lantern in sentence 29? (cause/effect)

The green spots probably got on the lantern when the alien shook it.

2 best evidence sentences: **18, 23**

The green glowing spots may have been baked on by the lantern's heat.

20. Farm Girl by Margaret Hockett

A [1]Step, slosh, step, slosh. [2]Gloria cautiously placed one foot in front of the other, just like Papa showed her, her left arm outstretched to balance her burden. [3]At 15 pounds, the pail of life-giving liquid weighed nearly a fifth of her own weight. **B** [4]She had left her father 20 yards behind, where he was transferring the big sucking machine from Betsy to Moovystar. [5]The end of the barn was still a good thirty yards away. [6]There she would steel herself for the effort of pouring out her pail in the milkhouse. [7]She knew she would struggle to raise the pail high enough, without spilling a drop, to empty it into the bulk tank, its opening just above the level of her shoulders. [8]She paused to catch her breath and wipe off the sweat that trickled down her neck. [9]It was hard work for a girl of her age.

C [10]Even so, she looked protectively at the farm product in the bucket at her side. [11]She knew every drop was precious, and would become money used to buy any of the food they did not grow themselves, any clothes they did not make at home. [12]Each drop would also help her older brother finish college; eventually, it would allow her, too, to go to college.

1. What sentence from paragraph B suggests that the pail contains milk? (conclusion)

Sentence **6** (**7** acceptable for those familiar with a dairy)

Sentence 6 says that she is going to the milkhouse to dump her pail. (If students are familiar with a dairy, sentence 7 may be their best clue because a bulk tank is used to store milk.)

2. Choose the two best answers to complete the following sentence: Gloria most likely felt that her work was (inference)

A. hard but worth the effort.

B. a necessary thing.

C. something to do for fun.

D. a waste of time.

2 best evidence paragraphs: **A, B**

There is no evidence for choice C.

Paragraph B demonstrates the difficulty of Gloria's chore, and sentence 11 shows that the work is necessary for the family's living. Therefore, choices A and B are correct, and choice D is incorrect.

3. Which of these actions was completed within the story? (sequence)

   A. carrying the pail to the end of the barn

   B. entering the milkhouse

   C. dumping the milk in the bulk tank

   D. carrying the milk twenty yards

1 best evidence sentence: **4**

From sentence 5, we know Gloria has not reached the end of the barn; there is evidence only that she stops after leaving her father 20 yards behind (4).

4. You can conclude that Gloria is probably (conclusion)

   A. a preschooler.

   B. a preteenager.

   C. a high school senior.

   D. a college freshman.

1 best evidence sentence: **3**

Since the 15-pound pail is a fifth of her weight, she weighs about 75 pounds; it is therefore unlikely that she is a high school senior or college freshman. On the other hand, most preschoolers would not be able to carry a 15-pound pail of liquid through the barn, not to mention lifting it above the shoulders, without spilling it.

5. The contents of the bulk tank most likely will be (predict outcome)

   A. fed to farm animals.

   B. donated to the homeless.

   C. sold for money.

   D. fed to the family.

1 best evidence sentence: **11**

They are in the dairy business.

6. Why did Gloria walk so carefully? (inference)

   A. to protect the product she carries

   B. to keep herself from getting hurt

   C. so her father wouldn't criticize

   D. so her walk would take longer

1 best evidence paragraph: **C**

Paragraph C describes the value of the contents of the pail, explaining *why* Gloria is careful.

7. As used in sentence 6, the word *steel* most likely means (vocabulary)

   A. strengthen

   B. remind

   C. sneak away

   D. cover with a metal

B could be possible, but the evidence for A is much stronger. We can tell that Gloria will need strength (A) because she will lift the heavy pail. We can tell that she feels her task is important to the family (paragraph C), so she would not sneak away (choice C) without performing her chore. D makes no sense in context; there is no reason she would cover *herself* with metal.

21. Riddle Time by Margaret Hockett

A ¹Greg and Nan enjoy making up games. ²Yesterday, they played DescriptoPict, in which one would draw an object and the other would guess it. ³Today, they were playing DescriptoRhyme. ⁴It was Nan's turn.

B ⁵"It's often wide but very long; it's hard to see the end. ⁶It can be curved, but sometimes straight; it often needs a mend.

⁷Sometimes it comes, sometimes it goes; it crosses many others. ⁸Use it on vacation or go home to see your mother."

C ⁹Greg took only a minute to recognize what she was describing.

D ¹⁰"It's the road!" he shouted.

E ¹¹"Right! ¹²Now you have to try your hand at it," Nan said, eager to guess his riddle.

F ¹³It took Greg a few minutes because, of course, he had to plan it so it would rhyme. ¹⁴Finally, he started:

G ¹⁵"It carries several members; all end in something hard. ¹⁶It hangs around in all the joints and sometimes in the yard. ¹⁷A tool you use in many ways, you raise it for attention; it should be easy now to guess—it's something you just mentioned!"

H ¹⁸Nan was stumped at first. ¹⁹She racked her brain thinking of different parts of her "road" riddle. ²⁰A road is hard, but what are the joints? ²¹The road crossings? ²²No—you raise it for attention. ²³Road workers raise flags…but she never mentioned those. ²⁴She gazed at her fingers as they drummed on the table. ²⁵Fingers…are attached with joints…to hands…which are raised for attention…

I ²⁶"I've got it!" she exclaimed.

1. What clue probably gave Nan the answer to Greg's riddle? (cause/effect)

   Looking at her fingers made her think of the answer.

   3 best evidence sentences: **24, 25, 26**

2. Which of the following are rules of the game Greg and Nan were playing? (Choose all that apply.) You have to (conclusion)

   A. describe an object.
   B. draw an object.
   C. make the clues rhyme.
   D. use at least 5 sentences.

3 best evidence paragraphs: **B, F, G**

3. What is the answer to Greg's riddle? (reading for detail)

   a hand

   List 2 evidence sentences in which Nan mentions the answer to Greg's riddle. **12, 25**

4. Which one of the following is NOT referred to in Greg's rhyme? (Hint: some of these are referred to by other names.) (reading for detail)

   A. fingernails
   B. joints
   C. bones
   D. hand

   Fingernails were referred to as "something hard" in sentence 15. Joints are referred to by name in sentence 16. A hand is referred to by the word "it" in sentences 15–17, and by the word "tool" in sentence 17.

5. In general, Nan and Greg (generalization)

   A. try to outdo each other.
   B. make up and play games.
   C. play DescriptoRhyme.
   D. draw objects for each other.

   B is the best answer because sentence 1 states that they enjoy making up games. There is no evidence for choice A. Though they have played DescriptoRhyme and also DescriptoPict, there is no evidence they have played those particular games before or will again. Therefore, choices C and D are incorrect.

6. If Nan and Greg made up a game called DescriptoSong, what would the players have to do? (prediction)

They would have to make up a song to describe something.

1 best evidence sentence from paragraph A: **2**

We can tell by the names of their games that the first part tells that they must *describe* something and the last part tells *how* they must describe it. For example, in DescriptoPict, they draw pictures. In DescriptoRhyme, they make rhymes. Therefore, one can predict that, if they made a game called DescriptoSong, they would have to sing their descriptions.

7. In sentence 18, "Nan was stumped" meant that Nan (figurative language)

   A. needed to make a choice.
   B. was sitting on a tree.
   C. had stubbed her toe.
   D. couldn't think of an answer.

There is no evidence for choices B or C. Nan did need to make a choice, but sentence 18 includes the words "stumped *at first*" so choice A makes no sense. We can tell by paragraph I that Nan couldn't think of the answer at first; she was thinking how her road riddle might contain the answer and couldn't make anything fit. Therefore, choice D is correct.

8. Number the following according to the order given in the passage. (sequence)

   5 Nan wonders about Greg's riddle.
   2 Greg guesses "the road."
   4 Greg describes a hand.
   1 Nan gives a description.
   3 Greg thinks about his riddle.

22. Pet Overpopulation
by Carrie Beckwith

Dear Editor:

A [1]Dog and cat overpopulation is a serious problem. [2]Most people don't realize that every day in the United States, almost 100,000 puppies and kittens are born. [3]Compare this to the 11,000 humans that are born each day. [4]As you can see, there simply aren't enough homes for them all.

B [5]An easy way to lessen the problem of pet overpopulation is to have your pets spayed or neutered, or "fixed." [6]Spaying or neutering an animal is a simple surgery that prevents your pet from having a litter of kittens or puppies. ([7]Females are spayed and males are neutered.)

C [8]I know some people argue that fixing a pet is dangerous to the animal. [9]They believe that it shortens the animal's life and causes health problems. [10]They also worry that the surgery itself is too risky. [11]However, studies have shown that animals who are fixed live just as long and are just as healthy as animals who have not been fixed. [12]There will always be some risk with surgery, but fixing a pet is a fairly simple operation. [13]The real risk is *not* spaying or neutering your animal and having to find homes for 6 to 8 new puppies or kittens!

D [14]If you still haven't been convinced to have your pets spayed or neutered, imagine this: You purchase a cat at the pet store. [15]Your new cat, Fluffy, has a litter of 6 kittens. [16]If each of those 6 kittens has 6 kittens, there will be 36 new kittens. [17]If those 36 kittens each have 6 kittens, there will be 216 new kittens! [18]Female cats as young as 6 months of age can give birth to kittens. [19]That means that after only a year and a half, Fluffy could have 258 offspring! [20]As you can see, the problem can get out of hand very quickly.

E [21]So become a solution to the problem of pet overpopulation—spay or neuter your animal friends!

Sincerely,
A concerned
member of the
community

1. What is the writer trying to convince you to do? (author's purpose)

   The author is trying to convince you to spay or neuter your pet.

   2 best evidence sentences: **14, 21**

2. Using paragraph A, give the numbers of the two sentences that best support why the author believes you should have your pets fixed. (supporting detail)

   Sentences **1, 4**

3. What can you conclude from the example of Fluffy in paragraph D? (conclusion)

   A. Cats should be left indoors.
   B. Cats reproduce quickly.
   C. Cats can't have kittens until age one.
   D. Cats should be watched carefully.

   There is no evidence for A, C, or D.

4. Give two reasons why people might NOT spay or neuter their pets. (supporting detail)

   1. They think that it will shorten the animals' lives.
   2. They worry about the risk of surgery to their pets.

   2 best evidence sentences: **9, 10**

5. What type of math did the author do to find out Fluffy could have a total of 258 offspring? (application)

   A. addition and subtraction
   B. multiplication and addition
   C. multiplication and division
   D. square root

   $6 + 36 (6 \times 6) + 216 (36 \times 36) = 258$

6. What do you think would happen to the problem of pet overpopulation if more people spayed/neutered their pets? (prediction)

   A. Pets would have more litters.
   B. The problem would get worse.
   C. More animals would end up in shelters and pounds.
   D. The problem would get better.

   1 best evidence sentence: **5**

   D is the best answer because sentence 5 states that spaying and neutering would lessen the problem. A is incorrect because spaying and neutering prevents animals from having litters (6). B is incorrect because the author states that the solution to the problem is spaying or neutering our pets (5, 21). There is no evidence for C.

7. Why does the writer bring up the views of people who disagree with having their pets fixed? (point of view)

   A. He wants to defend their position.
   B. He doesn't know how to make an argument.
   C. He doesn't understand their views.
   D. He wants to explain why he thinks they're wrong.

   The purpose of the passage is to convince you to spay/neuter your pet; therefore, A is incorrect. There is no evidence for B. C is incorrect because the author does understand their views—he just doesn't agree with them.

23. A Tale of Two Boarders
by Margaret Hockett

A [1]I, Su Kapo, was ready for a change. [2]My skateboard was only two months old but I was tired of it. [3]At first, I loved the blue design highlighted with bright colors. [4]After awhile, the graphics "got old" and everyone else's board looked better to me. [5]What could I do? [6]I couldn't afford a new one. [7]Then I saw it! [8]An ad for a used skateboard that sounded really cool.

B **[9]Check out the hottest skate in town! [10]Gold and crimson bands form a dragon that appears and disappears in the misty aqua background of this rolling winner. [11]Only $85! [12]Call 303-6578.**

C [13]I called the number. [14]Like me, the owner was tired of her board, and she suggested a trade! [15]If she liked my board and I liked hers, we would exchange boards and both be happy.
D [16]Skating to her house, I gazed at the top of my board. [17]Maybe the idea that someone else might want my board made me see it in a new light. [18]I had never noticed how those yellow and red stripes curved back and forth through the blue-green haze. [19]Or how they could come together to form the shape of some kind of…beast?
E [20]I was at her front door. [21]Before I could knock, the door swung open and revealed a girl about my age and size. [22]We both shouted with surprise as we each looked at the other's skateboard.

1. What is the best explanation for the girls' surprise? (conclusion)

A. Their boards looked alike.
B. The girls were the same size.
C. They didn't expect to see each other.
D. The door swung open too suddenly.

2 best evidence paragraphs: **B, D**

You can tell that the boards were probably alike by the similarities in the descriptions in paragraphs B and D: gold and crimson stripes could be described as red and yellow bands, misty aqua could be described as hazy blue-green, and a disappearing dragon could be seen as a beast.

2. In sentence 4, Su says the graphics "got old," though the board was only two months old. What do you think she really meant? (figurative language)

She was bored with or tired of the design.

1 best evidence sentence from paragraph C: **14**

3. Explain why Su didn't recognize the description of the board in the ad. (inference)

The graphic was described in a way that was different from how Su saw it. She had never looked closely at the graphic design.

3 best evidence sentences: **17, 18, 19**

4. What was the "beast" mentioned in sentence 19? (conclusion)

A picture of a dragon.

5. In sentence 2, Su says she was tired of her board after only two months. If she also said "I never finish books because I lose interest," you might say

that Su is a person who (generalization/character trait)

A. keeps her interest in things.
B. becomes bored quickly.
C. takes good care of things.
D. sticks to her decisions.

By the words "only" and "but," in sentence 2 the author implies that Su is tiring of her board unusually quickly. This, as well as the "book" statement, provides contrary evidence for A and D. C has no evidence.

6. The word *reveal,* in sentence 21, most nearly means (vocabulary)

A. hit.
B. uncover.
C. hide.
D. enclose.

There is no evidence that the girl was hit or enclosed by the swinging door. She may have been hidden by the door *until* it was open, but since the door swung open *to reveal* the girl, only "uncover" makes sense here.

7. Predict what Su will likely do next. (predict outcome)

She probably will not trade with the girl if their boards are the same. She will probably decide to keep her board, now that she sees it differently.

3 best evidence sentences: **17, 18, 19**

8. Describe two ways the writer of the ad tries to persuade the reader to buy the board. (author's purpose)

(Accept any two)

1. She gets the reader's attention with the first line. 2. She makes the board sound exciting. 3. She

makes the price sound low by writing "Only $85!"

24. Little Squirt, Big Squirt by Carrie Beckwith

A [1]I was facing another hot, boring day in the valley. [2]Normally, I didn't allow my little brother to step one foot near me, but I decided this day would have to be different. [3]I came up with the idea of turning Mom's clothesline into a theatre of sheets, and I let A.J. help me. [4]"This time," I told him, "I will be a beautiful Arabian belly dancer." [5]With golden bells around my waist and billowy lavender pants, I danced to the snakes. [6]They coiled themselves as if to attack, but were powerless under the spell of my dancing. [7]"Hissss…"

B [8]"Stop! [9]You're spitting on me." [10]My brother screamed and fell backwards in a fit of laughter, knocking over the picnic bench that was supposed to be front row seating.

C [11]"You have no imagination, A.J." [12]Of course, why did I expect an eight year old to know raw talent when he saw it?

D [13]"Well maybe if you did something besides squirm around with the garden hose I'd be interested!" A.J. joked. [14]Then he picked himself up and began cartwheeling around the yard, amused by his own humor.

E [15]I did not take kindly to insult, especially from my own brother. [16]So I did what any self-respecting sister would do to keep her brother in line…I played a little trick on him. [17]"You're right, A.J," I said. [18]"I'll start over. [19]This time I'm going to enter the stage from behind this bush. [20]You won't be able to see me right away, but just sit on the bench and wait, okay? [21]I'm going to act out a mystery, and I want you to be part of it, too."

F [22]When A.J. heard he could participate

in one of my plays, he raced to the picnic bench, sat down, and folded his hands. [23]Within seconds, I had the hose. [24]POW! [25]Right to the gut! [26]Front row seating was soaking wet. [27]"How did you like that mystery, A.J.?" I cackled. [28]But A.J. was quick. [29]He leaped up, grabbed the hose at its neck, and squirted it right back at me. **G** [30]"Not as much as I like squirting you with this hose, Tameeka!"
H [31]Nothing was left dry when we were through. [32]As I look back now, maybe it wasn't such a boring day after all.

1. Why do you think Tameeka "allowed" A.J. to play with her? (inference)
   A. She always played with her brother.
   B. She needed an actor for the play.
   C. She didn't have anything better to do.
   D. She liked A.J.'s ideas.

   1 best evidence sentence: **1**

   C is the best answer because Tameeka states in sentence 1 that it was a boring day. A is incorrect because sentence 2 states that Tameeka didn't normally allow her brother to play with her. B is incorrect because Tameeka never uses A.J. as an actor. D is incorrect because sentence 11 states that Tameeka doesn't think A.J. has any imagination.

2. From whose point of view is the story written? Explain your answer. (point of view)
   A. An unnamed narrator
   B. A.J.'s
   C. Mom's
   D. Tameeka's

   A.J. calls the narrator "Tameeka."

3. What caused A.J. to race back to the picnic bench? (cause/effect)

He thought his sister was going to let him participate in the play.

1 best evidence sentence: **22**

4. What does A.J.'s. reaction to being in his sister's play tell you about how he is feeling? (inference)
   A. He is afraid of his sister and will do whatever she wants.
   B. He is excited about being part of the play.
   C. He is angry and has his own plan to trick his sister.
   D. He's not sure if he wants to be part of his sister's play.

   1 best evidence sentence: **22**

   B is the best answer because sentence 22 explains that he rushed to the picnic bench and sat down with his hands folded (in full attention). There is no evidence for A , C, or D.

5. Compare Tameeka's opinion of the day at the beginning of the story to her opinion at the end. (compare/contrast)

   In the beginning of the story, she describes the day as boring. By the end of the story, she has changed her mind and thinks that maybe it wasn't such a boring day after all.

   2 best evidence sentences: **1, 32**

6. Put the following events in their correct order. (sequence)
   4 A.J. sprays Tameeka with hose.
   2 A.J. knocks the bench over.
   1 Tameeka pretends to be a belly dancer.
   3 Tameeka tells A.J. she will act out a mystery.

7. What conclusion about Tameeka is NOT supported in the story ? (conclusion/character traits)

   A. She likes to dance.
   B. She is shy.
   C. She is playful.
   D. She is imaginative.

   A is incorrect because we know that Tameeka dances (5). C is incorrect because much of the story is about playing. D is incorrect because sentences 4–7 illustrate Tameeka's imagination. There is no evidence to conclude that Tameeka is shy; therefore, B is correct.

8. Using paragraph A, describe the setting of the story. (setting)

   The story takes place on a hot day in the valley. A.J. and Tameeka are playing outside, using the clothesline and sheets to construct a theatre.

   2 best evidence sentences: **1, 3**

25. No Show by Margaret Hockett

A ¹"Look," I said, sitting on Jeremy's bed, "everyone's going to be there. ²And Mr. Grimes says some kid is doing some really cool magic tricks this year." ³But my best friend was making some lame excuse about going to the library first. ⁴I was afraid he was going to miss "Talent on Tap" at the high school gym. ⁵The variety show was so funny last year we both thought we'd bust a gut laughing.
B ⁶I tried once more. ⁷"Come on! ⁸"You even have your dress shoes on—and shined," I said. ⁹"Let's go now!"
C ¹⁰"Nah, I'll catch up with you later, Sid."
D ¹¹I gave up and left to meet Andy. ¹²Come to think of it, I'd been doing a lot with Andy lately. ¹³Jeremy had missed

baseball and dinner at my house last week. ¹⁴And he seemed thoughtful—he hadn't flashed his crinkly grin in days.
E ¹⁵We found our seats as the Master of Ceremonies began. ¹⁶After a few warmup jokes, he introduced The Dipsy Doodle Talking Poodles. ¹⁷They were only mildly funny. ¹⁸But by the time the Door Jams finished, we were rolling on the floor! ¹⁹Time for mystery and drama: the Magic Moment act was about to commence…
F ²⁰I looked around anxiously, hoping Jeremy had finally made it, because this act looked like it would be really big.
G ²¹KaBoom! ²²There was a bright glow, then a figure in black arose out of a mist. ²³His back was to us, and I caught a reflection of light off his glossy heels. ²⁴He slowly turned, one hand on the brim of his top hat, as his face crinkled into a grin…

1. Who is Sid's best friend? (inference)

   Jeremy

   1 best evidence sentence: **3**

   Sentence 3 says his best friend was making an excuse; this refers to the person he is now talking to.

2. What was Sid's conflict with Jeremy in paragraphs A and B? Sid was trying to (conflict)

   A. convince him to go to the show.
   B. make up with him after fighting.
   C. get him to go to the library.
   D. ask him to come to dinner.

   1 best evidence sentence from paragraph A: **4**

3. What persons are meant by "We" in sentence 15? (conclusion)

   the narrator (Sid) and Andy

4. Sid uses the phrase "rolling on the

floor" to show that they (figurative language)

A. thought the act was very funny.
B. were tired of sitting.
C. were too bored to watch.
D. had been scared.

Rolling on the floor is an idiom—a phrase used to communicate a figurative meaning. The word "But" of sentence 18 contrasts with the words "mildly funny" in sentence 17, so "rolling on the floor" is understood to mean *more* than mildly funny.

5. What does the word *commence* mean as used in sentence 19? (vocabulary)

A. bomb
B. cancel
C. begin
D. end

Sid hopes that Jeremy has arrived because this act looks like it will be big; therefore it hasn't happened yet so D is ruled out. Also, "Time for...," in sentence 19, implies a beginning. There is contradictory evidence for choices A and B because the magic act is described in paragraph G.

6. Give two clues from paragraph G that support the idea that Jeremy was the magician in the show. (inference)

glossy shoes, crinkly grin

1 best evidence sentence for each clue: **8, 14**

7. Assuming that Jeremy was the magician, when do you think he found time to practice his magic act? (inference)

Jeremy probably missed baseball and dinner with Sid in order to practice his magic act.

1 best evidence sentence: **13**

26. Truth or Dare
by Carrie Beckwith

A [1]Ann approached the house timidly. [2]Her first instinct was to run back to the safety of the tree house where Neve and Drew were waiting for her. [3]But this was a dare for her membership test, and that meant serious business.
B [4]"The house has been abandoned for over a hundred years," Ann remembered Neve telling her.
C [5]"The McWilliams family just picked up and left. [6]People said there was something strange about the way it all happened. [7]Since then, no one has set foot in the house," Drew had explained.
D [8]Ann held her breath and placed one foot on the paint-chipped steps of the front porch. [9]Every step closer to the front door made her heart pound faster and louder. [10]Her cold, sweaty hand clenched and twisted the knob. [11]The door swung open with unexpected ease. [12]"Maybe it was the wind," Ann tried to reason.
E [13]Her steps were cautious as she entered the dining room. [14]She stopped, her eyes darting wildly around the room. [15]Old, worn linens hung over the cherry wood tables and chairs. [16]Behind the cabinets, long-stemmed wine goblets were neatly arranged in rows, like little glass armies.
F [17]Ann crept towards the winding, red-carpeted staircase. [18]*Were those pictures of the McWilliams family lining the walls of the hallway upstairs?* [19]Her curiosity was piqued. [20]She walked upstairs and gazed at the yellowed portraits of a family long gone. [21]Just down the hallway, an open door with a stream of light caught her attention. [22]The wood floors creaked as she walked down the hall. [23]The words came ringing back to her, "The McWilliams

family just picked up and left. ²⁴People said there was something strange about the way it all happened."

G ²⁵Ann couldn't take it anymore. ²⁶She raced down the stairs, out the back door, and straight to the tree house. ²⁷Nearly out of breath, she hollered, "Drew, Neve, I'm back! ²⁸I made it!" ²⁹The girls tried to hold back their amusement, but couldn't.

H ³⁰"You're right. ³¹You did make it, Ann. ³²Welcome to our Tree House Club! ³³And if it makes you feel any better, that old house isn't really abandoned. ³⁴It's going to be part of the new town museum called Village of Our Past!"

1. Which two sentences in paragraph A best support the idea that Ann was nervous about going into the house? (supporting details/character trait)

Sentences **1**, **2**

2. Which sentence in paragraph E uses a simile to describe something? Write the sentence. (figurative language)

Behind the cabinets, long-stemmed wine goblets were neatly arranged in rows, like little glass armies.

Sentence **16**

3. In paragraph F, Ann decided to go upstairs because she noticed (cause/effect)

   A. the portraits of the McWilliams family.
   B. the long-stemmed wine goblets.
   C. the stream of light just down the hallway.
   D. the worn linens.

   2 best evidence sentences: **18**, **19**

   The portraits of the McWilliams family interested Ann and made her decide to go upstairs (18–19). Ann did

notice the wine glasses (16) and worn linens (15) before she went upstairs, but they did not cause her to go upstairs, so B and D are incorrect. She did not see the stream of light in the hallway (21) until she had already gone upstairs, so C is incorrect.

4. The word *piqued*, as used in sentence 19, means (vocabulary)

   A. controlled.
   B. stopped.
   C. mistaken.
   D. excited.

   In sentence 18, Ann thinks she sees pictures of the McWilliams family upstairs. Sentence 19 explains that Ann is curious. In sentence 20, she decides to go upstairs. Her curiosity, then, must have been excited.

5. Put the following events in the order they happened in the story. (sequence)

   3 Ann goes upstairs.
   1 Ann is dared.
   4 Ann runs out the back door.
   2 The front door swings open.

6. Using paragraphs E and F, list the numbers of the 2 sentences that best show that Ann was careful. (character trait/inference)

   Sentences **13**, **17**

   In sentence 13, Ann's steps were *cautious*. In sentence 17, Ann *crept* towards the staircase, suggesting that her steps were slow and cautious.

7. Which two paragraphs best describe the way the house looks inside? (setting)

   A. Paragraphs F and G
   B. Paragraphs A and E
   C. Paragraphs E and F
   D. Paragraphs F and H

8. Which of the following can you conclude about Neve and Drew? (Choose all that apply.) (conclusion)

  A. They were relieved to see Ann come back.

  B. They knew what was going on all along.

  C. They have asked Ann to tell the truth about something.

  D. They are members of the Tree House Club.

2 best evidence sentences: **33, 32**

There is no evidence for A and C. They knew the house wasn't abandoned, and they were both members of the club.

27. Case of the Missing Diamond by David White

[1]No one spoke in the small, hot room. [2]They all knew each other too well.

[3]Inspector Graham questioned each person in turn, making notes on a thin, white pad.

[4]The man in the striped trousers shifted in his chair, gripping his briefcase tightly. [5]The teenaged boy in the blue blazer leaned against the bookcase, trying to look bored.

[6]The woman in the red dress stood up and stretched. [7]Realizing she was being watched, she sat back down quickly and wrapped her hands around her purse. [8]When she was sure no one was looking, she opened the purse. [9]She looked inside, smiled, and snapped the purse shut.

[10]The man seated on the couch wiped his sweaty hands on his handkerchief. [11]He tapped his hearing aid in response to a question from the inspector. [12]When the question was repeated more loudly, he nodded his head. [13]His wife was sitting straight up at the end of the couch. [14]She stared at the wall and barely responded to the inspector's questions. [15]Her heavy earrings jingled over her knees.

[16]The antique clock struck two. [17]Everyone jumped. [18]The silence returned.

[19]"It's all clear to me now," the inspector said loudly. [20]"Mrs. Page's diamond has been missing for eighteen hours. [21]You have all remained here in this house. [22]One of you has that diamond right now."

[23]The suspects looked quickly at one another, then back at the inspector.

[24]The teen was the first to speak. [25]"When can I get out of here?" he said loudly, putting his hands back in his pockets. [26]"I have a date tonight."

[27]The woman in the red dress turned pale. [28]"You don't think it's me, do you?" she said softly. [29]Her hands were pale as she clutched her purse.

[30]The man in the striped trousers stood up angrily. [31]"You're mad, Graham," he said. [32]"I'm leaving."

[33]"This is an outrage!" the woman on the couch said, standing up suddenly. [34]Her left earring fell off and hit the floor, shattering into a dozen pieces. [35]The room was suddenly abuzz.

[36]"Good thing it's a fake," Inspector Graham whispered.

[37]"It is not a fake!" the man on the couch roared. [38]"We paid good money for those earrings!"

[39]"So," the inspector said with a smile, "you don't need the hearing aid after all. [40]In fact, the missing diamond is about that size."

1. Where do you predict the diamond will be found? (predict outcome)

  A. in a purse

  B. in the clock

C. in a briefcase
D. in the hearing aid

2 best evidence sentences: **39, 40**

Since the man with the hearing aid didn't appear to need it (he quickly responded to a whisper), and since the missing diamond is about the size of a hearing aid, we can predict that the diamond may be inside the hearing aid.

2. In sentence 17, why did everyone jump when the clock struck two? (inference)

They were nervous. It was quiet. The sudden sound took them by surprise.

3. What caused the earring to fall off? (cause/effect)

The woman's earring fell off when she stood up suddenly. Sentence 15 mentions that the earrings were heavy.

2 best evidence sentences: **15, 33**

4. Which is true of *all* the suspects? (generalization)

A. They are all sitting down.
B. They are all holding something.
C. They all know one another.
D. They all work for Mrs. Page.

1 best evidence sentence: **2**

5. How did the setting, as described in sentence 1, affect the suspects? (setting/inference)

The room is small and hot. This makes the suspects even more nervous and uncomfortable.

6. Give one example of how the man in striped trousers revealed his

nervousness through his actions. (supporting detail/character trait)

He kept a tight grip on his briefcase. Also, he shifted in his chair.

1 best evidence sentence: **4**

7. Give two examples of how the woman in the red dress acts suspicious of other people. (inference)

She sits down quickly and wraps her hands around her purse. She makes sure no one is looking before she opens her purse.

2 best evidence sentences: **7, 8**

28. Buttered Up
by Margaret Hockett

A [1]It was a very hot day, and Pa and I were weary after driving Uncle Charlie to the train station in our new Model T Ford. [2]On the way back home, Pa pulled into the gravel drive by Sickle Tree. [3]The sprawling oak had got that name because of the rusty old sickle* trapped within its trunk. [4]A farmer had hung it on the tree before heading off to the Civil War, from which he had never returned.

B [5]As we neared the stout woman minding a churn**, I could see what Pa had in mind. [6]There was nothing he loved better than a big old glass of buttermilk on a good hot day.

C [7]"I'll give ya five cents for a glass of that," he told her. [8]But the good-hearted woman offered us both buttermilk in exchange for gossip, as she "didn't get to town much."

D [9]We sat under the tree and enjoyed our cool, rich drinks while the woman churned. [10]She and Pa chatted pleasantly about the weather, farming, and life in general. [11]I was the first to notice the mangy looking yellow cat sneaking up to the churn as the woman removed the churn lid.

E [12]I was too fascinated to make a sound as the cat jumped up on the edge of the churn and promptly fell in.

F [13]When Pa and I realized how that dirty old cat would affect the woman's wonderful buttermilk, we felt sorry for her. [14]But the woman didn't seem too disturbed. [15]She just pulled out the cat, held him up with one hand, and wrung him out into the churn. [16]"You fool cat!" she scolded. [17]"That's the third time you've been in there today!"

G [18]We left shortly after that. [19]Pa thanked the woman politely, but I noticed that it was the first time he had ever left a glass of buttermilk unfinished.

   * sickle: a tool used for cutting grain

   **churn: (1) a container in which milk is made into butter by stirring, (2) the act of stirring milk until it becomes butter

1. The story most likely takes place (setting)

   A. in the present time.
   B. just after the Civil War.
   C. in the early 20th century.
   D. in the future.

   2 best evidence sentences: **1, 7**

   C is the best answer because Model T cars were new in the early 1900s, and a nickel might have been a reasonable price to pay for a glass of buttermilk in that era. Since Model T cars are not new today, A is incorrect. B is incorrect because there would have been no Model T's at all. There is no evidence for D.

   Note: Students may say B is unlikely because the tree might not have had

time to grow around the sickle right after the Civil War.

2. As used in sentence 5, what does the word *minding* mean? (vocabulary)

   A. tending
   B. baby-sitting
   C. being bothered by
   D. guarding against theft

   There is no evidence for C or D. Sentence 9 indicates the woman was working with the churn, not just baby-sitting it, so B is incorrect.

3. Why does the narrator call the woman "good-hearted" in paragraph C? (inference/character trait)

   She would not accept money for the buttermilk.

   1 best evidence sentence: **8**

4. Why do you think the farmer never removed the sickle from the oak tree described in paragraph A? (inference)

   The farmer who hung it there had never returned from the Civil War. (Also acceptable: He may have died in the Civil War.)

5. As used in sentence 11, the word *mangy* is used to suggest that the cat is (vocabulary)

   A. groomed.
   B. bright.
   C. mean.
   D. unclean.

   There is no evidence for A, B, or C. The description of the cat as "dirty" in sentence 13 is a clue to the meaning of *mangy*.

6. Pa probably left his glass unfinished because he realized that (inference)

A. he was too full.
B. they would be too late getting home.
C. he didn't like cats.
D. the cat had probably been in his milk.

1 best evidence sentence: **17**

There is no evidence for A, B, or C. We can infer from 17 that D is true, since Pa's milk was probably in the churn when the cat was in it earlier.

7. Do you think Pa will stop for buttermilk at Sickle Tree again? Why or why not? (prediction)

No. He doesn't want buttermilk if the cat's been in it. The cat might get in it again.

2 best evidence sentences: **17, 19**

8. The woman seems most concerned about (inference)

A. cleanliness.
B. losing buttermilk from the churn.
C. keeping the cat from drowning.
D. health.

1 best evidence sentence: **15**

There is no evidence for A, C, or D. Since she squeezes the liquid from the cat back into the churn (15), she probably wants to save the buttermilk.

29. It's All Downhill
by David White

[1]"Slow down, Brad, you're blowing dirt in my face!"

[2]"Hey, if you were ahead of me like you're supposed to be, you wouldn't even see this dirt," Brad yelled back, bracing himself as he skidded through more dirt.

[3]"Well, I'm not the one screaming around curves, nearly wiping out every minute."

[4]"Eric, those girls are ahead of us. [5]It's time to catch up."

[6]They zigzagged down a narrow stretch of trail, their eyes focused on the rocks and roots beneath them.

[7]"Maybe if you hadn't had that flat at the top—"

[8]"We fixed it in no time, didn't we? [9]Besides, it's not like we're racing them."

[10]"Yeah, but we will be soon," Eric said as he braked and turned the handlebars to avoid another rock. [11]"This is a training ride. [12]That race is in two weeks."

[13]"That's exactly why I want to go fast down this hill."

[14]Brad shifted into a higher gear and zoomed ahead, managing to keep one foot on the pedals as he swerved around another curve. [15]Eric carefully kept close behind. [16]Like a yo-yo, he soon caught up.

[17]"What are you, some kind of stuntman? [18]You're out of control, Brad. [19]I'm right behind you, and I'm in control. [20]You've got maybe 2 or 3 seconds on me at the most."

[21]They pedaled through grassland and across a shallow stream and then back into the trees. [22]Brad let out a whoop and zoomed ahead. [23]Bending to avoid hitting his head on a low branch, he came up too late to see a big rock in the middle of the trail. [24]He hit the rock, and bike and rider went airborne. [25]Fortunately, no branches hung low on the downward side. [26]The landing jolted him hard, but Brad stayed aboard. [27]He stopped to catch his breath. [28]Eric stopped right behind him.

[29]"Don't you remember that rock from the trip up?" Eric said. [30]His face was a mixture of laughter and concern. [31]"Who are you trying to impress? [32]The girls are way ahead of us now. [33]Be careful."

[34]"I didn't wipe out, did I? [35]Besides, it was a big rock."

³⁶"Yeah, well, I'm not picking you up if you fall down. ³⁷See you at the bottom."
³⁸"See you there!"

1. Which quote from the passage best sums up the main idea? (main idea)

   A. "Be careful."
   B. "See you there!"
   C. "It's time to catch up."
   D. "This is a training ride."

   1 best evidence sentence: **11**

   A, B, and C are details. C seems plausible, but Eric's comments throughout reinforce the need to be careful because it is only a training ride. Only D describes the main idea.

2. Which is the correct order for the following events? Choose A, B, C, or D. (sequence)

   1. Brad has a flat tire.
   2. Brad shifts into a higher gear.
   3. Brad blows dirt in Eric's face.
   4. Brad goes airborne after hitting a rock.

   A. 1, 2, 3, 4
   B. 1, 3, 2, 4
   C. 4, 1, 3, 2
   D. 4, 3, 2, 1

3. Why did dirt blow in Eric's face? (cause/effect)

   A. He was riding behind Brad.
   B. He was riding carefully.
   C. He stopped right behind Brad.
   D. He turned his handlebars to avoid a rock.

   B, C, and D are things that Eric does, but only A is a direct effect.

4. Based on the conversation the cyclists have, do you think Eric will stop to help Brad if Brad falls down? Explain your answer. (prediction)

No. Eric will probably not stop and help Brad if Brad falls down. He is worried at first, but then he says he won't help Brad up if he falls down.

1 best evidence sentence: **36**

5. Contrast the way the two riders go down the hill. To support your answer, list three sentences for each rider. (compare/contrast)

Brad goes fast around the curves. He shifts into a higher gear and zooms ahead. He brags about hitting a rock. Eric stays in control. He brakes and tries to avoid a rock. He stays close behind Brad.

3 best evidence sentences for each rider: Brad **3**, **22**, **34**; Eric **19**, **10**, **15**

6. Which of these is the best reason why Brad wanted to go fast? (inference)

   A. He had a flat tire.
   B. He shifted into a higher gear.
   C. He was trying to show off in front of Eric.
   D. He knew his friends were ahead.

   2 best evidence sentences: **4**, **5**

7. Sentence 16 contains which kind of figure of speech? (figurative language)

   a simile ("like a yo-yo")

8. Which of these quotes from the story is an opinion? (fact/opinion)

   A. "That race is in two weeks."
   B. "Besides, it was a big rock."
   C. "You're out of control, Brad."
   D. "Eric, those girls are ahead of us."

   A, B, and D are facts. Only C is something that one of the characters thinks, feels, or believes.

30. Teacher Turns Eleven
by Margaret Hockett

A [1]Ms. Henson thought she was getting too old. [2]She was annoyed that she couldn't see without her bifocals—"Those are for old 'folkles,'" she'd say—and that she had trouble bending to pick up papers. [3]"I'm just going to have to start getting younger," she finally said.

B [4]First, we noticed a new sparkle in her eye. [5]A couple of days later, it looked as if someone had erased her mouth wrinkles. [6]Her walk seemed bouncier, and she started wearing teenagers' clothes. [7]It was all pretty odd, but when she got shorter and started talking funny it got scary.

C [8]We could barely see her over the books on her desk. [9]A high-pitched voice would pierce the room with "Time for social studies, class." [10]The sight of this small creature acting like a teacher was even stranger than the voice. [11]It would have been funny except for that no-nonsense attitude in her voice and manner. [12]We got used to the changes, and class was pretty much "business as usual."

D [13]Ms. Henson showed her usual talent for problem solving. [14]When she couldn't reach the top of the blackboard, she declared "We'll just have to lower it." [15]After we helped her do that, she proceeded to fill it entirely with chalk marks. [16]Math, social studies, reading assignments—all appeared under her childish yet capable fingers.

E [17]Things went well until Genie Pix came to school. [18]On Genie's first day, we had a substitute for the morning since Ms. Henson was at the dentist and wouldn't be back until recess. [19]It was obvious that Genie was a "do righter." [20]She scolded Won and me for passing notes. [21]She gave threatening looks to the girls who were making faces in class. [22]Anyway, during recess, Genie came in to the classroom to get her sweater. [23]She found Ms. Henson taking the field trip money out of her special locked drawer. [24]Well, when Genie found what appeared to be a student thief, she got all bent out of shape. [25]She yelled and tried to grab the money bag. [26]Ms. Henson held on tight, but when Genie gave a second yank, Ms. Henson went flying backward! [27]She ended up with four stitches and a whole bunch of bruises. [28]That's when she decided that being eleven was too dangerous.

F [29]Before long, Ms. Henson's head appeared higher and higher behind her desk. [30]A familiar quality came back to her voice. [31]The childish clothes and smooth skin went away. [32]But one thing that never did go away was that mischievous gleam in her eye.

1. Choose the main idea of the passage. (main idea)

   A. The teacher learns a lesson.
   B. The teacher gets hurt.
   C. The class learns to cope.
   D. The new student takes a stand.

   B, C, and D may be thought of as supporting ideas or detail. A gives the overall idea.

   1 best evidence sentence from paragraph E: **28**

2. From sentence 5, which of the following is reasonable to conclude? (conclusion)

   A. A sketch of Ms. H had been changed.
   B. Ms. H's wrinkles were disappearing.
   C. Some of Ms. H's makeup was removed.
   D. Ms. H had just gotten into a fistfight.

   Explain your answer.

The word "erased" is used as a figure of speech to mean that the lines around the teacher's mouth were disappearing.

3. Put the features of Ms. Henson in the order they appear in the story. (sequence)

   3 Short height
   1 Sparkle in her eye
   2 Bounce in her step
   4 Bruises

   Ms. Henson gets a sparkle in her eye in sentence 4, a bounce in her step in sentence 6, shorter height in sentence 7, and bruises in sentence 27.

4. What was the one change that remained with Ms. Henson at the end of the story? (reading for detail)

   a gleam, or sparkle, in her eye

   2 best evidence sentences: **4, 32**

5. Based on her actions from the story, what do you think Genie Pix would do if she found someone cheating on a test? (character trait/prediction)

   A. Talk them out of it.
   B. Point it out.
   C. Wait until after class to discuss it.
   D. Ignore it.
   1 best evidence paragraph: **E**

   Choices A, C, and D are not supported. From her behavior in sentences 19, 20, 21, and 25, Genie doesn't seem like the type of person who ignores behavior or stops to think before reacting. She also usually scolds or yells, rather than discusses.

6. As a result of Genie's letting go of the money bag, Ms. Henson (cause/effect)
   A. yelled loudly.
   B. held on tight.

C. knocked Genie over.
D. lost her balance.

7. The narrator is (inference/point of view)

   A. a student in Ms. Henson's class.
   B. a teacher in Ms. Henson's school.
   C. the new student.
   D. an observer outside the class.

   1 evidence sentence from paragraph E: **20**

   A is the best answer because the narrator includes her/himself in the story. The narrator is part of the classroom and Mrs. Henson is her/his teacher. There is no evidence for B, C, or D.

8. Which could be the theme of this story? (theme)

   A. New students imagine things.
   B. Being young makes things better.
   C. Getting old is worse than anything.
   D. With change comes knowledge.

   1 best evidence sentence: **28**

NONFICTION

31. "Pokey-pines" by Margaret Hockett

A [1]Do you like getting stuck with thorns? [2]Then you probably won't enjoy getting too close to the "thorn pig," or porcupine.
B [3]The word porcupine comes from two Latin words, *porcus* and *spina*. [4]*Porcus* means pig, though the porcupine is not a pig. [5]Spina means thorn, though the porcupine has no real thorns. [6]Porcupines are slow and clumsy, and they can't see well. [7]How then does a porcupine protect itself?
C [8]The answer lies in the weapons on its body. [9]The porcupine carries about 30,000 little "darts," ready to pierce an enemy. [10]These darts are really stiff hairs called

quills. ¹¹Quills grow out of the back, sides, and tail of the porcupine. ¹²A porcupine cannot shoot quills. ¹³Instead, it whirls around and flicks its tail back and forth. ¹⁴Anyone coming too close to the rear end of the porcupine will be stuck with quills. ¹⁵A quill can't be pulled out easily because its barbs point backwards. ¹⁶Because of these quills, many animals have learned to stay far away from the porcupine!

Closeup of a porcupine quill

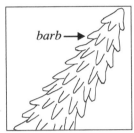

barb→

1. Why do you think the Latin word *spina* was used in naming the porcupine? (conclusion)

   The word *spina* means thorn. The porcupine has quills, which are like thorns (they are sharp and can stick in the flesh).

   1 evidence sentence from paragraph B: **5**

2. Which sentence best sums up the reasons a porcupine needs the protection of quills? (conclusion)

   Sentence **6**

   The details of sentence 6 show a porcupine's weaknesses (it can't see well and is slow and clumsy). Therefore, quills would be very helpful in its defense.

3. In sentence 9, the word *pierce* means to (vocabulary)

   A. stab
   B. tickle
   C. protect
   D. stroke

Quills are being compared to darts, so only "stab" makes sense.

4. How does an enemy get stuck with quills? (reading for detail)

   A. The enemy gets shot by quills.
   B. The enemy moves away.
   C. The enemy gets near the porcupine's rear.
   D. The enemy stands in front of the porcupine.

   1 best evidence sentence: **14**

   A is contradicted by sentence 12. There is no evidence for B or D.

5. Explain why a quill can be painful to remove. (cause/effect)

   The quill goes one way but the barbs point the opposite way. So, when you try to pull the quill out, barbs get caught and keep the quill from sliding out.

   1 best evidence sentence: **15**

6. The main idea of the passage is to describe how the porcupine can (main idea)

   A. get food.
   B. protect itself.
   C. move around.
   D. grow quills.

   Sentence 7 gives the main idea in the form of a question ("how…does a porcupine protect itself?"). That question is answered in the second paragraph.

32. Making "Sense" Out of Poetry
by Carrie Beckwith

A ¹Writing a poem that uses your senses is a great way to express your feelings and ideas to the reader. ²Not only does it let the reader see what you're talking about, it also lets him or her smell, touch, taste, and hear it! [3]Just follow these easy steps, and you'll be on your way to writing your own unique poem for the senses.

B [4]First, pick something you are familiar with to write about. [5]For example, you may want to write about your favorite sport, your little sister, or chocolate chip cookies! [6]Next, describe your chosen subject using some or all of your senses: taste, touch, sight, hearing, and smell. [7]You don't have to use all five senses in your poem—using two or three is fine. [8]The important thing is to be specific in your choice of details. [9]For example, if you were to write about baseball, you could describe the sound of the bat hitting the ball as a "loud crack." [10]Or you might say that the air in the field smelled "like it was thick with dirt."

C [11]Here is one example from 5th grade student Juan Gonzalez:

SOCCER
[12]People in the stands. [13]Black and white balls flying through the air. [14]Kids charging at me.
[15]People shouting "Move the ball upfield!" [16]Kids saying "Pass the ball!"
[17]Coach yelling plays.
[18]Feel the ball banging against my feet as I move it upfield.
[19]Taste the dirt as I hit the ground.
[20]Taste the salty sweat that rolls down my face.
[21]Smell the victory as my team shoots the goal for the winning point!

1. The purpose of the passage is to show you how to (author purpose)
    A. describe something you want to write a poem about.
    B. write a poem using your senses.
    C. use your sense of smell and taste to describe cookies.

D. get started on a poem.

1 best evidence paragraph: **A**

A is close to being correct, but it is only one step in the whole process, so it is not the best answer. C is a detail. D is incorrect because it is too broad and doesn't mention the senses.

2. What is the first step in writing a sense poem? (sequence)
    A. Be specific with your details.
    B. Choose a subject.
    C. Use your senses.
    D. Write an example of a poem.

1 best evidence sentence: **4**

A and C do not take place until you have started to write a poem. There is no instruction to write an example of a poem, so D is incorrect.

3. Why is it a good idea to write about something you know well? (conclusion)

A sense poem asks you to tell how something feels or smells. When you know something well, it is easier to describe it in detail.

2 best evidence sentences: **5, 6**

4. In general, poems using the senses (generalization)
    A. describe sight and hearing only.
    B. make comparisons.
    C. describe chocolate chip cookies.
    D. make words come to life.

2 best evidence sentences: **1, 2**

D is the best answer because sentence 2 tells us that a sense poem describes actual sounds, smells, and tastes. A, B, and C give only specific parts of the poem-writing process.

5. Fill each blank with the letter of the line from the poem (given below) that best describes the sense. The first one has been done for you. (reading for detail)

e smell
b touch
c sight
d hearing
a taste

a. Taste the dirt as I hit the ground.
b. Feel the ball banging against my feet as I move it upfield.
c. Black and white balls flying through the air.
d. Kids saying "Pass the ball!"
e. Smell the victory as my team shoots the goal for the winning point!

6. What 3 sentences, or lines, from the poem support Juan's idea that soccer is a loud sport? (supporting detail)

Sentences **15, 16, 17**

33. Defining Geometry by David White

[1]Geometry is a branch of mathematics that focuses on shapes. [2]A large part of geometry is the study of the lines, points, and angles used to form these shapes. [3]A line is a set of points that extend forever in two directions. [4]A line segment can be thought of as a part of a line joining two end points. [5]If two lines join at one point, they form an angle. [6]An angle is two rays* that extend from the same point. [7]Two rays that intersect at a right angle (90-degree) are called **perpendicular**.

[8]Lines can be joined to form geometric figures. [9]A three-sided figure is a **triangle**. [10]There are several different types of triangles, which vary according to the length and angles of the lines that form them. [11]Here are some definitions.

[12]**Equilateral triangle:** a triangle with three equal sides

[13]**Isosceles triangle:** a triangle with two equal sides
[14]**Scalene triangle:** a triangle with no equal sides

[15]A four-sided figure is called a **quadrilateral**, which is four points joined by four lines to produce four sides. [16]The following are definitions of specific types of quadrilaterals:

[17]**Parallelogram:** a quadrilateral that has opposite sides that are parallel and equal in length
[18]**Rectangle:** a parallelogram that has four right angles
[19]**Square:** a rectangle that has four equal sides

[20]The last basic geometric figure to define is the **circle**, a perfectly round enclosed shape made by a curved line. [21]All points on the line are the same distance (equidistant) from a fixed point in the center of the circle.

*ray: a half line that extends forever in one direction from a point

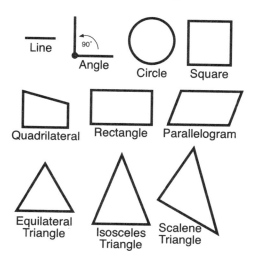

Line   Angle   Circle   Square

Quadrilateral   Rectangle   Parallelogram

Equilateral Triangle   Isosceles Triangle   Scalene Triangle

1. According to the diagram, which of the following figures has the most right angles? (diagram use)

A. circle
B. square
C. parallelogram
D. scalene triangle

2. Using the diagram, choose the figure listed below that does NOT contain perpendicular lines. (diagram use)

   A. angle
   B. square
   C. rectangle
   D. parallelogram

3. Choose the statement that is accurate. (supporting detail)

   A. All circles have sides.
   B. All squares are rectangles.
   C. All triangles are equilateral.
   D. All quadrilaterals have right angles.

   1 best evidence sentence: **19**

4. How does an equilateral triangle differ from a scalene triangle? (compare/contrast, reading for detail)

   An equilateral triangle has three equal sides while a scalene triangle has no equal sides.

5. "A rhombus has four equal sides but no right angles." In which section of the passage would this sentence best fit? (application)

   A. sentences 1–6
   B. sentences 7–11
   C. sentences 12–15
   D. sentences 16–21

   Sentences 16–21 describe four-sided figures, of which a rhombus is one.

6. Which of these best describes the purpose of the passage? (author purpose)

   A. to show similar things
   B. to match pictures to words
   C. to define triangles and circles
   D. to describe geometric shapes

   There is no evidence for B. A and C are supporting details for the main idea.

34. Cesar Chavez: A Biography
by Carrie Beckwith

A [1]Cesar Chavez was a very important leader to Mexican and Mexican-American farm workers. [2]He had been a farm worker himself, and he knew firsthand the unfair treatment they faced. [3]Chavez led protests and strikes against farm owners for higher wages. [4]He also boycotted companies that did not treat their workers fairly.

B [5]Chavez began his political career working for a group that helped Mexican-Americans in California. [6]Chavez helped people sign up to vote and talked to them about their rights. [7]Chavez strongly believed that farm workers needed a union,* so he started the United Farm Workers Union and got many people to join.

C [8]Chavez's first strike with the union was against owners of grape farms in California. [9]The strike was a protest against the low pay farm workers received. [10]Chavez's strike kept union workers out of the fields, and many of the crops rotted. [11]The farm owners lost a lot of money. [12]Some farm workers were beaten for going on strike. [13]When people found out about the strike and the beatings, they decided to do something. [14]Buyers, shipping companies, and store owners boycotted the grape growers by refusing to buy, ship, or carry grapes. [15]Finally, after five years of bargaining with the union, farm owners raised the farm workers' pay. [16]It was a great victory for the workers and the union.

D [17]Chavez led many strikes and marches before his death in 1993. [18]He traveled all over the world, talking about the rights of farm workers. [19]The message that was first delivered in California spread throughout the entire world. [20]To this day, Cesar Chavez's life continues to have a powerful effect on the well-being of the farm worker.

*union: an organization that brings workers together to improve working conditions and wages

TIME LINE

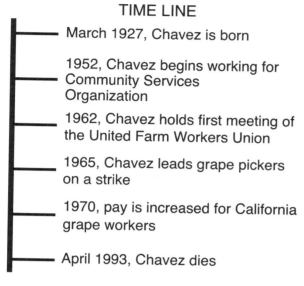

March 1927, Chavez is born

1952, Chavez begins working for Community Services Organization

1962, Chavez holds first meeting of the United Farm Workers Union

1965, Chavez leads grape pickers on a strike

1970, pay is increased for California grape workers

April 1993, Chavez dies

1. Which of the following sentences gives the main idea of the passage? (main idea)

   A. Chavez helped people sign up to vote.
   B. Chavez traveled the world to speak about farm workers' rights.
   C. **Chavez accomplished much for farm workers.**
   D. Chavez organized a successful strike in California.

   2 best evidence paragraphs: **A, D**

   Choices A, B, and D are details within the passage that support the main idea.

2. As used in paragraph C, the word *strike* means (vocabulary)

   A. stopping of payment.
   B. notice of leaving.
   C. **stopping of work.**
   D. firing of a worker.

   Sentence 10 explains that the strike kept farm workers *out of the fields*. If

the workers are out of the fields, they are no longer working; therefore, C is the correct answer. A, B, and D do not make sense in the context of the passage.

3. What was the final result of the strike against owners of grape farms in California? (cause/effect)

   The owners of grape farms gave the workers a pay raise.

   1 best evidence sentence: 15

4. How long did it take before grape farm owners came to an agreement with the union? (supporting detail, use of time line)

   5 years

5. How old was Chavez when he died? (use of time line)

   66 years old (1993 − 1927 = 66)

6. Why did many people refuse to buy, ship, or carry grapes? (cause/effect)

   They found out about the strike and the beatings.

   2 best evidence sentences: **13, 14**

7. List the two sentences in paragraph D that support the fact that Chavez was an active union leader. (supporting detail)

   Sentences **17, 18**

   Chavez led many strikes and marches before his death in 1993 (17). He traveled all over the world, talking about the rights of farm workers (18).

35. How to Make Dough Ornaments by Carrie Beckwith

A [1]Making ornaments couldn't be easier!

²Just follow these quick and easy directions for dough-making fun.

B ³Before you begin, you will need the following ingredients:

> 1 cup salt
> 1 1/2 cups hot tap water
> 4 cups flour

C ⁴Combine salt and hot water in a large bowl. ⁵Stir the mixture until the salt dissolves into the water. ⁶Then add flour to the salt water mixture and stir thoroughly. ⁷Next, knead the flour and salt water until it becomes a soft and spongy dough. ⁸Place your dough in a plastic bag and let it rest for several hours so that it can thicken. ⁹After letting it rest, take the dough out of the bag.

D ¹⁰Preheat your oven to 300° Fahrenheit. ¹¹You can then roll out the dough and use cookie cutters to make shapes, or you can use your own two hands to make whatever you like. ¹²Be careful not to make your dough ornaments too thick (no more than 1/2"), or they won't cook properly. ¹³Once you are done crafting your ornaments, place them on a cookie sheet and bake them in the oven for about one hour to harden them. ¹⁴Let them cool for at least another hour.

E ¹⁵The last part of making ornaments is the best. ¹⁶Now it's time to get your watercolors out and paint your ornaments. ¹⁷When the paint has dried, you can glue buttons, flowers, or glitter onto the ornaments. ¹⁸You can also glue ornaments together, attach ribbons, or even glue a magnet to the back. ¹⁹Be as creative as you like, and, most important, have fun!

1. The purpose of the article is to (author purpose)

    A. explain all the different things you can add to your ornament.

    B. explain how fun and easy it is to make ornaments.

C. explain how to make the dough.

D. explain how to decorate your home.

1 best evidence paragraph: **A**

A and C are not correct because they explain only a portion of what the whole article is about. Nothing is ever mentioned about decorating a home, so D is incorrect.

2. What warning does the article give? (reading for details)

The article warns you not to make the dough ornaments too thick.

1 best evidence sentence: **12**

3. What would happen if you didn't preheat the oven before putting in the dough ornaments? (prediction)

The ornaments would not be fully cooked in the time given.

Since the oven would not be hot when you put the ornaments in to bake, it would take several extra minutes to heat up the oven. You have to subtract this time from the overall cooking time. If you followed the time given in the recipe (which includes preheating), the ornaments would not be fully cooked.

4. What do you think causes the dough to get soft and spongy? (cause/effect)

The kneading probably causes the dough to get soft and spongy.

The signal word is *until;* you knead *until* the dough is soft.

1 best evidence sentence: **7**

5. Is the following sentence a fact or an opinion? "The last part of making ornaments is the best." (fact/opinion)

opinion

Sentence 15 is a value judgment. Someone else might think differently about painting the ornaments.

6. In what order does the author present the information? (sequence)

   A. by importance
   B. randomly
   C. step-by-step
   D. by difficulty

   A is not correct because one step is not more important than another; they must all be performed in order to make dough ornaments. B is not correct because the steps are given in an order that progresses as you go. D is incorrect because people might differ on which step is more difficult.

7. What must you do just after your mixture has become a dough? (sequence)

   A. Preheat the oven.
   B. Place the dough in a bag and let it rest.
   C. Roll out the dough and begin making ornaments.
   D. Stir the mixture thoroughly.

   1 best evidence sentence: **8**

   A and C do occur after the mixture has become a dough, but not *just after*. D is incorrect because it occurs before the mixture has become a dough.

36. All Around the Sun
by David White

A [1]One way to study the planets in our solar system is by their distance from the Sun. [2]Mercury is closest to the Sun, with Venus not far behind. [3]Earth is the third planet out from the Sun. [4]From there outward, it's Mars, Jupiter, Saturn, Uranus, Neptune, and Pluto. [5]Pluto is farthest, more than 3 billion miles from the Sun.

B [6]A planet's distance from the Sun influences its surface temperature and atmosphere. [7]The closer a planet is to the Sun, the hotter that planet is. [8]Earth's average temperature is 57 degrees Fahrenheit. [9]Mercury can get as hot as 625 degrees. [10]Faraway Pluto, on the other hand, has an average temperature of 300 degrees below zero.

C [11]The number of moons a planet has also seems to be related to its distance from the Sun. [12]Generally, the closer a planet is to the Sun, the fewer moons it has. [13]Mercury and Venus, which are closest to the Sun, have no moons. [14]Earth has only one moon. [15]Saturn, which is much farther from the Sun, is believed to have 18 moons. [16]The only exception to the rule is Pluto, which has just one moon.

D [17]The closer a planet is to the Sun, the fewer days (or years) it takes for that planet to orbit (go once around) the Sun. [18]Earth's orbit is 365 days, or one year. [19]Mercury's orbit is only 88 days. [20]The largest planet, Jupiter, takes 11.86 Earth years to complete one orbit. [21]It's not just the large planets that have long orbits, though. [22]Tiny Pluto takes about 248 years to go once around the Sun.

The Nine Planets

Planet	Miles from Sun
Mercury	36 million
Venus	67 million
Earth	93 million
Mars	142 million
Jupiter	484 million
Saturn	888 million
Uranus	1.78 billion
Neptune	2.79 billion
Pluto	3.66 billion

1. List the six planets closest to the Sun in order from nearest to farthest. (sequence, diagram use)

Mercury, Venus, Earth, Mars, Jupiter, Saturn

2. Which sentence in Paragraph A best supports the idea that the solar system is huge? (inference)

Sentence **5**

Pluto, the farthest planet from the Sun, is more than 3 billion miles away from it.

3. Name two things that are related to a planet's distance from the Sun. (reading for detail)

Accept any two of the following: **A planet's distance from the Sun is related to that planet's atmosphere, temperature, number of moons, and length of orbit**.

1 best evidence sentence for each example given: **6, 11**, or **17**

4. Which of these planets is closest to Earth? (application)

A. Mars
B. Venus
C. Mercury
D. Jupiter

Earth is 93 million miles from the Sun. Mars is 142, Venus is 67, Mercury is 36, and Jupiter is 484. The difference is least between 93 and 67, so B is correct.

5. If scientists discovered a tenth planet 1.1 billion miles away from the Sun, to which two planets would it be closest? (diagram use, prediction)

A. Uranus and Neptune
B. Saturn and Uranus
C. Neptune and Pluto
D. Jupiter and Saturn

The new planet would fall between Saturn, at 888 million miles, and Uranus, at 1.78 billion miles (888 < 1.1 < 1.78).

6. Give two examples from paragraphs C and D that show how Mercury and Earth are different. (compare/contrast)

1. Earth has a moon; Mercury has none. 2. Mercury takes less time to orbit the Sun.

2 best evidence sentences for each example: **13, 14; 18, 19**

7. The closer a planet is to the Sun, (generalization)

A. the smaller it is.
B. the more moons it has.
C. the thicker its atmosphere is.
D. the hotter it is.

1 best evidence sentence: **7**

There is no evidence for A or C. B is contradicted by sentence 12.

37. What Do Owls Eat? by Cheryl Block

A [1]Owls are carnivores, animals that eat other animals. [2]In the wild, their diet is mainly small mammals such as mice and squirrels, and birds. [3]You can look at an owl's actual diet by studying an owl pellet. [4]An owl pellet is food that an owl has eaten but could not digest. [5]An owl usually coughs up one pellet a day. [6]The owl forms the pellet in its stomach and then coughs it up, similar to a cat's coughing up a hairball after grooming itself. [7]These pellets are usually found below the owl's roosting place.

B [8]Dissecting a pellet will tell you what

an owl has eaten. [9]Begin by placing the pellet in a bowl and adding a small amount of water to make it easier to remove the outer coating. [10]You should use forceps or tweezers to make it easier to remove the outer coating. [11]This coating is made up of the fur and feathers of animals the owl has eaten.

C [12]Now carefully begin to break the pellet open. [13]Inside you will find bits and pieces of animal bones. [14]You may even find a tiny rat skull. [15]Place these skeletal parts on a sheet of paper or cardboard. [16]You might want to try to piece the bones together to determine what kind of animal the owl ate. [17]Parts of several animals may be found inside one pellet.

D [18]When you are done dissecting the owl pellet, record the types of bones you found (leg bone, jawbone, etc.) and what kind of animal you think they belonged to. [19]You now have a record of an owl's diet.

Owl Pellet Remains

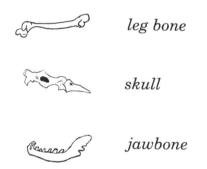

leg bone

skull

jawbone

1. What coats the outside of an owl pellet? (reading for detail)

the fur and feathers of the animals the owl has eaten

1 best evidence sentence: **11**

2. According to paragraph A, why does an owl cough up a pellet? (cause and effect)

It can't digest certain parts of the animals it eats.

1 best evidence sentence: **4**

3. Looking at the skull pictured in the diagram, how might you determine that it belongs to a bird? (diagram use)

You can see the shape of a bird's beak.

4. Why would it be helpful to identify what kind of body parts are in the pellet? (as shown on the diagram) (diagram use)

It may help you figure out from what kind of animal the part comes.

5. How does a cat's hairball compare to an owl pellet? (compare/contrast)

The owl pellet is food that the owl can't digest. A hairball is fur that a cat licks off while grooming.

2 best evidence sentences: **4, 6**

Like the owl, the cat is probably unable to digest the fur, so it coughs it up.

6. As used in sentences 8 and 18, what does the word *dissecting* most closely mean? (vocabulary)

A. giving an estimate
B. putting together
C. separating into pieces
D. cleaning thoroughly

In paragraphs B and C, you remove the coating from the pellet and separate the contents of the pellet. There is no evidence to support A or D. B is incorrect based on sentences 9 and 12.

7. Why do you think owl pellets are commonly found beneath an owl's roosting place? (inference)

A. This is the place an owl rests and sleeps during the day.

B. The pellets are used to make the owls' nests.

C. Owls toss them out when they clean their nests.

D. The pellets are used to attract prey.

A is the best answer because an owl would return to its roosting place after eating. There is no evidence to support B, C, or D.

38. Comanche Horsemen
by Carrie Beckwith

[1]The North American tribe called the Comanche were known for their outstanding skill with horses. [2]As early as age four or five, Comanche children—boys and girls—were given ponies. [3]Young boys, in particular, were trained for war. [4]They were taught how to pick up objects from the ground while riding their ponies at full speed. [5]Gradually, the objects increased in size until the rider was able to pick up another man! [6]This skill was necessary in battle when a rider would have to rescue an injured tribe member.

[7]The Comanche also learned how to ride alongside the horse's flank. [8]The rider was able to ride this way by hooking his heel over one side of the horse and resting his elbow in a rope looped round the horse's neck. [9]This position protected him from enemy arrows. [10]The rider was still able to shoot his own arrows from either above the horse's back or underneath its neck.

[11]Part of the Comanche's success with horses was due to their skill at horse-breeding. [12]Their horses came from the half-Andalusian, half-Arab horses that the Spaniards brought over in the 16th century. [13]After many years of breeding only their finest stallions, the Comanche produced what is now known as the Indian pony, a very strong and responsive horse.

[14]In addition to being skilled riders and breeders, many of the Comanche were also skilled horse thieves! [15]For the Comanche, wealth was measured by the number of horses they had, and no other tribe owned more horses than the Comanche. [16]One Comanche band of 2000 owned close to 15,000 horses!

[17]The Comanche's skill in horse riding, horse breeding, and even horse stealing helped them to become one of the most successful tribes of the Plains.

1. What is the main idea of the passage? (main idea)

   A. The Comanche were skilled at horse stealing.

   B. The Comanche were skilled with horses.

   C. The Comanche were trained to ride horses.

   D. The Comanche children were trained for war.

   1 best evidence sentence: **1**

   A, C, and D are all details of the passage. Only B gives the overall idea.

2. Which detail from the story best supports the idea that the Comanche were talented horse riders? (supporting detail)

   A. Comanche children were given ponies at an early age.

   B. The Comanche measured wealth by the number of horses they had.

   C. The Comanche learned how to ride alongside a horse's flank.

   D. The Comanche helped develop the Indian pony.

3. Why was it necessary for riders to

learn how to pick up objects from the ground? (cause/effect)

The Comanche warrior had to be able to pick up fallen and wounded tribe members while riding a horse.

1 best evidence sentence: **6**

4. Why was it helpful to be able to ride alongside the horse's flank? (supporting detail)

Riding alongside a horse's flank let the Comanche use their horses as shields. It also helped them shoot arrows from above a horse's back or underneath its neck.

2 best evidence sentences: **9, 10**

5. "One Comanche band of 2000 owned close to 15,000 horses!" According to the passage, what can you conclude about this band? (conclusion)
   A. The band was wealthy.
   B. The band stole the horses.
   C. The band had the same number of horses as other tribes.
   D. The band trained all 15,000 of the horses.

1 best evidence sentence: **15**

There is no evidence for B. C is not correct because we do not know how many horses other tribes had. D is incorrect because there is no evidence for it. We know from sentence 15 that the Comanche measured wealth by the number of horses one had. Given this, we can conclude that this band was wealthy.

6. What can you conclude about the Comanche's horses? (conclusion)
   A. They required little care.
   B. They were hard to train.

C. They were dressed and painted for war.
D. They were important to the tribe.

1 best evidence sentence: **17**

There is no evidence for A, B, or C.

39. Blowing Hot and Cold
by David White

A [1]Differences in air temperature can tell us which way the wind blows. [2]Hot air is lighter than cold air. [3]So, the colder the air is, the heavier it is. [4]The heavier it is, the more pressure it has (and the more it pushes downward).

B [5]A difference in air pressure, created by differences in air temperature, causes wind. [6]Air in a high-pressure area (cold air) will move to a low-pressure area (hot air). [7]So, if a large pocket of cold air is east of a large pocket of hot air, the wind will blow west.

C [8]Also, the greater the difference between the temperatures of the two pockets of air, the faster the wind blows. [9]If the cold air is biting cold and the hot air is blazing hot, then the wind will blow at a high rate of speed between those two pockets of air.

D [10]Wind is especially noticeable near the oceans. [11]In the daytime, the temperature of seawater is usually lower than the temperature of land at the seashore, so people on the coast almost always feel a sea breeze coming inland. [12]At night, the temperature of the land may become cooler than the water (ocean). [13]The breeze then switches directions and blows from land to ocean—a land breeze.

E [14]Wind, the movement of air around us, is caused by differences in air temperature and pressure.

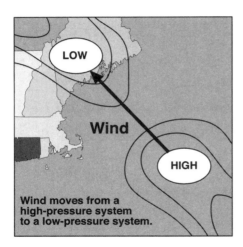

1. What causes wind? (cause/effect)

Wind is caused by differences in air pressure.

1 best evidence sentence: **5**

2. What is the main idea of the passage? (main idea)

A. to describe how wind blows
B. to compare hot air and cold air
C. to describe how temperature and air pressure affect wind
D. to describe the range of air temperatures throughout the day

A, B, and D are details. The passage tells the most about C.

3. Why does the wind along the seashore change direction at night? (conclusion)

The wind along the seashore will change direction at night if the temperature over the land becomes cooler than the temperature over the water.

2 best evidence sentences: **11, 12**

4. If the wind is blowing south toward you, what does that suggest about the air pressure to the north of you? (inference)

The air pressure to the north

would be higher than the air pressure where you are.

1 best evidence sentence: **6**

Air moves from a high-pressure area to a low-pressure area.

5. Look at the diagram below. Between which two points is the wind blowing more quickly? (diagram use)

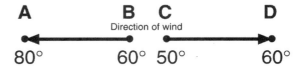

The wind is blowing more quickly from Point B to Point A because the difference in temperature is larger than between Point C and Point D.

1 best evidence sentence: **8**

6. In the diagram above, the air above Point B is colder than the air above Point A. What two other comparisons can be made about the air above Point B and Point A? (diagram use, compare/contrast)

The air above Point B is heavier and pushes downward more than the air above Point A.

2 best evidence sentences from paragraph A: **3, 4**

7. How do the words "biting" and "blazing" in sentence 9 help to describe how the air might feel? (figurative language)

"Biting cold" sounds like it would be cold enough to hurt. "Blazing heat" sounds like a fire, which would be very hot.

40. The *Challenger* Disaster
by Carrie Beckwith

[1]On January 28, 1986, the space shuttle *Challenger* was getting ready to blast off into space. [2]Inside the shuttle were seven astronauts, one of whom was a school teacher, Christa McAuliffe. [3]Christa was the first private citizen in the entire history of space travel to be chosen for a space flight. [4]She was chosen from more than 11,000 teachers. [5]NASA officials felt that Christa would be able to capture the experience of space travel and put it into words for students all over the world. [6]While aboard the *Challenger*, McAuliffe's duties were to include presenting two "live" lessons: one on the roles and duties of all the astronauts aboard the *Challenger* and the second on the purpose of space exploration.

[7]Students and faculty members from McAuliffe's school were watching the event on television. [8]They held big signs that said "We're with U Christa." [9]It was a dangerous mission and the astronauts understood that, but they were confident and excited. [10]McAuliffe hoped students would get excited about space exploration as a result of seeing her, an "ordinary person," in space.

[11]The countdown began: "T minus 10, 9, 8, 7, 6, we have main engine start, 4, 3, 2, 1, and lift-off." [12]Shouts and happy cheers rang out from the auditorium of McAuliffe's Concord, New Hampshire, elementary school. [13]Seventy-three seconds later, an explosion lit up the sky. [14]Someone yelled to quiet the cheering. [15]"The vehicle has exploded," the voice from the television said. [16]Some people cried; others stared at the television in disbelief. [17]The excited cheers and happy faces of McAuliffe's students and coworkers quickly disappeared.

[18]Afterwards, many national leaders spoke about the event. [19]In a memorial service for the astronauts, President Reagan remembered Christa McAuliffe, who he said had "captured the imagination of the entire nation."

[20]The next six months were spent investigating the cause of the disaster. [21]As a result of the investigation, several changes were made to ensure a safer, more reliable space shuttle. [22]Since then, NASA has launched many successful shuttles into space.

1. What was the author's main purpose in writing this article? (author's purpose)

   A to describe the *Challenger* disaster and members of the crew

   B. to explain how the shuttle exploded

   C. to describe the *Challenger* disaster and Christa McAuliffe's role in the mission

   D. to call attention to the importance of space exploration

   A is partly correct, but no description of the other crew members is given. There is no evidence for B or D.

2. Give two examples of how Christa McAuliffe was different from the other astronauts. (compare/contrast)

   1. She was a school teacher.

   2. She was the first private citizen chosen for a space flight.

3. List the numbers of the two sentences that best support the idea that the people watching were excited about the *Challenger* mission. (supporting detail)

   Sentences **8, 12**

4. What was going to be one of

McAuliffe's duties while aboard the *Challenger?* (reading for detail)

One of McAuliffe's duties while on board the *Challenger* was to give two "live" lessons. (It is also acceptable for students to list either of the individual lessons.)

1 best evidence sentence: **6**

5. What did McAuliffe hope would get students excited about space exploration? (conclusion)

    McAuliffe hoped they would get excited because an "ordinary person" like herself was going into space.

6. From the last paragraph of the article, you can conclude that the space program (conclusion)

    A. is in danger of being done away with.
    B. has had several disasters.
    C. is safer than it was.
    D. is larger than it was.

    1 best evidence sentence: **21**

    There is no evidence for A, B, or D.

41. Little Green Food Factories by Cheryl Block

[1]Humans and animals must eat plants or other animals to get energy. [2]They cannot make their own food. [3]Plants are able to make their own food through a process called photosynthesis. [4]Most of this process takes place in the plant's leaves.

[5]A plant is like a little green food factory. [6]Just as a factory uses raw materials to make a product, a plant uses raw materials to make its food. [7]These raw materials are carbon dioxide and water. [8]Leaves take in carbon dioxide from the air through their pores (tiny openings in the surface). [9]Roots take in water from the soil; the water passes up through the stem to the leaves. [10]The plant leaves will convert, or change, these raw materials into food.

[11]Both a factory and a plant need energy to convert raw materials. [12]The energy for photosynthesis comes from sunlight. [13]Chlorophyll, the pigment that gives plants their green color, absorbs the sunlight and then changes it into chemical energy.

[14]Using this chemical energy, the plant combines water and carbon dioxide to make sugar. [15]At the same time, the plant gives off oxygen we need to breathe. [16]Sugar is the food that a plant needs to survive. [17]The sugar is carried from the leaves to other parts of the plant and stored. [18]During winter, plants that lose their leaves must rely on this stored food until they regrow their leaves in the spring.

[19]Green plants are the only living things that are able to make their own food. [20]Even animals who eat only other animals depend on plant-eating animals for food. [21]Humans and animals could not survive if the little green food factories stopped producing food.

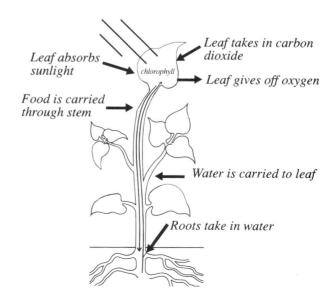

Leaf absorbs sunlight

Leaf takes in carbon dioxide

chlorophyll

Leaf gives off oxygen

Food is carried through stem

Water is carried to leaf

Roots take in water

1. Besides providing food, what is another way that plants help us? (conclusion)

Plants provide oxygen for us to breathe.

1 best evidence sentence: **15**

2. Which of the following occurs first after chlorophyll converts sunlight to chemical energy? (sequence)
   A. The plant absorbs water through its roots.
   B. The plant combines water and carbon dioxide.
   C. The chemical energy turns leaves green.
   D. Sugar is transported throughout the plant.

1 best evidence sentence: **14**

B is supported by sentence 14. A is incorrect because the roots provide water for the plant, but this is not caused by chemical energy. C is incorrect because chlorophyll turns leaves green. D is incorrect because it occurs later, after the sugar is made.

3. What is the meaning of the word *pigment* in sentence 13? (vocabulary)
   A. A kind of chemical used on plants.
   B. A kind of sugar produced by the plant.
   C. A substance that produces color.
   D. A kind of energy.

There is no evidence for A or B. In D, the pigment chlorophyll helps to convert energy, but is not a kind of energy itself. Chlorophyll gives the plant its green color.

4. Where is most of the chlorophyll in a plant located? (diagram use)

It is found in the plant's leaves.

5. Which of the following gives the main idea of the passage? (main idea)
   A. Both a factory and a plant use energy to convert raw materials.
   B. Humans and animals must eat plants or other animals.
   C. Plants make their own food through a process called photosynthesis.
   D. Chlorophyll absorbs sunlight and then changes it into chemical energy.

C is supported by paragraphs B, C, and D, which describe the photosynthesis process. A and D refer to steps in the process. B refers to animals.

6. The article compares a plant to a factory. Give two examples that show how they are alike. (compare/contrast)

Both a factory and a plant use raw materials to make a product. Both a plant and a factory need energy.

2 best evidence sentences: **6, 11**

42. Ancient Egyptian Hieroglyphs by Cheryl Block

A [1]The writing system of the early Egyptians was tied to their religious beliefs. [2]Ancient Egyptians used a form of picture writing called hieroglyphs. [3]In early hieroglyphic writing, a picture symbol stood for the object shown. [4]A picture of an owl meant an owl.
B [5]Eventually, the Egyptians began to develop an alphabet. [6]The picture symbol came to stand for the sound of the letter the word began with, rather than the object itself. [7]For instance, the symbol of an owl came to represent the sound of the letter *m*, with which the Egyptian word for owl begins. [8]Symbols could now be

combined to represent more complex words and ideas.

C [9]Hieroglyphic writing was an important part of the Egyptians' belief in life after death. [10]Egyptians believed that written words had magical powers that captured the spirit of a person or object. [11]If a person's name was written or carved, the person's spirit would remain within that writing forever after death. [12]They also believed that if they wrote an object's name on the object itself and on the walls of the tomb, they would have that object in their next life. [13]Names were also written on the walls in case the actual objects were removed by robbers. [14]As a result, there are examples of hieroglyphic writing on the walls of tombs and temples, on statues, and on ordinary items such as mirrors.

D [15]Because of their magical powers, hieroglyphs were also considered a powerful weapon. [16]Removing a person's name from the tomb erased not only all memory of the person, but also his or her chance for an eternal life. [17]When Queen Hatshepsut died in 1470 B.C., her stepson Tuthmosis II, who had always hated her, took his revenge by having her name and pictures removed from all her temples. [18]To him and other Egyptians, it was as if she had never existed.

EGYPTIAN HIEROGLYPHS

Symbol	Object	Letter
(a foot symbol)	a foot	B as in bat
(a snake symbol)	a snake	F as in fat
(an owl symbol)	an owl	M as in mummy

1. How was early hieroglyphic writing different from later hieroglyphic writing? (compare/contrast)

   In early hieroglyphic writing, a picture stood for the object. In later hieroglyphic writing, the pictures came to represent letter sounds.

   2 best evidence sentences: **3, 6**

2. In paragraph B, how did the development of an alphabet help the Egyptians? (conclusion)

   Symbols could be combined to represent more words and more complex ideas than just the names of objects.

   1 best evidence sentence: **8**

3. Egyptian alphabet symbols represented (reading for detail)

   A. the sound of the first letter in a word.
   B. the sound of the vowel in a word.
   C. the sound of the last letter in a word.
   D. the first syllable in the word.

   1 best evidence sentence: **6**

4. What did Egyptians think would happen if a person's written name were erased? (cause/effect)

   A. The gods could not find that person.
   B. The person would die sooner.
   C. The person's spirit would be erased.
   D. The person would live eternally.

   1 best evidence sentence: **16**

   There is no evidence for choices A or B. Choice D is contradicted by sentence 16. Egyptians believed that if a person's name were carved or written, his spirit would remain there forever after death. (11)

5. How did writing an object's name on the wall allow the person to have that object in the next life? (inference)

Egyptians believed that the spirit of an object was captured in the writing itself. If the actual object disappeared, the spirit of it still remained in the written word.

1 best evidence sentence: **11**

6. The main idea of the passage is that hieroglyphic writing was (main idea)

A. commonly used in the Egyptians' daily lives.
B. found on the walls of tombs.
C. important to the Egyptians' belief in the afterlife.
D. used mainly to decorate homes.

There is no evidence for A or D. B is a detail in the passage. C is supported by paragraphs C and D.

43. Almonds for Sale
by Margaret Hockett

A ¹DELICIOUS...and so <u>NUTRITIOUS</u>!
²Buy Heart Almonds—They Have It All.

B Bone-Building Calcium: ³Maintain strong bones, teeth, and nails—almonds have about twice the calcium of milk!
C Tasty Treat: ⁴Each nut rewards you with a delicate flavor you won't forget!
D Convenient Snack: ⁵Grab a handful on your way out the door each morning. ⁶They pack a big nutritional punch but are small enough to take anywhere.
E Choice of Blanched or Unblanched: ⁷Blanched almonds cost a

little more, but you'll be sure of a tasty, nutritional snack that has no prussic acid.* (⁸If you choose almonds that have not been blanched, we recommend that you remove the skins yourself—see below for instructions.)

F ⁹To remove the skins from a handful of almonds, start by boiling a cup of water. ¹⁰Drop almonds carefully into the water and soak them for 20 to 30 seconds. ¹¹Drain and rinse with cold water. ¹²Finally, squeeze each almond between your thumb and finger. ¹³Be careful—the slippery almonds may try to escape by shooting out in any direction! ¹⁴But they can't escape giving you plenty of calcium for healthy bones, teeth, and nails.

*prussic acid: another name for hydrocyanic acid, a poisonous chemical

1. Why is the word *nutritious* shown as it is in paragraph A? (inference)

The author wants to emphasize that the word *nut* is contained in the word *nutritious*.

It is being used as an advertising trick.

2. From paragraph B, you CANNOT conclude that (conclusion)

A. calcium builds strong bones.
B. milk contains calcium.
C. almonds have more vitamins than milk.
D. milk has less calcium than almonds.

Though sentence 3 says that almonds have about twice the calcium of milk, there is no indication that almonds have more *vitamins* than milk. Therefore, choice C cannot be concluded.

3. Based on the information in the passage, you can conclude that prussic acid (inference)

A. is a nutrient.
B. is good for the stomach.
C. is in milk.
D. is in the almond skin.

2 best evidence sentences **7, 8**

There is no evidence for A, B, or C. Sentence 7 suggests that blanched almonds have no prussic acid, and sentence 8 suggests that blanching removes the skins; therefore the skins probably contain the prussic acid.

4. If you are "careful" as it warns in sentence 13, you will most likely (application)

A. avoid the hot water.
B. hold a knife correctly.
C. keep the almond skin out of your food.
D. prevent the nut from escaping.

1 best evidence sentence: **12**

By sentence 13, you are done with the hot water, so A makes no sense. There is no knife involved, so B is wrong. The warning given in 13 is about almonds escaping and is related to the squeezing described in sentence 12. Keeping the skin out of your food (C) makes no sense. Only D would prevent the loss of almonds.

5. In section F, you are told to do five different things to the almonds after boiling the water. List these five actions in the correct order. (sequence)

1. <u>drop</u>
2. <u>soak</u>
3. <u>drain</u>
4. <u>rinse</u>
5. <u>squeeze</u>

6. The author's main purpose is to (author purpose)

A. educate you about health.
B. convince you to buy almonds.
C. describe how to remove skins.
D. entertain you with descriptions.

1 best evidence sentence: **2**

7. In general, you could say that almonds are (generalization)

A. good for you.
B. difficult to eat.
C. inexpensive.
D. full of iron.

A is correct based on paragraphs B, D, and E. B is incorrect based on Section D. There is no evidence for C or D.

44. The Food Chain
by Cheryl Block

A [1]What is a food chain? [2]All organisms are connected by their need for food. [3]Food provides energy. [4]A food chain shows how the living things in a community are connected by who eats what. [5]Each link in the chain represents an organism in the community. [6]Energy is transferred through the chain as one organism feeds on another.

B [7]All food chains begin with the producers, which are the plants. [8]Plants are able to produce their own food. [9]The animals in a community are called consumers. [10]There are two types of consumers, primary and secondary. [11]Primary consumers are animals that eat only plants. [12]Secondary consumers are animals that eat smaller animals or both plants and animals. [13]Consumers cannot make their own food; they must rely on plants and other animals for energy.

C [14]Let's look at a woodland community as an example. [15]In the woodland, grass, trees, and other plants are the producers.

¹⁶Rabbits are primary consumers; they eat the grass and plants. ¹⁷Foxes are secondary consumers; they eat the rabbits. ¹⁸This is how a food chain is linked together. ¹⁹One organism feeds on another.

D ²⁰At the end of each food chain are the decomposers. ²¹All living things die. ²²The decomposers feed on waste products and dead matter, both plant and animal. ²³Fungi and bacteria are the main decomposers. ²⁴As they break down dead material, they add nutrients* to the soil. ²⁵These nutrients help the plants to grow, and the chain continues.

*nutrient—a substance, such as a mineral or vitamin, found in food and needed for health

SIMPLE FOOD CHAIN

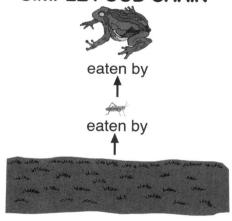

eaten by

↑

eaten by

↑

1. How is a primary consumer different from a secondary consumer? (compare/contrast)

   A primary consumer eats plants. A secondary consumer eats animals or both plants and animals.

   2 best evidence sentences: **11, 12**

2. You can conclude that plants are self-supporting because they (conclusion)

A. produce food for animals.
B. produce their own food.
C. get energy from the Sun.
D. feed on dead matter.

1 best evidence sentence: **8**

Although A and C are facts, they do not give evidence that plants are self-supporting. There is no evidence for D.

3. Which of the following is the correct sequence in a food chain? (sequence/diagram)

A. A secondary consumer is eaten by a primary consumer.
B. A secondary consumer is eaten by a producer.
C. A decomposer is eaten by a producer.
D. A producer is eaten by a primary consumer.

2 best evidence sentences: **7, 11**

D is correct because producers are plants, and primary consumers are animals that eat plants. A is incorrect because primary consumers eat only plants (11). B and C are incorrect because producers make their own food (7–8).

4. Which animal shown in the diagram is a primary consumer? (diagram use)

   The grasshopper

5. How are all organisms in a community connected? (reading for detail)

   All organisms are connected by their need for food.

   1 best evidence sentence: **2**

6. In an ocean community, which of the following would be a producer? (application)

A. whale
B. tuna fish
C. clam
D. seaweed

1 best evidence sentence: **7**

7. What might happen if the rabbits disappeared from the woodland community ? (prediction)

A. The grass would stop growing.
B. The foxes would have to eat grass.
C. The foxes would have to find other food.
D. There would be too many foxes.

1 best evidence paragraph: **C**

8. Part of a decomposer's role in the food chain is to (supporting detail)

A. add nutrients to the soil.
B. produce its own food.
C. eat plants.
D. feed other animals.

2 best evidence sentences: **24, 25**

45. Who Was Benjamin Banneker? by David White

[1]In the 18th century, when most African-Americans were considered second-class citizens or property, Benjamin Banneker was making a name for himself.

[2]Born a free man in 1731, Banneker showed an early interest and skill in math and science. [3]He was also good at designing and building things. [4]Seeing a pocket watch for the first time when he was 19, Banneker decided to build a clock of his own. [5]This remarkable hand-carved clock was made entirely of wood, and it kept accurate time for more than 40 years.

[6]Banneker also developed a strong interest and skill in astronomy. [7]In fact, he correctly predicted a solar eclipse for April 14, 1789, proving wrong many well-known astronomers. [8]His successful prediction made him famous.

[9]Banneker's scientific ability and new-found fame led to his publishing an annual almanac, beginning in 1791. [10]Each year, people of all races would read the almanac for its information on medicine, weather, moon phases, and times for sunrise and sunset.

[11]The almanac's accuracy and its wide audience disproved a common belief of the day—that African-Americans were inferior to European-Americans. [12]When Thomas Jefferson publicly made racist remarks, Banneker sent a strongly worded response to Jefferson along with a copy of his almanac. [13]Jefferson was so impressed with Banneker's scientific accuracy that he sent the almanac to European scientists. [14]Thus, Banneker's fame spread to Europe.

[15]From such widespread recognition came the opportunity for Benjamin Banneker to make his most lasting impression. [16]In 1791, President George Washington appointed Banneker to the engineering group that was designing the city of Washington, D.C. [17]Banneker thus became the first African-American to receive a presidential appointment. [18]Pierre Charles L'Enfant, the head of the group, quit in 1792 after a disagreement and took his plans back to France. [19]Banneker reproduced those plans from memory, and the new capital was born.

[20]Benjamin Banneker published his almanac until 1802, when he was physically unable to continue. [21]He died four years later, a famous and well-respected African-American.

1. What were the gears of Benjamin Banneker's clock made of? (conclusion)

wood

1 best evidence sentence: **5**

2. What is the main idea of the passage? (main idea)

    A. to show how hard work can pay off
    B. to tell how to predict a solar eclipse
    C. to describe the problems that African-Americans faced
    D. to describe a remarkable African-American's accomplishments

3. Put these accomplishments by Benjamin Banneker in their correct time order. (sequence)

    1 creates clock
    3 publishes first almanac
    5 reproduces Washington, D.C., plans
    4 writes letter to Thomas Jefferson
    2 predicts solar eclipse

4. How often did Benjamin Banneker publish his almanac? (read for detail)

    A. once a day
    B. once a week
    C. once a month
    D. once a year

    1 best evidence sentence: **9**

5. Which of these would Benjamin Banneker NOT have witnessed in his lifetime? (sequence/setting)

    A. The Revolutionary War (1775–1783)
    B. The Louisiana Purchase (1803)
    C. The completion of Washington, D.C. (1800)
    D. The War of 1812 (1812–1814)

    2 best evidence sentences: **20, 21**

6. List one accomplishment of Benjamin Banneker in each of the following fields: (read for detail)

    Astronomy   **predicted eclipse**

    Architecture   **designed D.C.**
    Writing   **published almanac**

7. Why did Thomas Jefferson send Benjamin Banneker's almanac to European scientists even though he knew the book was written by an African-American? (supporting detail)

    Jefferson was impressed by Banneker's scientific accuracy.

    1 best evidence sentence: **13**

46. The Land Down Under by Cheryl Block

[1]The smallest of the seven continents and the only continent that is an island, Australia is unique in many ways. [2]Located between the Indian Ocean and the Pacific Ocean, Australia is sometimes called the land "Down Under" because of its location in the Southern Hemisphere. [3]In fact, the name Australia comes from a Latin word meaning "southern."

[4]While Australia has rain forests, plains, and mountains, nearly a third of Australia is desert. [5]It has a larger percentage of desert land for its size than any other continent and is also the driest, except for Antarctica. [6]The largest desert in Australia is called the Outback. [7]In over two-thirds of the country, the average annual rainfall is less than twenty inches.

[8]Australia is also the flattest continent. [9]This is the result of millions of years of erosion by wind, rain, and heat. [10]The world's largest coral reef, the Great Barrier Reef, is located in the Coral Sea off the coast of Australia. [11]It measures about 1250 miles (2,025 km) in length. [12]Because Australia was geographically isolated for millions of years, unique varieties of animals have developed there.

¹³Australia has pouched mammals (marsupials) such as the kangaroo and the wallaby, and egg-laying mammals like the duck-billed platypus. ¹⁴Only in the last two hundred years have new animal species been introduced by settlers from Europe and Asia.

¹⁵Given all of its unusual features, Australia would be a fascinating place to visit.

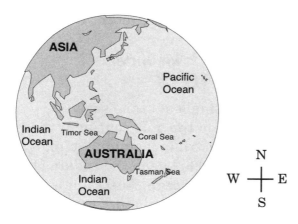

1. Which two statements support the idea that Australia is unique compared to other continents? (compare/contrast)

   A. Australia is flattest.
   B. Australia is in the Southern Hemisphere.
   C. Australia is an island.
   D. Australia has rain forests.

   1 best evidence sentence for each: **8, 1**

   B is incorrect because the fact that Australia is located in the Southern Hemisphere does not make it unique; there are other continents in the Southern Hemisphere. D is incorrect because this feature is not unique to Australia.

2. Which of the following was the greatest influence in the development of Australia's unusual animal population? (cause and effect)

   A. Australia lies in the Southern Hemisphere.
   B. Australia was isolated for millions of years.
   C. Australia has a large percentage of desert.
   D. Australia has the world's largest coral reef.

   1 best evidence sentence: **12**

3. Where does the name *Australia* come from? (reading for detail)

   The name comes from a Latin word meaning "southern."

   1 best evidence sentence: **3**

4. Which of the following statements from the passage is an opinion? (fact/opinion)

   A. While Australia has rain forests, plains, and mountains, nearly a third of Australia is desert.
   B. Australia is also the flattest continent.
   C. Only in the last two hundred years have new animal species been introduced by settlers from Europe and Asia.
   D. Given all of its unusual features, Australia would be a fascinating place to visit.

   The first three sentences give factual information about Australia. The fourth sentence makes a personal judgment about visiting Australia.

5. The author's main purpose in writing this article is to (author purpose)

   A. show how geographic isolation has affected Australia in many ways.
   B. describe how Australia is different compared to other continents.

C. show that Australia is the smallest of the continents.

D. describe how unique Australia's animal life is.

3 best evidence sentences: **1, 5, 8**

1, 5, and 8 make a direct comparison between Australia and other continents.

6. Which sea is located to the northeast of Australia? (map reading)

A. Timor Sea

B. Coral Sea

C. Tasman Sea

D. Pacific Ocean

47. Dress Like an Egyptian by Margaret Hockett

A [1]Early Egyptians dressed according to their wealth and their role in society. [2]Those who did common work wore what was practical, and those who were rich wore what was beautiful.

B [3]The clothing of servants and laborers was simple and inexpensive. [4]It was usually white in color and rough in quality. [5]Not only was simple dress cheaper, it was easier to work in. [6]Men wore a cloth like a Scottish kilt. [7]Women wore long skirts with plain shawls or dresses without sleeves, and no jewelry. [8]Children often wore nothing at all. [9]Even their scalps were bare because they were shaved to prevent lice.

C [10]Wealthy people dressed differently. [11]They wore colorful clothing, though fabric dye was expensive (the vibrant colors, such as gold and yellow were especially costly). [12]They could afford delicate linens of fine quality (so fine that some were as transparent as a screened window.) [13]The rich sometimes wore pleated and loosely flowing robes that would have ruled out hard work. [14]The

rich also wore wigs, eye makeup, perfume, and jewelry. [15]Even children wore jewels about the neck.

D [16]Yes, the dress of the poor was practical for labor while the decorations of the rich were not. [17]However, these rich decorations did serve at least two purposes. [18]They made the wearer feel beautiful. [19]They also reminded the working-class Egyptians of the rank and majesty of those who were wealthy.

1. Choose the ending that completes the main idea of the passage: Early Egyptian dress style was (main idea)

A. based on wealth.

B. too expensive.

C. beautifully displayed.

D. often simple and rough.

1 best evidence sentence: **1**

2. Why do you think the lower class wore mostly white clothing? (inference)

A. White was a symbol of innocence.

B. Colored cloth was not permitted.

C. Rough cloth came in white only.

D. Fabric dyes were too expensive.

1 best evidence sentence from paragraph C: **11**

3. As used in sentence 11, the word *vibrant* means (vocabulary)

A. bright.

B. dull.

C. many.

D. dark.

Sentence 11 suggests that gold and yellow dyes were used to make the vibrant clothes, so only choice A makes sense.

4. The very wealthy Egyptians dressed splendidly for several reasons. Which

of the following was NOT a reason for their style of dress? (inference)

A. It made them feel beautiful.
B. It showed their majesty.
C. They could buy it cheaply.
D. They did not have to work hard.

Sentence 18 shows that A is true. Sentence 19 shows that B is true. Sentence 13 implies that D is true since only those who didn't have to labor could wear fine dress. Sentences 11 and 12 suggest that the clothes were expensive.

5. You can tell from sentence 12 that transparent clothing is easy to (vocabulary)

A. recognize.
B. clean up.
C. do work in.
D. see through.

Since the clothing is compared to a screened window, we infer that the author is stressing the ability to see through the material.

6. Why might it have been difficult for a servant to work in clothing like that of the wealthy? (prediction)

She or he might get the clothes caught and either ruin them or hurt him/herself.

The clothes were often loose and flowing, according to sentence 13.

7. Why do you think a pharaoh (ruler) might dress even more elaborately than the wealthy class? (application)

He would have wanted to set himself apart as more important so they would respect him as their superior.

(Students can answer this by taking

the information in sentence 19 one step further.)

48. Natural Rhythm
by Margaret Hockett

A [1]Many of us think of rhythm as the regular patterns of sound in music. [2]But where did rhythm come from? [3]Rhythm has been around since there have been ears and minds to appreciate it. [4]For example, within our bodies, our hearts beat with a regular tha-thump, tha-thump. [5]From the world around us come the flap-flap of bird wings and the steady pelting of rain accented by the baBOOM of thunder. [6]These patterns of sound fascinate us humans. [7]We create various rhythms with our voice, with our hands, and with objects.

B [8]Early rhythm was primitive. [9]The first planned rhythms were probably made by clapping hands and pounding sticks on logs. [10]The pattern would have been simple, with one hit as hard as the next and equal time between hits: whack-whack-whack-whack. [11]Before long, other objects would have been added and the patterns would have grown more complex: da-da WHACK adeedle, da-da WHACK adeedle.

C [12]Humans have developed the "logs" into hundreds of percussion* instruments from bongos to snares. [13]Modern recording artists use a number of complex rhythms within a single work of music. [14]These days, most of us are content to listen to their recordings instead of playing instruments of our own.

D [15]Does this mean we have left our own natural rhythm-making ability behind? [16]Can we no longer relate to our rhythmical roots? [17]Let's try a test and see:

[18]1) Play a recording of your favorite music.

¹⁹2) Close your eyes as you listen to
     the rhythm.
²⁰3) Check your body.

E ²¹Chances are, you're tapping your feet
and swaying back and forth! ²²Yes, you've
picked out a simple, regular pattern in
that music—and you've still got that
natural human rhythm.

*percussion: hit or struck to make
sound

1. Describe how the cymbal in an
   orchestra could be compared to
   thunder. (compare/contrast)

   **Both make loud, crashing sounds.
   Both occur occasionally rather
   than steadily. Both add accent to
   surrounding sounds.**

   Sentence 5 describes how thunder is
   loud and occasionally accents the
   steady sound of the rain. A cymbal in
   an orchestra has a similar effect.

2. The author uses the made-up word
   "baBOOM" in sentence 5. From
   paragraph B, give another example of
   made-up word. (figurative language)

   whack, da-da WHACK adeedle

   Explain why you think these "words"
   are used.

   **The words are used to describe
   actual sounds. The words
   themselves sound like what they
   are describing.**

3. As used in sentence 8, *primitive*
   means (vocabulary)
   A. simple.
   B. loud.
   C. grunted.
   D. early.

   There is no evidence for B or C. It

would make no sense to say "Early
rhythm was early," so D is probably
incorrect; the author probably
intended another meaning of the
word. A makes more sense in the story
context.

4. The "logs" mentioned in sentence 12
   refer to what kind of instruments?
   (figurative language)
   A. wind instruments
   B. drums
   C. organs
   D. brass instruments

   1 best evidence paragraph: **B**

   Sentence 12 says the logs were refined
   into *percussion* instruments. Given
   the definition for *percussion* (hit or
   struck to make sound), only choice B
   makes sense. Paragraph B describes
   logs in a way that can be understood
   as "drums." Also, bongos and snares
   are types of drums.

5. In sentence 15, why does the author
   ask whether we have left our rhythm-
   making ability behind? Choose all of
   the following that apply. (inference)
   A. She doesn't know the answer.
   B. She wants to introduce a test.
   C. She wants to make us think.
   D. She stresses an earlier question.

   Choices B and C are the best answers
   because the author does introduce a
   test shortly after the question, and she
   does want to make us think, as
   evidenced by the question and the test.
   A is contradicted by the "test" she gives
   you and the results she predicts: that
   we are tapping and swaying (21), and
   that we still *do* have our natural
   rhythm (22). There is no evidence for D.

6. The purpose of paragraph B is to describe how (author's purpose)

   A. rhythm became more complicated.
   B. objects were used to make rhythm.
   C. rhythm could make us healthy.
   D. particular patterns were created.

   Choices B and D give only details of paragraph B. D refers to examples of how the patterns went from simple to complex. There is no evidence for choice C.

7. Paragraph A gives an example of rhythm that occurs in our bodies. What is that example? (reading for detail)

   Our heartbeat is given as an example of rhythm.

49. Jackie Robinson, All-star by Margaret Hockett

A [1]Jackie Robinson was a superb baseball player. [2]However, in the 1940s, a black man had little hope of playing in the major leagues. [3]Little hope, that is, until Branch Rickey came along.
B [4]Branch Rickey was general manager for the Brooklyn Dodgers. [5]After World War II, the Dodgers needed to rebuild their team. [6]Rickey decided to tap a new source of talent and hire the Dodgers' first black player. [7]He found Jackie Robinson.
C [8]Rickey knew that many people would object to Jackie's presence and would try to get him to quit. [9]He told Robinson he'd need "guts enough not to fight back" when people said or did mean things to him. [10]He would be accepted only if he were *more* of a gentleman than anyone else in baseball.
D [11]Robinson understood. [12]He knew it would be hard, but he agreed to take the taunts without fighting back.

E [13]At first, some of his own teammates were against him. [14]Restaurants refused to serve him. [15]Both fans and players called him names. [16]Some opposing players even tried to "spike" Jackie at first base by stepping on his foot. [17]But when Jackie wanted to fight back, he remembered his promise. [18]He remained silent.
F [19]Jackie Robinson concentrated on playing ball. [20]He was bold and speedy, and he stole more bases than anyone else. [21]His teammates came to like and respect him. [22]His daring moves brought excitement to the games. [23]Fans came especially to watch Jackie. [24]He played so well, in fact, that by the end of his first season he was named Rookie of the Year. [25]Robinson went on to play nine more seasons for the Dodgers.
G [26]It was largely because of his self-control that Jackie Robinson was accepted in major league baseball. [27]In fact, he paved the way for many black athletes whose skill and sportsmanship we admire today.

1. From paragraph A, you can tell that Jackie Robinson probably started playing for the Dodgers during what decade? (reading for detail)

   1940s

   2 best evidence sentences: **2, 3**

   Saying that black people had little hope in the 1940s before Rickey came along implies that it was in the '40s that he found and hired Robinson. This is also supported by sentence 5 referring to the period after World War II.

2. As used in sentence 12, what could the word *taunts* mean? (vocabulary)
   A. pitches

B. jobs
C. insults
D. offers

1 best evidence paragraph: **C**

Paragraph C shows that the reason Jackie needed to be tough was that people would say and do mean things to make him quit. In this context, only choice C makes sense.

3. Which of the following was probably NOT an important ingredient of Jackie Robinson's success? (conclusion)

   A. strong self-control
   B. ability to steal bases
   C. ability to fight back
   D. advice from Rickey

   It was not his ability to fight back, but rather his ability to control the desire to fight back, that helped Jackie succeed (sentences 9, 10, 26).

4. By "having guts enough *not* to fight back," Rickey probably meant that Jackie would have to (inference)

   A. claim rights.
   B. remain calm.
   C. lecture others.
   D. argue back.

   1 best evidence sentence: **10**

   By "guts enough *not* to fight back" in Sentence 9, we can understand that Rickey means not to argue or fight when people say or do mean things. Only choice B is similar.

5. Number the following events in the order they occur in the passage. (sequence)

   5 A. Jackie is Rookie of the Year.
   4 B. Fans are impressed with Jackie's skill.
   1 C. World War II ends.

   2 D. Jackie is told to be gentlemanly.
   3 E. Jackie's self-control is challenged.

6. Why did Branch Rickey look for a black baseball player for the Dodgers? (cause/effect)

   The team needed to rebuild, and he decided to draw from a new source of talent.

   2 best evidence sentences: **5**, **6**

7. What caused Jackie to remain silent when players tried to "spike" him? (cause/effect)

   Remembering his promise not to fight back kept Jackie silent.

   2 best evidence sentences: **17**, **18**

50. Magellan's Voyage Around the World by David White

[1]Ferdinand Magellan was the first explorer to lead a voyage that circled the globe. [2]In doing so, he helped prove once and for all that the world was round.

[3]Magellan was 12 when Christopher Columbus first landed in the New World in 1492. [4]Magellan went to school to learn how to be a page—an assistant at the royal court of Portugal. [5]While in school, he learned celestial navigation, which is how to find your way in uncharted water or open seas by following the stars. [6]His studies created in him a lifelong desire to explore. [7]After several years as a page, he left the Portuguese court for a life at sea.

[8]Magellan wanted to lead his own voyage and tried unsuccessfully to persuade the king of Portugal to finance it. [9]He finally won financial support from the king of Spain. [10]In 1519, Magellan set off as captain of a five-ship Spanish

expedition. [11]The goal was to find a way to Asia by going west.

[12]Legends told of El Paso—a water passage that went through the newly discovered American continents. [13]A year into the voyage, Magellan found this passage. [14]It was at the southern tip of South America.

[15]The sailors were not happy with Magellan because the water and winds were very cold. [16]Still, they sailed on. [17]After making it through the passage, Magellan and his men sailed 98 days across the Pacific Ocean without once seeing land. [18](Maps at the time showed the ocean to be small.)

[19]Finally, Magellan reached Guam. [20]It was 1521—two years after the voyage had begun. [21]Their food supply had long since run out, and the sailors were famished. [22]The people of Guam gave the sailors lots of exotic foods and fresh water. [23]They rested for a few days. [24]Some would have been happy to stay, but Magellan wanted to go on. [25]Nine days later, they reached the Philippines.

[26]While there, Magellan tried to spread his religion to anyone who would listen. [27]He was successful in converting the natives of one island, but he was killed by natives on another island. [28]The voyage continued without him, though. [29]Only one ship was left in the end. [30]The *Victoria* returned to Spain in 1522. [31]The voyage around the world was complete.

[32]Even though Magellan himself did not survive the voyage, his discovery did. [33]The world was indeed round.

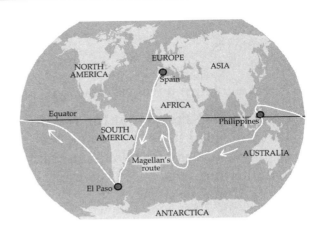

1. How long did the voyage last? (reading for detail)

   The voyage lasted three years.

   2 best evidence sentences: **10, 30**

   The voyage ended in 1522 and began in 1519. 1522–1519 = 3.

2. According to the passage, which of these was NOT a part of Magellan's many travels? (supporting details)

   A. sailing the seas
   B. exploring the world
   C. spreading religion
   D. conquering countries

   A (7), B (6), and C (26) are mentioned in the passage as being purposes of Magellan's travels. There is no evidence for D.

3. Why did Magellan ask the king of Spain to send him on a voyage? (cause/effect)

   He was unable to get financial backing from his own king.

   1 best evidence sentence: **8**

4. Number these events in correct time order as performed by Magellan. (sequence)

   5 lands in Philippines
   2 finds El Paso

4 reaches Guam
1 studies to be a page
3 sails into the Pacific Ocean

5. What is Magellan's voyage famous for? (main idea)

The voyage proved once and for all that the world was round.

2 best evidence sentences: **2, 33**

6. What could have convinced Magellan to continue sailing the Pacific Ocean even though the crew had gone for days without seeing land? (inference, cause/effect)

Maps of the time showed the Pacific Ocean to be small. Magellan thought land was just ahead.

1 best evidence sentence: **18**

7. Which of these words is closest in meaning to *famished,* as used in sentence 21? (vocabulary)

A. lost
B. sore
C. tired
D. hungry

Since their food supply had run out, the sailors were probably hungry. This is supported by sentence 22, also.

8. Explain why celestial navigation, as described in sentence 5, was useful to sailors. (conclusion)

It was useful because you could find where you were at sea even if you didn't see land.

GLOSSARY OF TERMS

character trait: A person's individual qualities, such as greed or kindness.

conflict: The tension or opposition between two characters, or between a character and some opposing force, such as society.

figurative language: Words and phrases used to compare two unlike things or to mean something other than their actual meaning. Similes and metaphors are types of figurative language.

generalization: A broad statement that is made about a group of things in general, based on one or more samples from the group.

inference: Information that is suggested in a story, but not directly stated.

metaphor: A comparison between two things which says that one thing is another.
> Example: The <u>flowers were bright flags</u> signaling the return of spring.

narrator: The person or character who is telling the story.

plot: The structure of the story around which events occur. Most plots begin with a problem or conflict that builds to a high point and is then resolved.

point of view: The narrator's focus in telling the story. In a first person viewpoint, the narrator is a character in the story. In a third person viewpoint, the narrator is observing the story characters.

resolution: Solving the problem or conflict in a story.

setting: The particular time and place in which a story occurs.

simile: A comparison of two things, using the words *like* or *as*.
> Example: His <u>nose glowed like a lantern</u> in the night.

theme: The underlying meaning of the story. It is a comment or view about life or human nature in general that is woven throughout the story. It may be stated directly or revealed through the character's words and actions and the story's events.

LITERATURE CITATIONS

Fudge-a-mania
From FUDGE-A-MANIA by Judy Blume, copyright (c) 1990 by Judy Blume. Used by permission of Dutton Children's Books, a division of Penguin Putnam Inc.

Mr. Popper's Penguins
From MR. POPPER'S PENGUINS by Florence & Richard Atwater. Copyright (c) 1938 by Florence Atwater and Richard Atwater; copyright (c) renewed 1966 by Florence Atwater, Doris Atwater and Carroll Atwater Bishop. By permission of Little, Brown and Company (Inc.).

Maniac Magee
From MANIAC MAGEE by Jerry Spinelli. Copyright (c) 1990 by Jerry Spinelli. By permission of Little, Brown and Company (Inc.). World publication by permission of Ray Lincoln Literary Agency.

Owls in the Family
From OWLS IN THE FAMILY by Farley Mowat. Copyright (c) 1961 by Farley Mowat Ltd.; copyright (c) renewed 1989 by Farley Mowat Ltd. By permission of Little, Brown and Company (Inc.).

Where the Red Fern Grows
From WHERE THE RED FERN GROWS by Wilson Rawls. Copyright (c) 1961 by Sophie S. Rawls, Trustee, or successor Trustee(s) of the Rawls Trust, dated July 31, 1991. Copyright (c) 1961 by The Curtis Publishing Company. Used by permission of Dell Publishing, a division of Random House, Inc.

Island of the Blue Dolphins
Excerpt from ISLAND OF THE BLUE DOLPHINS. Copyright (c) 1960, renewed 1988 by Scott O'Dell. Reprinted by permission of Houghton Mifflin Company. All rights reserved.

Blue Willow
From BLUE WILLOW by Doris Gates, copyright 1940 by Doris Gates, renewed (c) 1968 by Doris Gates. Used by permission of Viking Penguin, a division of Penguin Putnam Inc.

The Witch of Blackbird Pond
Excerpt from THE WITCH OF BLACKBIRD POND. Copyright (c) 1958, renewed 1986 by Elizabeth George Speare. Reprinted by permission of Houghton Mifflin Co. All rights reserved.

Charlie's House
From CHARLIE'S HOUSE by Clyde Robert Bulla Copyright (c) 1993 by Clyde Robert Bulla. Reprinted by permission of Alfred A. Knopf, a division of Random House, Inc.

READING DETECTIVE ™ B SAMPLE ACTIVITY

On the following pages is a sample activity from our popular reading series, *Reading Detective*™. There are currently three books in the series, *Beginning Reading Detective*, grades 3–4, *Reading Detective A1*, grades 5–6, and *Reading Detective B1*, grades 7–8. The following sample is from the *Bl* book.

- *Reading Detective* ™ is based on national and state reading standards. These books, however, go beyond current reading comprehension materials by requiring 1) a higher level of analysis and 2) evidence to support answers. Students are asked to read a passage, then answer a variety of questions, supporting their answers with specific evidence from the passage. This skill, required by most state standards, is not often addressed in the available reading materials.

- Skills covered include basic reading skills such as reading for detail and identifying the main idea, literary analysis skills such as analyzing character traits and identifying setting, and critical thinking skills such as making inferences and distinguishing between cause and effect.

- Each book includes excerpts from works of award-winning authors and original fiction in a variety of genres: mystery, fantasy, adventure, humor. Nonfiction articles cover topics in science, social studies, math, and the arts that coincide with classroom curriculum.

- For further samples and information on the *Reading Detective*™ series, see our web site at www.criticalthinking.com.

20. Old Woman of the Oak
by Margaret Hockett

[1]I crossed the stream, wound my way through the bushes, and came to a clearing. [2]The oak sprawled before me.

[3]I pressed a dark knot on the pale gray trunk. [4]A rope ladder immediately snaked its way down through rustling red leaves. [5]A note had been tacked to the third rung: CAREFUL, JUDE. ROPE WET. [6]That was Old Meg, never one to waste words.

[7]Soon, I was swinging my legs into the entrance. [8]Meg sat in her "living room" in the oak she called home. [9]She was as gnarled as the tree, but her eyes usually crackled with fire. [10]Today they were flat.

[11]"Won't be much longer," she said. [12]"They're going to bulldoze the field for the new road."

[13]"No way!" I said in disbelief. [14]"We'll stop them—" [15]She held up her hand.

[16]"But where will you go…?" I started.

[17]She was moving her rocker back, baack, baaack—until it was on the edge of the runner and you thought she was going all the way over!—and then forward. [18]She'd do that when she was making up her mind.

[19]"Been here 'bout long enough. [20]Seen the sun set nine thousand times, and ain't none of them been the same as the one before." [21]I followed her gaze past dewy leaves, a patch of meadow, and jutting rocks of the coast. [22]An inky line was forming a boundary between sea and sky. [23]Suddenly, it spread, as if an artist were washing the scene with a dark tint. [24]My mood darkened with it as Meg's meaning came home to me.

[25]"I'm leaving you my Oak Log," she announced. [26]Her precious journal! [27]Meg thought the road project was a sign that her time had come, that her life was over! [28]I couldn't accept that.

[29]As I walked back to town, I ignored the slapping branches, the wet stream, and the cold night. [30]I was making a plan.

SAMPLE QUESTIONS

2. Paragraph B suggests that Meg's speech is

   A. brief.
   B. lengthy.
   C. mean.
   D. descriptive.

   Give the number of the sentence that best supports your answer. ____

3. In sentence 9, the word "gnarled" most likely means

   A. hard.
   B. twisted.
   C. tall.
   D. awesome.

4. Why did Jude need to be careful in climbing to Meg's home?

   _____

6. Jude is most likely to make a plan to

   A. force Meg to move.
   B. move in with Meg.
   C. get the Oak Log.
   D. stop the bulldozing.

   List the numbers of the 2 sentences that best support your answer. ____, ____

10. In sentence 24, what does Jude infer from Meg's comments?

    _____

    _____

    _____

    Give the number of the sentence that confirms Jude's inference. ____

SAMPLE ANSWERS

2. **Paragraph B suggests that Meg's speech is (character trait)**

    A. brief.
    B. lengthy.
    C. mean.
    D. descriptive.

    1 best evidence sentence: **6**

3. In sentence 9, "gnarled" most likely means (vocabulary)

    A. hard.
    B. twisted.
    C. tall.
    D. awesome.

    Since "gnarled" is contrasted with the liveliness of her eyes, the author probably wants to show that Meg's body is aged, as a tree with knots and twisted branches.

4. Why did Jude need to be careful in climbing to Meg's home? (reading for detail)

    The rope was wet.

6. Jude is most likely to make a plan to (predict outcome)

    A. force Meg to move.
    B. move in with Meg.
    C. get the Oak Log.
    D. stop the bulldozing.

    2 best evidence sentences: 13, 14

    Choice D is supported by sentences 13 and 14, which show that Jude has strong feelings against the bulldozing. B is unlikely because there is no evidence that moving in with Meg would help. Since Meg is already going to give Jude the Oak Log, C is incorrect. A is a possibility but is unsupported.

10. In sentence 24, what does Jude infer from Meg's comments? (inference)

    He probably infers that Meg thinks her time has come to leave or die or both.

    1 best evidence sentence: **27**